Ergonomics: A Practical Approach

Ergonomics: A Practical Approach

Calum Blackwell

MURPHY & MOORE
www.murphy-moorepublishing.com

Ergonomics: A Practical Approach
Calum Blackwell
ISBN: 978-1-63987-198-8 (Hardback)

MURPHY & MOORE

Published by Murphy & Moore Publishing,
1 Rockefeller Plaza,
New York City, NY 10020, USA

Cataloging-in-Publication Data

Ergonomics : a practical approach / Calum Blackwell.
p. cm.
Includes bibliographical references and index.
ISBN 978-1-63987-198-8
1. Human engineering. 2. Industrial engineering. I. Blackwell, Calum.

T59.7 .E74 2022
620.82--dc23

For more information regarding Murphy & Moore Publishing and its products, please visit the publisher's website www.murphy-moorepublishing.com

Table of Contents

Preface

The purpose of this book is to help students understand the fundamental concepts of this discipline. It is designed to motivate students to learn and prosper. I am grateful for the support of my colleagues. I would also like to acknowledge the encouragement of my family.

Ergonomics is the use of physiological and psychological principles for the designing and engineering of products, systems and processes. It deals with the interactions among humans and other aspects of system. It uses theories, principles and methods to optimize overall system performance and at the same time ensure human well-being. It focuses on finding the right fit between the equipment, user and the environment. This discipline is further divided into three types. These are cognitive, physical and organizational ergonomics. Some of the common methods used in this field are ethnographic analysis, meta-analysis, human performance modelling, kansei method, focus groups and macroergonomic analysis of structure. This field combines the concepts of various other fields such as anthropometry, biomechanics, psychology, visual design, user interface design and engineering. The topics covered in this extensive book deal with the core aspects of ergonomics. Also included herein is a detailed explanation of the various concepts and applications related to this field. For all those who are interested in this discipline, this book can prove to be an essential guide.

A foreword for all the chapters is provided below:

Chapter – Introduction

Ergonomics refers to the physiological and psychological principles that are applied to the design and engineering of products, processes, and systems. It is done in order to optimize human well-being. Its three major types are physical, cognitive and organizational ergonomics. This is an introductory chapter which will briefly introduce about ergonomics.

Chapter – Physical Ergonomics

Physical ergonomics deals with the physical activities that are related to human anatomical, physiological, anthropometric, and biomechanical characteristics. Some of the equipment used under it are ergonomic keyboard, datahand, velotype, microwriter, frogPad, etc. This chapter has been carefully written to provide an easy understanding of physical ergonomics.

Chapter – Organizational Ergonomics

Organizational ergonomics deals with the optimization and modification of organizational policies, structures and processes. Crew resource management, work design, participatory design, community ergonomics, cooperative work, virtual organizations, telework, etc. are a few of its concepts. This chapter discusses the subject of organizational ergonomics in detail.

Chapter - Occupational Safety and Ergonomics

Occupational safety in ergonomics deals with ergonomic hazards and risk assessment, work related musculoskeletal disorders and ergonomics training. Carpal tunnel syndrome, repetitive strain injury, etc. are some of the injuries related to ergonomics. This chapter delves into the subject of occupational safety and ergonomics for a thorough understanding of it.

Chapter - Cognitive Ergonomics

Cognitive ergonomics is the discipline that is associated with the evaluation and designing of tasks, products and environment as well as their interaction with humans. It can be applied in different sectors of aviation, transportation, healthcare system, nuclear power systems and product design. The topics elaborated in this chapter will help in gaining a better perspective of cognitive ergonomics.

Calum Blackwell

1

Introduction

Ergonomics refers to the physiological and psychological principles that are applied to the design and engineering of products, processes, and systems. It is done in order to optimize human well-being. Its three major types are physical, cognitive and organizational ergonomics. This is an introductory chapter which will briefly introduce about ergonomics.

ERGONOMICS

Ergonomics is the process of designing or arranging workplaces, products and systems so that they fit the people who use them.

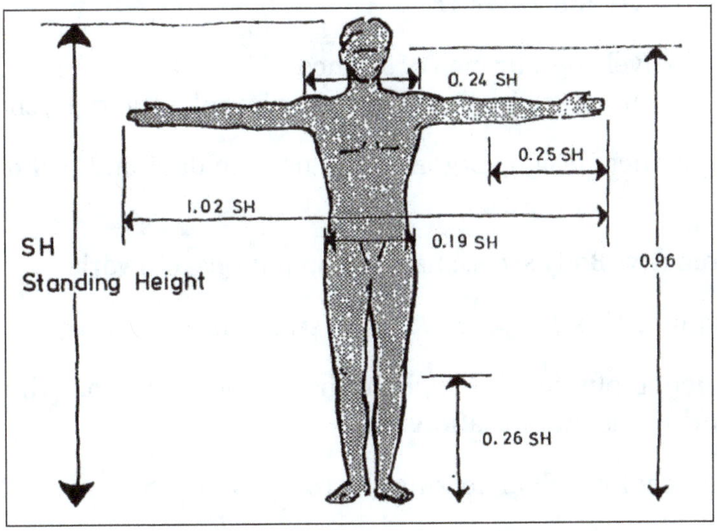

Most people have heard of ergonomics and think it is something to do with seating or with the design of car controls and instruments – and it is but it is so much more. Ergonomics applies to the design of anything that involves people – workspaces, sports and leisure, health and safety.

Ergonomics is a branch of science that aims to learn about human abilities and limitations, and then apply this learning to improve people's interaction with products, systems and environments.

Ergonomics aims to improve workspaces and environments to minimise risk of injury or harm. So as technologies change, so too does the need to ensure that the tools we access for work, rest and play are designed for our body's requirements.

Importance of Ergonomics

- In the workplace: The total economic cost of work-related injuries and illnesses is estimated to be $60 billion dollars. Research has shown that lower back pain is the world's most common work-related disability – affecting employees from offices, building sites and in the highest risk category, agriculture.

  Ergonomics aims to create safe, comfortable and productive workspaces by bringing human abilities and limitations into the design of a workspace, including the individual's body size, strength, skill, speed, sensory abilities (vision, hearing), and even attitudes.

- In the greater population: The number of people in Australia aged 75 and over is forecast to double over the next 50 years. With this, equipment, services and systems will need to be designed to accommodate the increasing needs of the ageing population, applying to public transport, building facilities, and living spaces.

How does Ergonomics Work?

Ergonomics is a relatively new branch of science which relies on research carried out in established scientific areas, such as engineering, physiology and psychology.

To achieve best practice design, Ergonomists use the data and techniques of several disciplines:

- Anthropometry: Body sizes, shapes; populations and variations.
- Biomechanics: Muscles, levers, forces, strength.
- Environmental physics: Noise, light, heat, cold, radiation, vibration body systems: hearing, vision, sensations.
- Applied psychology: Skill, learning, errors, differences.
- Social psychology: Groups, communication, learning, behaviours.

HUMAN FACTORS AND ERGONOMICS

Human Factors, as the definition goes, "refer to environmental, organisational and job factors, and human and individual characteristics," and these factors/characteristics can affect people's health and safety. In other words, human factors is consist of but not limited to physical, cognitive, psychomotor, behavioral and usability categories, in order to improve humans' safety and productivity. The design and engineering part, as most people have known of, is in fact just an application of the Human factors study and research. HF itself is much more than that.

This picture shows how people are evolved: biologically from monkeys to human beings, and ergonomically from performing in awkward positions to better ones.

It is "an applied science concerned with designing and arranging things people use so that the people and things interact most efficiently and safely." Looking into the dictionary, it seems like Ergonomics can also be seen as Human Factors, with "ergon" meaning work and "nomoi" meaning natural laws. It describes the science of work and a person's relationship to that work.

After understanding the definition of these two important words, it is necessary to shift gears to the main elements of them: the job, the individual, and the organization. Human Factors focus on people, not only employees but also employers. It is a study of what workers are being asked to do, who will be doing it, and who they are working for. Thus HF and Ergonomics might be broader and more influential than the general public thinks.

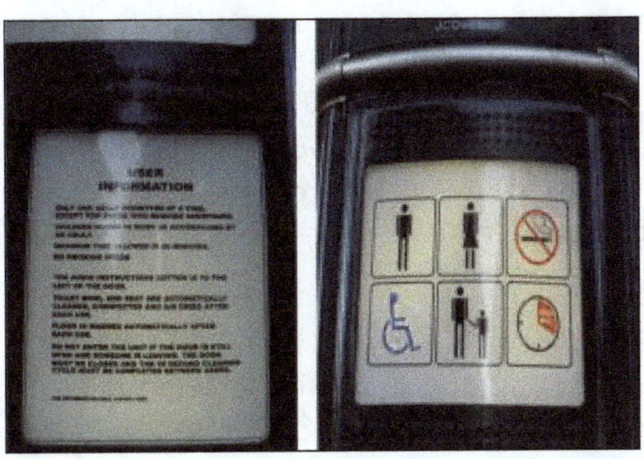

An example of signs on the public bathroom doors showing how visual images are clearer than tons of words and sentences.

As Human Factors and Ergonomics become more and more important these days, tons of examples, no matter how big or small, appeared in real life. The public restroom information mentioned in class is very appropriate. Before using Ergonomics, the information was written in long and capitalized sentences, making it difficult to read; after Ergonomics, however, the same information is presented in a much more straight-forward way, using pictures. While same instructions are mentioned, the latter one is definitely more efficient and causing peoples less time to read.

Ergonomics Education for Office Computer Workers

One of the contemporary health issues in today's society is work-related musculoskeletal disorders (WMSDs). Musculoskeletal disorders (MSDs) are injuries and illnesses that affect the muscles, nerves, tendons, ligaments, joints, or spinal discs. According to the United States (US) Bureau of Labor Statistics, MSDs include pinched nerve, herniated disc, meniscus tear, sprains, strains, tears, hernia (traumatic and nontraumatic), pain, swelling, numbness, carpal or tarsal tunnel syndrome, and Raynaud's syndrome; when the event or exposure leading to these injuries or illnesses is overexertion, bodily reaction, repetitive motion involving microtasks, and vibration. Work-related disorders are prevalent among myriad occupational groups such as factory workers, truck drivers, hair dressers, allied health professionals, field workers, and computer workers. The regions that are prone to developing musculoskeletal injuries are the lower back, upper back, neck, and upper extremities.

WMSDs have enormous economic implications. The Institute of Medicine estimates that the total economic burden of WMSDs could be as high as $54 billion annually. Ergonomic injuries related to computer work constitute a significant portion of WMSDs. The US Occupational Safety and Health Administration (OSHA) estimated that employers are "spending $20 billion a year on worker's compensation costs related to ergonomic injuries and illnesses".

Occupational injuries and illnesses have many direct and indirect cost implications. When calculating cost implications of WMSDs, one must give due consideration to all factors. Workers' compensation costs and charges involved in medical care and rehabilitation are considered direct costs, while lost productivity, lost time, training new staff, administrative costs, and temporary staffing are considered indirect costs. Web resources may assist employers to calculate cost implications of occupational injuries. For example, the OSHA Safety Pays website calculates the estimated total costs (direct and indirect) of common work-related injuries based on national worker's compensation data of the US.

In today's age, computer use has become an integral part of daily life. People use computers for various work-related and non–work-related tasks (social media, banking, shopping, etc.). Office computer workers (OCWs) use computers on an average of 6-12 hours a day. The surge in computer use has also created a surge in computer work-related MSDs. Rehman et al. stated that around 27% of computer users report backaches or discomfort. The chance of sustaining WMSDs is high when computer workers spend long hours on their computers.

Risk Factors

Factors that make a worker prone to developing WMSDs are called risk factors. Table lists various risk factors associated with WMSDs. Risk factors related to office computer work are classified into postural risk factors, environmental risk factors, individual risk factors, psychosocial risk factors, and risk factors associated with duration and intensity of office work.

Risk Factors for WMSDs

- Awkward and prolonged static postures.
- Bending and twisting.
- Excessive work.
- Force.
- Glare.
- Job strain.
- Lifting.
- Monotonous activity.
- Pace of work.
- Repetition.
- Vibration.

Postural Risk Factors

Posture is the carriage of a body as a whole, the attitude of the body, or the position of the limbs. The literature showed an established link between MSDs and improper posture at computer workstations. Sauter et al. found that arm discomfort increased when keyboard height was above the elbow level. Chiu et al. reported a significant association between head posture during computer work and neck pain. Eltayeb et al. highlighted the significant associations between irregular "head and body posture" and "neck, shoulder and forearms/hands complaints."

Awkward and prolonged static postures contribute to musculoskeletal discomforts among OCWs. Twisting the torso to reach file cabinets, cradling the phone between the neck and shoulder, curved sitting (bending the torso toward the monitor), slouched sitting with legs placed on an object under the work surface, and sitting on a high chair with dangling feet are some examples of awkward postures during office computer work. Postures with elevated or abducted shoulders are also considered awkward postures. These postures, when sustained, strain the lower back, shoulders, and neck muscle groups.

As computer workers often engage in tasks that demand high level of concentration, they get absorbed in their work and assume a given posture for long periods of time.

During prolonged static sitting, the muscles that sustain body posture undergo a prolonged state of contraction, leading to decreased transportation of sugar and oxygen to dynamically contracting muscles. This causes an accumulation of waste products such as lactic acid and carbon dioxide in those muscles, leading to muscle spasms and fatigue. Prolonged sitting also contributes to myriad health issues such as low back pain, coronary artery disease, and kidney disease.

Environmental Risk Factors

Poor work environments augment the risk of WMSDs. Office work environments that are not conducive to their users can be referred to as "poor work environments." For instance, a workstation where the keyboard and mouse are placed at different levels, causing the user to elevate/abduct shoulders can be considered a poor workstation. A workstation without adjustable components (work surface, office chair, etc.) and necessary accessories (hands-free phone, document holder, etc.) can also be construed as a poor work environment. Further, environments with the heightened noise level, increased glare, and extreme temperatures are considered as poor work environments.

Individual Risk Factors

A computer worker may also become prone to developing WMSDs due to personal factors such as health history and poor work behaviors. Individual-related factors contribute to WMSDs through their effect on body structure, function, and posture. Some of the individual-related risk factors are obesity, pregnancy, arthritis, trauma, and endocrinal disorders. Working without rest breaks, binge working, ignoring the body's warning signs such as pain and discomfort, ignoring flexibility/stretching exercises, failing to alternate work tasks, following poor working techniques, and failing to adjust workstation components as needed are the examples of some maladaptive work behaviors.

Gender has also been hypothesized as a risk factor. Women are at a relatively higher risk than men. This could be due to differences in anthropometrics and physiology in women. Also, women often assume responsibilities of non–work-related activities such as household tasks, which may add to muscle strain and make them more vulnerable to WMSDs.

Psychosocial Risk Factors

Psychological variables such as work pressure and job strain may also contribute to WMSDs. Hannan et al. found a correlation between increased job strain and neck musculoskeletal symptoms. Perceived inadequate support from managers, low level of control, and information overload were also identified as psychosocial risk factors. With information overload, a worker spends an increasing amount of time using electronic gadgets and ignores proper work posture, thereby developing his/her risk for WMSDs.

Mental stress can also augment the physical load during computer work because a computer worker with mental stress may exert more force on mouse or keyboard.

Risk Factors Associated with Duration and Intensity of Work

Working on computers for long hours is a risk factor. A correlation between the duration of computer use and upper extremity (UE) pain, back pain, and eye strain. Repetitive hand, wrist, and finger movements (e.g., typing for extended periods of time), speedy/jerky movements, and force applied while typing may also contribute to UE pain and musculoskeletal discomforts. The demand for productivity and time pressure in today's work culture demand increased keying and extended hours of work from OCWs, thereby making them susceptible to WMSDs. Repetitive motions result in the vasoconstriction of arteries causing ischemic injury and edema due to anoxic damage.

Prevention of Work-related Musculoskeletal Disorders

To prevent WMSDs, measures must be taken to avoid exposure to risk factors. These measures could be technical such as an elevated work surface for a tall worker, organizational such as conducting ergonomic workshops, and personal such as working with rest breaks. Some of the WMSD prevention strategies in practice include workstation modification, task modification, and provision of necessary ergonomic accessories. However, "for these prevention measures to work, proper knowledge/awareness about how (a) the work-related factors contribute to WMSDs, (b) to carry out the work tasks safely, and (c) to effectively use the equipment, are essential". Robertson et al. stated that the availability of adjustable office furniture alone cannot reduce or prevent musculoskeletal injuries. For instance, a lot of computer workers sit on adjustable chairs without adjusting them due to lack of knowledge. Similarly, though many computer users know that bad posture is a risk factor, they continue to assume awkward and risky postures. Hence, to prevent WMSDs among OCWs and ensure their well-being, it is critical to educate them on "ergonomics" and "risk factors associated with WMSDs." An evidence-based strategy to impart this education is Ergonomics Education.

Ergonomics Education

Ergonomics means the science of fitting the job to the worker. In the context of office computer work, it refers to the computer user-workstation fit. Interventions that aim to enhance this fit are called ergonomic interventions. Ergonomic interventions differ from traditional therapeutic interventions because they target work posture, work habits, behaviors, and the environment. They range from modifying workstations to long-term educational interventions with the aim of preventing and treating WMSDs.

Ergonomics is a recognized intervention strategy. Several occupational health and safety agencies across the world advocate for ergonomics. Many mid- and large-size technology companies offer ergonomic training to their employees as ergonomic interventions have been found to enhance productivity, improve worker well-being, and reduce WMSDs.

One of the well-documented ergonomic interventions is ergonomics education. Ergonomics education is a strategy in which an ergonomic expert educates participants (workers) on ergonomic principles and other necessary ergonomic information either on-site or virtually. The aim is to enhance participants' knowledge on WMSD risk factors, WMSD prevention strategies, and effective work behaviors. There are two primary objectives for any ergonomics education program. One is to help participants become aware of the risk factors and the other is to encourage participants to modify their work behavior.

Types

Ergonomics education can be classified into traditional and participatory ergonomics education. In traditional ergonomics education, the information is presented via lectures, seminars, handouts, videos, etc., and participants assume a passive role. In participatory ergonomics education, participants interact with and learn from the expert using adult learning models. The difference between these two types of ergonomics education is the high level of interaction, which is present in the latter. Participatory ergonomics education was reported to achieve better outcomes than the traditional type.

Anatomy and Biomechanics

Ergonomics education programs for computer workers typically include content on biomechanics and anatomy of the back, neck, and upper extremities, as they are the body parts that are commonly affected during office computer work. When reviewing the anatomy and biomechanics of the back, ergonomic experts discuss the anatomy of the spinal curves and biomechanical alterations on the spine and intervertebral discs due to postural modifications. Experts also review the anatomy of two major muscles (trapezius and latissimus dorsi) that get used during office computer work and emphasize how these muscles get stretched or strained when a worker cradles the phone between the neck and shoulder, elevates the shoulders to reach high work surfaces, abducts the shoulders to reach the mouse and keyboard, hunches over computers, or reaches overhead to retrieve items.

When reviewing the anatomy of the upper extremities, ergonomic experts place a major emphasis on shoulder joints since awkward shoulder positions contribute significantly to WMSDs related to office computer work. They highlight three most common shoulder positions (elevated shoulders, rounded shoulders, and abducted shoulders) that contribute to UE/neck pain and discomfort. Ergonomic experts also review wrist and hand joints and underscore the importance of keeping wrists in a neutral position while working on computers, as incorrect position of these joints may lead to forearm and wrist pain, discomfort, or injury. Further, they review the impact of repetitive wrist and hand movements on forearm muscles and tendons. Information on conditions like muscle strain and carpal tunnel syndrome (a condition that occurs due to increased pressure on the median nerve at wrist) is also presented during these sessions.

Mechanism of Injury

Ergonomics education sessions highlight the mechanism of injury behind WMSDs. It has been a generally accepted notion that the theoretical mechanism behind WMSDs is repetitive microtraumas and their cumulative damage on musculoskeletal tissues. Ergonomic experts educate participants on various risk factors and how they affect musculoskeletal tissues and contribute to WMSDs. They explain how sustained muscle activity leads to muscle spasms, how back rest angle of less than 95° adds pressure on ischial tuberosities, etc. In addition, they highlight the health issues associated with maladaptive work behaviors such as back pain, visual fatigue, visual dryness (due to constant watching of monitors), headaches, and weight gain.

Ideal Work Posture and Workstation

The content related to ideal work posture and workstation forms the core of ergonomics education programs for OCWs. The ideal work posture is the one where the back is straight or slightly reclined (95–110°), the shoulders are abducted less than 20°, the elbows are flexed at 90–100°, and the forearm is pronated with the wrist, hand, forearm in a straight line with the work item. Wrist extension or deviation of more than 15° must be avoided. For lower extremities, the legs need to be perpendicular to the floor, the thighs should be parallel to the floor, and the hip joint should be slightly higher than the knee joint. The feet should rest flat on the floor or a footrest.

According to the US OSHA, an ideal workstation has an adjustable work surface, a keyboard tray, a keyboard and input device (mouse) at the same level and frequently used items placed within easy reach. OSHA recommends a chair with adequate lumbar support, sufficient depth and width to accommodate the user, a seat front with a waterfall edge, and adequate thigh and knee clearance. In an ideal workstation, the top edge of the monitor lies at eye level or slightly below and is placed at a distance from the user so that the user does not have to bend or extend the neck/head to see and read the monitor (approximately at an arm's length from the user). The monitors are placed perpendicular to the window to minimize glare. An ideal workstation also provides adequate space under the work surface so that the user can get close to the work surface and can cross his/her legs without bumping. It is recommended to leave the area under the desk free of storage. OSHA recommends that all workstation accessories and components be well maintained and serviced.

Work Behaviors

Ergonomics education sessions also underscore the importance of work behaviors such as taking adequate rest breaks, engaging in exercise, being mindful of posture, and effectively arranging/adjusting the work surface. It is recommended that computer users take adequate rest breaks and vary their work tasks while working on computers. OSHA recommends rest breaks for jobs that require prolonged posture and repetitive tasks. Henning et al. highlighted the fact that frequent short rest breaks from computer-mediated work can benefit worker productivity and well-being. Galinsky found that taking four supplemental 5-min rest breaks and two conventional rest breaks of 15 min throughout the work day can minimize discomfort without impairing productivity. Microbreaks at 20-min intervals were also reported to be effective. During rest breaks, it is wise to step away from the workstation and walk around. Workers may visit a colleague's office, go to the print room, use the restroom or cafeteria, etc. To reduce eye discomfort and dryness, ergonomic experts recommend taking microbreaks to look 20 feet away from the monitor.

Ergonomic experts recommend that computer workers exercise at work, as the postural and proximal UE muscles undergo static loading during office computer work. They suggest that computer workers engage in stretching and flexibility exercises. Stretching exercises break cumulative musculoskeletal strain and relieve intervertebral disc pressure. Evidence supports the use of exercise to reduce musculoskeletal discomfort for computer workers. By engaging in exercises, OCWs can reduce perceived discomfort, improve posture, and minimize fatigue. Neck stretch, neck tilt, chin tuck, side stretch, and torso twist are some recommended exercises for the neck and upper body. Shoulder shrugs and rotations, wrist circles, and stretching the wrist flexors/extensors are some recommended exercises for the upper extremities. Hip marching, leg hug, leg extension, and ankle pumps are some of the exercises for the lower body. Stretching exercises also have psychological benefits. Stretching increases mental alertness while decreasing anxiety and stress. Table presents the stretching exercise guidelines.

Key Ergonomic Principles

Adequate clearance: Computer workers must have adequate thigh/knee clearance under their desk.

Adjustability: Computer workers must ensure that their workstation components, including the office chair, are adjustable.

Keep things within reach: Computer workers must keep frequently used items within forearm's distance and occasionally used items within arm's distance.

Minimize direct pressure: Computer workers must avoid resting their forearms/hands/thighs against sharp edges and hard surfaces.

Minimize fatigue: Computer workers must avoid prolonged work and sustained posture.

Work in good posture: Computer workers must be mindful of their posture and assume the ideal work posture at work.

Work at proper heights: Computer workers must adjust the workstation and chair as necessary to work at proper heights.

Stretching Exercise Guidelines

- Stretch the muscles slowly and avoid jerky movements.
- Stretch only to the point of comfortable stretch.
- Feel the stretch.
- Hold the stretch for 5-20 seconds.
- Repeat each stretching exercise 10 times or at least 3–4 times during each episode of exercise.
- Breathe slow, deep, and rhythmic while stretching.

In office work environments, workers start the work day with good posture, but eventually recline or bend throughout the course of the day assuming risky postures and enhancing their risk for WMSDs. Some workers habitually cradle the phone between the neck and shoulder so that their hands are free to type on the keyboard, thereby adding stress and strain to the lateral supporting muscles. Hence, ergonomic experts advise computer workers to be mindful of their posture when performing computer work. To help computer workers to be mindful of their posture, ergonomic experts suggest them to draw an imaginary line that connects the ears, shoulders, and hip joints and advise to maintain the line. Ergonomic experts also show participants examples of good (ideal posture) and bad posture (slouching, keeping feet on chair frame, elevating shoulders, etc.) during ergonomics education sessions.

When delivering ergonomics education, experts emphasize that ergonomics is nothing but a fit between worker and work environment. They offer information on arranging the workstation and adjusting its components. They suggest that computer workers keep work items within reach. It is generally recommended to keep frequently used items within forearm reach and less frequently used items within arm's reach. During ergonomics education sessions, experts show participants how to adjust manual and pneumatic office chairs in addition to other workstation components. When teaching chair adjustment, the emphasis is on properly adjusting the backrest because backrests that are tilted too far forward or backward may contribute to back issues.

Ergonomic Workstation Issues

The problems associated with poor office chairs (fixed backrests/arm rests, too low or too high, too wide or too narrow, and sharp edges), poor workstations (sharp edges), and poor work environments (bad lighting, glare, hot/cold environments) are reviewed during ergonomics education sessions.

Ergonomic Accessories

During ergonomics education sessions, ergonomic experts review various ergonomic accessories and their uses. Keyboard trays, footrests, glare protectors, document holders, large size mouse, hands-free telephones are some of the common accessories that are reviewed. According to ergonomic experts, there is no manufactured ergonomic device because what could be an ergonomically suitable device for a computer worker may not be suitable for another worker due to variations in anthropometric characteristics, nature of work tasks, and workstation arrangements.

Mode of Delivery

Ergonomics education is delivered to computer workers through didactic lectures, PowerPoint presentations, discussions, demonstrations, video, workstation visits, one-to-one consultations, provision of resources, etc.

Materials

Ergonomic checklists, session handouts, brochures, and pictures of ideal work postures and workstations are some of the commonly provided materials at ergonomics education sessions. Product manuals are also used as ergonomics education tools. These manuals describe the product's features/specifications and how to use/operate the product.

Efficacy of Ergonomics Education

Ergonomics education has been found to be an effective strategy. The literature supports the use of ergonomics education to improve computer workers' awareness of risk factor, reduce musculoskeletal injuries, improve workers' posture and workstation layout, increase perceived control over the physical environment, and improve workers' intrinsic motivation to alter posture and behaviors.

Ergonomics education enhances the knowledge about the risk factors associated with WMSDs.

Ergonomics education intervention was reported to be an effective intervention in reducing musculoskeletal pain and discomfort. Bohr stated that those who received ergonomics education reported less pain or discomfort. Ketola et al., through a randomized controlled trial, investigated the efficacy of ergonomics education on workstation changes and musculoskeletal disorders among computer users. Results identified that computer workers who underwent intensive ergonomics and ergonomics education interventions showed less musculoskeletal discomfort at the 2-month follow-up assessment post-intervention.

Several studies found that ergonomics education had a positive influence on the work posture of computer workers. Greene et al. evaluated the effectiveness of an ergonomics training program in computer workers and found that the risk factor exposure of the intervention group participants was significantly reduced. The Researchers asserted that participative training in workstation ergonomics can improve work postures and work practices. Mahmud et al. used a cluster randomized controlled trial design to investigate the effect of ergonomics education in reducing musculoskeletal disorders among computer users. When the outcomes were evaluated post-intervention, experimental group participants who received the ergonomics education demonstrated improved workstation habits and work posture. Through a cross-over trial that investigated the effectiveness of a 2-week workstation ergonomic intervention (consultation and provision of ergonomic accessories), the Researchers found that individualized ergonomic interventions may improve work-related posture and reduce low back pain. Esmaeilzadeh et al. examined the effect of ergonomic intervention on work-related UE MSDs among computer workers and found that the ergonomic training significantly improved participants' posture over 6 months.

Ergonomics education was reported to positively influence worker's behavior. Mani et al. stated that after 6 weeks of intervention, study participants demonstrated healthy work behaviors such as adjusting their workstation, taking rest breaks, and engaging in stretching exercises. Robertson et al. found that increased ergonomics knowledge resulted in behavioral translation. In their study, the experimental group participants demonstrated appropriate behavioral changes to their workstations when compared to the control group participants. The experimental group participants also adjusted their workstation and ergonomic accessories post-intervention. Esmaeilzadeh et al. also found a notable improvement in the workstation layouts of the experimental group participants 6 months post-intervention. Some studies reported less psychosocial stress and an increased sense of control as outcomes of ergonomics education.

Limitations of Ergonomics Education

One of the biggest limitations of any educational intervention is the retention of knowledge and ergonomics education intervention is not an exception. Studies that investigated the effectiveness of ergonomics education measured the outcome at different intervals that ranged from 1 week to as long as 30-month postintervention. Though the majority of the studies reported short-term improvements, evidence is scarce on long-term gains. One study reported improvements in work posture and reduction in pain during short- and long-term follow-ups. However, another study that reported a short-term gain (2-month follow-up), failed to report a similar outcome at the 10-month follow-up. Ongoing ergonomics education sessions at specified intervals and provision of ergonomic resources to employees may overcome the problems with latency of knowledge. Showing pictures that highlight good versus bad postures during ergonomics education sessions and encouraging participants to identify what is wrong and why it is wrong may also help solidify their knowledge.

Another limitation of ergonomics education is the lack of application of the learning.

Simply presenting the ergonomics information to employees does not solve the problem if they do not have the necessary ergonomic accessories. For instance, as a result of ergonomics education, an employee might become cognizant of the need to adjust his/her office chair to minimize the risk of WMSDs, but either does not have an office chair with adjustable components or has a chair with many adjustable features to the extent that he/she does not know how and what to adjust. Participatory ergonomics education, in which the participants are allowed to evaluate and modify their own workstation with the help of an ergonomic expert, may overcome this limitation to an extent.

Though ergonomics education reported to positively influence work behavior in a short term; in most instances, it fails to elicit the motivation required to induce permanent behavior change. Habits are powerful and difficult to overcome. Often, participants of ergonomics education were seen to resort to their old habits of work posture and behaviors. Ongoing participatory ergonomics education at specified intervals may overcome this limitation.

Role of Employers

To prevent WMSDs, employers must work collaboratively with their employees and ergonomic experts. Employers must make every effort to offer ergonomic training programs to their employees, as WMSDs related to computer work are preventable and may save a significant amount of money for them. As stated elsewhere, the economic benefits of ergonomics education programs can be realized by reviewing direct and indirect cost implications on OSHA Safety Pays website. There are myriad ways an employer can offer ergonomics education. One way to deliver ergonomics education is to make ergonomic resources easily accessible. For example, a company's intranet site may have a folder where employees can locate useful ergonomic information and resources. Recorded webinars can also be made available on the company's intranet site. Staff may be sent periodic e-blasts with ergonomic tips.

Role of Employees

The prevalence of WMSDs can only be mitigated if employees act in concert with employers' efforts toward WMSD prevention. Employees should educate themselves on ergonomics, cultivate healthy work behaviors, undergo training programs offered by the employer, and learn to use ergonomic software applications. A variety of public and private web resources offer useful information related to computer ergonomics such as OSHA, Cornell University Ergonomics web, Canadian Center for Occupational Health and Safety, Office-ergo, and Velocity EHS. Software applications such as Eyeleo, Workrave, and PC Work Break remind computer users to take a rest break, stretch break, and eye break during the work day. Some software applications also record the duration of computer usage. Employees may also download and use applications such as ErgoMinder and ergoffice on their personal digital assistants (smart phones/tablets) to cultivate effective work behaviors.

MACROERGONOMICS

Macroergonomics, is the field of science that concentrates on designing overall work systems (WS) by providing the knowledge and methods necessary for the improvement of work systems and, thus, developing the effectiveness and performance of companies.

The process typically involves designing, analysing, developing, and improving work systems. Macro-level problems cannot be solved by micro-level solutions, but micro-level problems can be solved with macro-level solutions.

In contrast with (micro)ergonomics, which deals with human-machine, human-task, human-interface, usability, and safety-type issues in the workplace, macroergonomics is a system-level approach to designing the interaction between humans and technology and to understanding how activities and processes are organized to produce products and services for customers.

Macroergonomics aims at a holistic understanding of how work is designed from the top-down, in such a way that macroergonomic design is considered first, work system design second, and microergonomic design last. The concept of socio-technical systems (STS) in organisational development provides a theoretical foundation for macroergonomics. STS explores how people and technology interact in the workplace.

The more complex work systems become, the more important it is to understand the interaction between humans and technology. The main concepts of STS are humans, tasks, structure, technology (hardware and software), and processes, as well as regulations, policies, and culture. According to macroergonomics, socio-technical work systems consist of five elements:

- Technology is needed to carry out the goals set for the work system. With the help of technology, tasks and problems can be solved.
- People (personnel) occupy a core role in work systems, since only people can achieve goals with the help of technology. Important aspects regarding people include competence, demographics, psychosocial factors, and teams.
- Organisational design specifies how technology and people are organised and managed together in work systems. Contemporary areas include lean processes and digitalisation.
- The external environment is something that cannot be influenced from inside work systems.
- The internal environment includes considerations such as the psychosocial and physical environment and cultures that are not part of the system design.

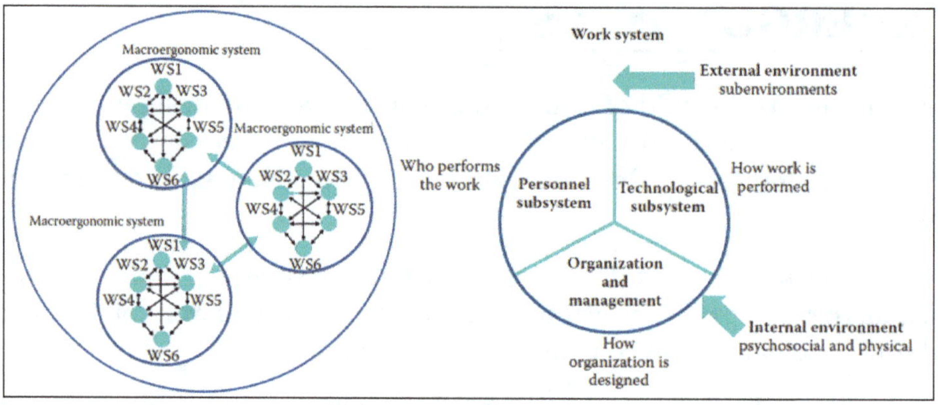

Different human factors and ergonomic theories and methods can be applied to various levels of the macroergonomic design process. A macroergonomic system may include several interconnected work systems. Interfaces are areas in which interactions between humans and machines and software occur. Interfaces are typically designed to support goal-oriented human being and activity.

Fundamental Principles of Macroergonomics

Macroergonomics, also known as organizational ergonomics, shares many of the principles of HFE at large:

- It takes a systems approach: Performance results from interactions in a sociotechnical system, of which the person is one component.
- It is design driven: Performance is improved by designing and redesigning systems to accommodate and support humans' capabilities and activities.
- It has a dual goal of improving performance and wellbeing: Outcomes to balance include "productivity, efficiency, effectiveness, quality, innovativeness, flexibility, systems safety and security, reliability, sustainability, health and safety, satisfaction, pleasure, learning, and personal development".

The systems perspective includes the concept of interactions between components of the system. Wilson argued that expertise in assessing and designing these interactions is a unique competence of the HFE discipline and Hendrick noted that a strength of macroergonomics is understanding these interactions in the context of a broader sociotechnical system, such as an organization or a community. The definition of sociotechnical systems varies from model to model, yet it is noteworthy that several models of systems include high-level community, political, regulatory, and sociocultural factors. For instance, in depicting the healthcare system, Karsh et al depicted people nested in work units, nested in organizations, nested in an external environment of industry and workforce factors and extra-organizational rules, standards, legislation, and enforcement. Karsh and colleagues' model and others like it (e.g., Moray) illustrate another fundamental principle of macroergonomics, which can be summarized as "context matters": lower-level systems are nested in and shaped by higher-level systems. Karsh wrote about the cross-level effects that describe the influence of context on a system and vice versa. The concepts of nesting and cross-level effects actually reveal a subtle point about the definition of macroergonomics: it is not concerned purely with high-level factors such as organizational safety culture but rather with multiple factors including high-level ones and the interactions within and between these multiple layers.

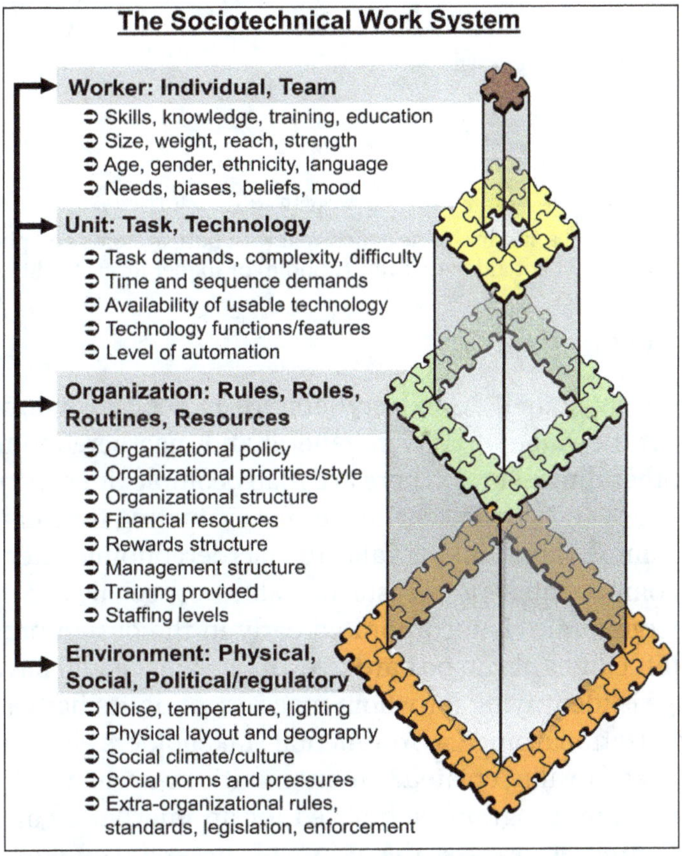

Depiction of the multiple-level sociotechnical work system.

Wilson argues that, when context is considered, the breadth and complexity of most systems of interest to HFE professionals cannot be replicated in the laboratory. Consistent with this, it is fair to say that most macroergonomic endeavors take place in the field of practice, where the complexity of systems is preserved and even embraced by researchers or practitioners. Furthermore, macroergonomic research and practice generally follows the principle of "multiple": using multiple methods including qualitative and quantitative ones, considering multiple levels of analysis, examining multiple actors and their multiple perspectives, designing a system for multiple users and tasks, measuring at multiple time points, and drawing on multiple disciplines. Finally, macroergonomics gives due concern to how HFE and other innovations are both designed and implemented; this is observed in the subdiscipline's development of participatory ergonomics approach.

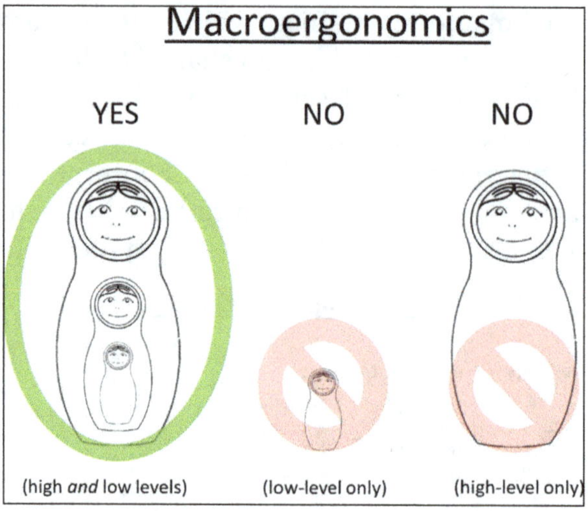

Macroergonomics as a subdiscipline concerned with both systems and phenomena across levels (left) not at lower levels (middle) or higher levels (right) alone.

Value of Macroergonomics

Hal Hendrick famously stated, "Good ergonomics is good economics." Others have urged evaluations of the value of HFE in general and macroergonomics in particular, on economic and other dimensions. There are many complexities to measuring the value of macroergonomics and specific challenges for evaluating the financial cost-benefit. Among them are defining value, linking value to macroergonomic interventions and specific intervention components, and measuring value—especially across settings. Moreover, when macroergonomics is incorporated early in the design process to eliminate future hazards or difficulties, it can be hard to estimate what could have gone wrong. An additional challenge is identifying for whom macroergonomics has value. For example, are employee, organizational, and environmental stakeholders equal recipients of value and at whose expense is value created? In an ambitious evaluation of the 3M Corporation's HFE intervention programs submitted for an internal ergonomics innovation award, Larson et al attempt to assess the nature of successful ergonomic interventions. They conclude that ergonomic interventions appear associated with both operational efficiency and WMSD reduction. This is a promising evaluation that bears repeating.

It is important to demonstrate and document value to key stakeholders, especially for a discipline that may not be a household name. Even for a well-publicized and large-scale national macroergonomic program, adoption and acceptance are not guaranteed and depend on stakeholder perceptions of the programs usefulness, and cost – i.e., value.

Macroergonomic Methods and Approaches

Methods and measures should be at least as diverse and complex as the phenomena they attempt to address. Having described the broad scope of macroergonomic and the complex sociotechnical systems where marcroergonomic phenomena occur, it is no surprise that macroergonomic methods are diverse, evolving, draw on many other fields of science and practice, and are often combined in a given project. Macroergonomic methods also range from broad approaches such as participatory ergonomics to step-by-step procedures for analyzing the structures and processes of work systems. Fray et al. use the Safety Culture Survey, developed by safety scientists. Weidman et al. leverage multiple useful theories and a standard scale development process to produce a measurement tool of large potential value for macroergonomics. Other papers describe the use of methods and approaches originating in macroergonomics, such as the Ergonomic Work Analysis in Sznelwar and Hubault, the mesoergonomic paradigm and the Tool for Risks Outstanding in Patient Handling Interventions (TROPHI) in Fray et al. or the Ergonomics Job Analysis (EJA) and Engineering Design Criteria (EDC) tools used in the 3M Corporation's risk reduction program in Larson et al.

We encourage both approaches: adapting what exists and developing and testing new methods, tools, and theories. Cognitive work analysis and many forms of cognitive task analysis are already well suited to macroergonomic pursuits. Other useful approaches are being newly developed, such as the Prevention by Design approach described by Weidman et al. and the Intervention Design and Analysis Scorecard (IDEAS). Future macroergonomic methods could focus on product design and evaluation, teamwork, virtual environments, and adaptive human activity.

Implementing macroergonomic methods, whatever their origin, can be its own challenge. In the field, even basic techniques such as audio or videorecording can be difficult or impossible. A decade ago, Karsh reflected on the challenges of conducting macroergonomic research in the field, the politics and social issues related to these studies, and the potential disruptiveness. He likened a macroergonomic project to any other change process, even when no intervention is introduced. Karsh concluded that if macroergonomic research is an organizational change, it can be managed as an organizational change. Thereafter, Karsh and colleagues described the principles of sociotechnical change management and practical considerations for ensuring the success of a macroergonomic research project. The 'change management framework for macroergonomic field research' has since been used to describe the challenges of conducting macroergonomic research in people's homes and communities, as opposed to institutional settings. Other models can be helpful to think about how macroergonomics and macroergonomic projects are innovations that must be diffused, accepted, and sustained.

ACTIVITY-CENTERED ERGONOMICS

The negative consequences of the accelerated changes that mark the world of goods and services production have been contributing decisively to investment in Quality of Working Life (QWL) in organizations. A global characterization of the limits of assistance-based approaches to QWL - of an individual, assistive, and hegemonic nature - provides the basis of reflection for thematic study in the field of Activity-centered Ergonomics Applied to Quality of Working Life. Effective and sustainable intervention in the field of QWL involves removing and mitigating the root causes of disaffection among workers toward conditions, the organization, and socio-professional workplace relations, and in particular, reversing the dominant paradigm of the "individual as an adjustment variable" in favor of the criteria of Ergonomics to "adapt the work to the human being." Limits and challenges are also presented for the consolidation of a theoretical-methodological approach of Activity-centered Ergonomics aimed at the Quality of Working Life.

Different actors working on organisations aligned with sustainability take into account aspects pertaining to environmental, economic, and social dimensions. This implies a complex system-of-systems approach that particularly involves social aspects. In this sense, according to both activity-centred ergonomics and the psychodynamics of work point of view, work activity can be interpreted in terms of human action, from the standpoint of sustainability for the individual as well as for collective life inside and outside the companies. This means work activity should be highlighted as vital not only for quality and productivity but also to workers themselves, including, ultimately, the development of society and culture. However, even organisations that claim to regard work activity as something that should be designed to provide meaning and purpose that helps to build both individuals' mental health and identity, these elements are still poorly developed in practice corporate actors perceived and implemented relevant issues related to internal social corporate sustainability (e.g. worker's health) and also the relationships between work activity and corporate sustainability.

Ergonomics Analysis of Work

Ergonomic analysis of work (EAW) is the main tool of the activity-centered ergonomic intervention. It can help to solve several problems related to working conditions or the design of tools and equipment.

- Aspects of health in work:
    - On the physical health including the musculoskeletal disorder (MSD) affecting 12 to 14% of employees.
    - On the mental health risks due to particular psycho-social (in stress) can cause anxiety-depressive syndromes (about 8% of employees).
- Aspects of performance:
    - Improving productivity.
    - Improving quality.

EAW - A Located Analysis

It is with the demand analysis and hypothesis he has made during the pre-diagnosis that the ergonomist will be able to choose situations to consider:

- Ensure sufficient mastery of technical data concerning the work situation.
- Build reference tools for description and interpretation of data.
- Give him a medium for demonstration and communication.

Different Elements of Influence on Work

The work activity is influenced by a multitude of facets. The ergonomist must rely on these aspects and compare the actual work for generating insights relevant to the problems posed:

- The technical process: These are views which focus on flows and processing steps of a product or information.
- The tools and media: An analysis of the means available to employees to obtain or receive information and act on the process to better prepare some investigations.
- The relationship between the variables of a device: In explanation with the operator or guidance, it is possible that reflected different variables to the settings or status of the device technology (e.g. quality). It is then possible to relate with each other.
- Procedures: The sequences of a process as provided corresponds only very rarely that transactions made by employees.
- Dependencies and stops time: The work activity may enroll in a timeframe more or less structured by the process, by advancing the work of other employees, or by events outside the company.
- The layout of the technical device: Often, initial plans of arrangement are now outdated. Indeed, subsequent implementations of equipment have been made.

Choice of the Situations to Analyze

It is rather difficult to extract a maxim or a rule in the choose of a situation that the ergonomist will do. The criteria he will use depending on the problem and the structure of the company. But it may be, for example, situations:

- Where complaints are most numerous?

- Where the consequences are more serious?
- Where the range of problems is the widest?
- Playing a central role in the functioning of the company.
- To be processing more or less long term.

Analysis by the Activity

At first glance, each is tempted by the establishment of relations of direct causation between working conditions and health consequences or effectiveness. A noisy situation makes deaf, carrying heavy loads of produce musculoskeletal disorder, bad lighting, eyestrain, etc. Unfortunately, this approach has important limitations: protection against noise may prohibit access to the machine, etc.

In fact, this approach neglects the fact that these relations necessarily pass through the activity of the employee. Indeed, it makes compromises with respect to constraints (it does not have them) to achieve the goals that are set and to limit the inconvenience caused by the tasks. For this reason, the ergonomist must focus its ergonomic analysis of work activity: it is in and by the activity of the operator in creating the effects of working conditions.

The role, in this context, analysis of the activity is not an evaluation (the workload for example) but the description and explanation of the mechanisms involved.

Tools Available to the Ergonomist

Observation

The observation is a specific feature in the Ergonomic analysis of work compared to other methods. This is to focus on the work as directed, whereas other approaches rely on "representations". Observation can be carried out openly or by focusing on the collection of certain categories of information with specific goals (we call then systematic observation).

- Broad observables categories: Travel, The direction of regards, Communications, Postures, The actions taken or information, Comments on the technical system and context, The collective.
- Technical statement, there exist a variety of techniques to conduct surveys. The choice is made by the ergonomist in the constraints and circumstances.

Verbalizations

To understand the activity, working conditions and their consequences, the verbalization of the employee is essential because: Activity can be reduced to what is observable;

The comments and actions take place at one moment, we must re-situate more broadly; The consequences of the activity are not all apparent.

However, there are limits to the verbalization to be taken into account:

- The employee described the work and its consequences in terms of what it believes to be the goals and interests of the speaker.
- The routine operations or learning old are not always mentioned spontaneously.
- Some aspects of the activities lend themselves well to verbal expression.

PARTICIPATORY ERGONOMICS

Participatory ergonomics means actively involving workers in developing and implementing workplace changes which will improve productivity and reduce risks to safety and health - or the "involvement of people in planning and controlling a significant amount of their own work activities, with sufficient knowledge and power to influence both processes and outcomes to achieve desirable goals". The underpinning assumptions are that: workers are the experts; and, given appropriate knowledge, skills, tools, facilitation, resources and encouragement, they are best placed to identify and analyse problems, and to develop and implement solutions which will be both effective in reducing injury risks and improving productivity and be acceptable to those effected. There are many types of participation, including consultative or representative participation where users or elected representatives respectively express ideas or opinions, and management makes decisions. We are more concerned with direct participation in which workers have some degree of influence over the decisions regarding workplace changes.

According to Noro, the term "participatory ergonomics" was coined in 1984, however it's antecedents are found in the management practices of quality circles and industrial democracy. A participatory ergonomics program typically employs one or more teams assembled for the purpose of improving the design of work, and the common element is to ensure utilisation of the expert knowledge that workers have of their own tasks by involving the workers, and others potentially affected by proposed changes. Although such programs have typically been primarily focused on reducing musculoskeletal injuries, participatory ergonomics programs have also explicitly aimed to create more human-centered work, to improve organisational climate, or been used as a framework for health promotion. Participatory ergonomics may be considered to be a method of work system design and thus, fundamentally, a macroergonomics technique.

Participatory ergonomics programs have been implemented across a large range of industries and organisations, including mining, domestic and civil construction, and office environments as well as diverse small businesses; newspapers, health care institutions and numerous manufacturing sites.

Perhaps as a consequence of the diverse settings in which programs have been implemented and the need for programs to "fit" each organisation or situation there are many variations in the program characteristics, such as the degree and nature of participation, extent of expert facilitation and assistance provided, the nature and extent of training provided to teams (in ergonomics methods and team work), and the tools employed to assist teams identify issues and develop solutions.

A conceptual framework for defining the range of variations found in participatory ergonomics programs has been proposed by Haines et al. The dimensions defined are:

- Location of decision making power: Whether retained by management and informed by consultation with individual workers or groups, or delegated to the workers.
- Mix of participants formed for the interventions: Front-line staff only, or including technical staff, middle management and senior management.
- Remit: That is, the extent of the participants' involvement in setting up and monitoring of the participatory ergonomics process, the identification of problems to be addressed, and the generation, evaluation and implementation of solutions.
- Role of 'ergonomics specialists': Acknowledged as potentially changing and evolving over time, ranging from being a facilitator or leader, trainer, expert team member, or available for consultation as required (or not involved).
- Nature of worker involvement: Varying from direct face-to-face involvement of all affected workers to representative participation of selected workers.
- Focus: Whether aimed at the level of design of tasks undertaken by individuals or teams, or broader work organisation issues or policies.
- Level of influence: Variations in the level of the organisation at which the intervention takes place, whether at the level of the work team or department, through to the entire organisation, or indeed, across an industry.
- Requirement: That is, whether the participation is undertaken by volunteers, or an expected part of a job role, noting that this may vary across group members.
- Permanence of the intervention: Ranging from a temporary program introduced as means of solving a particular problem, to programs intended to be permanently integrated into the ongoing continuous improvement activities of the organisation.

Participatory ergonomics programs may differ in terms of the complexity of the structures in which the activities are embedded. While a single layer structure involving work group/s only might be involved, more complex structures including, for example, a second layer of "steering committee" might well oversee the activities of multiple working groups; and more layers are also possible in large multi-site organisations.

The effectiveness of a participatory ergonomics intervention may well vary as a function of different combinations of these dimensions. The characteristics and level of commitment of the organisations in which such programs are implemented also varies considerably, and these factors are also very likely to influence the outcomes of such programs.

Effectiveness of Participatory Ergonomics Programs

Participative ergonomics is reported to have a range of benefits in addition to reduction in musculoskeletal injury risks, such as improved flow of useful information within an organisation, an improvement in the meaningfulness of work, more rapid technological and organisational change, and enhanced performance. As well as developing more effective solutions, the use of participative ergonomics techniques to derive solutions is believed to result in greater "ownership" by those affected, leading to greater commitment to the changes being implemented.

Psychosocial characteristics of work-places such as the workplace culture; high workloads; lack of control; high levels of interpersonal conflict; and poor change management both impact on the potential success of a participatory ergonomics intervention and may be influenced by such an intervention. A workplace with an existing culture of distrust and adversarial industrial relations, and without any history of worker involvement in decision making, is unlikely to be a fertile ground for participatory approaches to flourish without first addressing these issues. However, in absence of such a adverse context, the impact of a participatory ergonomics program in which management and workers work together to improve workplace conditions has potential to further improve the organisational culture and other aspects of the psychosocial work environment.

The economic impact of workplace ergonomic interventions (regardless of the process by which such interventions were devised) found the strength of the evidence to vary from strong in the manufacturing and warehousing sector, moderate in the administrative and support services sector, and health care sectors, and limited in the transportation industry. The implementation of a participatory ergonomics program at a Brazilian furniture manufacturer was report to lead to a 46% productivity increase attributable to a combination of reducing unnecessary load handling, waiting and transportation; and reduction in manufacturing time. Nagamachi reported similarly large productivity improvements in manufacturing case studies while Motamedzade et al. reported more modest productivity improvements (5% waste reduction, 8% reduction in rework) in a manufacturing context as consequence of introducing a participatory ergonomics program. Reynolds et al. reported a 17% increase in hourly earnings associated with changes made to a work-station at an apparel manufacturer.

While some research has demonstrated significant effects of implementing a participatory ergonomics program on physical risk factors associated with manual tasks most evaluations have focused on direct health effects. The effect of participatory ergonomics programs on musculoskeletal health have been the subject of three systematic reviews. The outcomes of individual evaluations are mixed. Silverstein and Clark noted this variability, concluding that participatory ergonomics programs were "often, but not always successful". Cole et al. reviewed 10 evaluations of the health effects of participatory ergonomics programs, concluding that the studies provided limited evidence that participatory ergonomics programs can have a positive impact on musculoskeletal injury symptoms and compensation costs. More encouragingly, Rivilis et al. concluded that the "12 studies that were rated as 'medium' or higher provided partial to moderate evidence that PE interventions have a positive impact on: musculoskeletal symptoms, reducing injuries and workers' compensation claims, and a reduction in lost days from work or sickness absence."

For example, Haukka et al. found no systematic effects of a participative ergonomics program involving six 3 h workshops at 119 Finnish kitchens, despite reporting the implementation of 402 ergonomic changes. Cole et al. reported a multiple case study involving programs of varying details across four production contexts. Production pressures were encountered as a barrier at each site and management commitment varied. Although changes were introduced at each site, no statistically significant effect on health outcomes could be detected. Driessen et al. reported that an intervention involving a single six hour meeting with 19 working groups in randomly assigned departments across four Dutch companies in diverse industries did not result in subsequently reduced low-back or neck discomfort compared to a control group of 18 departments, although a significant effect on recovery from back pain was noted. Dale et al. evaluated the implementation of a participatory ergonomics program consisting of six 10 min tool box talks in small construction firms. Issues with commitment to the program were encountered and while worker knowledge improved and changes to work practices and tools occurred, no changes in musculoskeletal symptoms were observed.

However, Rivilis et al. reported positive health effects of implementing a "ergonomic change team" including worker and management representatives, and an ergonomics facilitator, at one courier company depot compared with a referent depot. The team received four, 6 h training sessions covering ergonomics principles and tools required to develop and evaluate solutions. The team met weekly for seven months, and twice per month for the following seven months. Fourteen changes at the intervention depot were made during this period including new tools, workstation modifications and reduced conveyor speeds, while no changes were made at the referent depot.

Cantley et al. similarly reported positive outcomes from a 6 year evaluation of a large scale participatory ergonomics process at a multi-site aluminium manufacturer. Control measure implementation targets were set by senior management and the evaluation noted 204 control measures implemented across 123 jobs at 17 study sites, effecting the work of 14,540 workers. Jobs in which control measures were introduced were associated with significantly lower musculoskeletal injury risk and the authors concluded that the study "provides evidence that a systematic approach to ergonomic hazard identification, quantification and control implementation, in conjunction with requirements to establish an ergonomic process at each manufacturing plant, may be effective in reducing risk of MSD and acute injury outcomes among workers in targeted jobs".

The mixed nature of health effect evaluations is perhaps unsurprising given the diversity of program designs and the variety of organisational characteristics and contexts in which program implementation has been attempted. It is reasonable to conclude that, while participatory ergonomics programs have potential to reduce the incidence of musculoskeletal disorders, there are many potential barriers and success has not always been achieved. An examination of these potential barriers, and the lessons learned during the implementation of such programs, yields insights of value for the implementation of future programs.

SOFT ERGONOMICS

Soft Ergonomics is the study of designing virtual interfaces that cater towards the wellness of the human body, its emotional and cognitive abilities.

Soft Ergonomics is a subset of Ergonomics and Human Factors Engineering, a larger body of the study of human abilities for designing equipment and devices that fit the human body. Soft Ergonomics can be thus defined as the ability of any virtual interface(computer application, website, ATM options, parking meter etc.) to make it comfortable for the user to use the interface while working on the user's request.

Soft Ergonomics only deals with virtual interfaces. It tries to find a compromise between user expectations, system workflow and aesthetics. Users from various cultural and technological background are exposed to a common interface. The interface developer seeks to ensure that the interface does not harm the user psychologically, physiologically or emotionally. Soft Ergonomics generally takes into account the following human factors when building a virtual interface:

- Physical Limitations: Not all who use a virtual interface are physically equal. If the designed interface only caters to right-handed individuals, or people within a certain height range then the interface might need a redesign. One of the leading discussion is with respect to visually impaired users.
- Cognitive Abilities: If the product (software application, website) is designed for any casual user, then the designer should not expect that all users would be experts, with high cognitive abilities. The usage of the application should not need the user to know a lot of information prior to using the interface. For example, using an automated teller machine can require memorizing a pin number but not the account number.
- Emotional Needs: The interface should be 'designed for the occasion' or context. It should not leave the user confused, either how to start using the interface or what to do when an error occurs. Confusion leads to frustration, which eventually builds stress in the body causing long term emotional damage.

Criteria for Soft Ergonomics

The following lists(non-exhaustive) some of the most common criteria for evaluating soft ergonomics:

- Consistency: The design should be consistent across the entire application. Consistent sequence of actions, identical terminologies and platform conventions should be followed throughout the application.
- Efficiency: The virtual interface should allow efficient use of user's time. The screens should load and display content within acceptable amount of time. The more than expected time a user has to wait; more stress is built into the human body causing long term damage. The interface should also have functionality for advanced users. While being non-obtrusive to novice users, accelerators or shortcuts should be available for experienced users.
- Design: The system should preferably have minimalistic and aesthetically pleasing design. While this has no direct relation to the product or task in hand, minimalistic design help user easily consume the data and hence there is less stress on the human mind and aesthetically pleasing design increases the 'feel good' factor in the user. Following the principles of contrast, repetition, alignment and proximity will also help as they come naturally to humans.
- Memory: User's memory load should be minimized. All information that a user needs from the application to perform a task should be presented or easily retrievable by the user.
- Context Help: While the 'Help' menu and options should be non-obstructive to the user, context help should be always available to the user.

FUNDAMENTAL ERGONOMIC PRINCIPLES FOR BETTER WORK PERFORMANCE

Maintain Neutral Posture

Neutral postures are postures where the body is aligned and balanced while sitting or standing, placing minimal stress on the body and keeping joints aligned.

Neutral postures minimize the stress applied to muscles, tendons, nerves and bones and allows for maximum control and force production.

The opposite of a neutral posture is an "awkward posture." Awkward postures move away from the neutral posture toward the extremes in range of motion. This puts more stress on the worker's musculoskeletal system, is a contributing risk factor for Musculoskeletal Disorders (MSDs), and should be avoided.

Following are examples of Neutral vs. Awkward postures for the wrist, elbow, shoulder and back. When you put on your "ergo eyes", you'll immediately begin to notice when workers are in awkward postures and when they are maintaining a neutral posture.

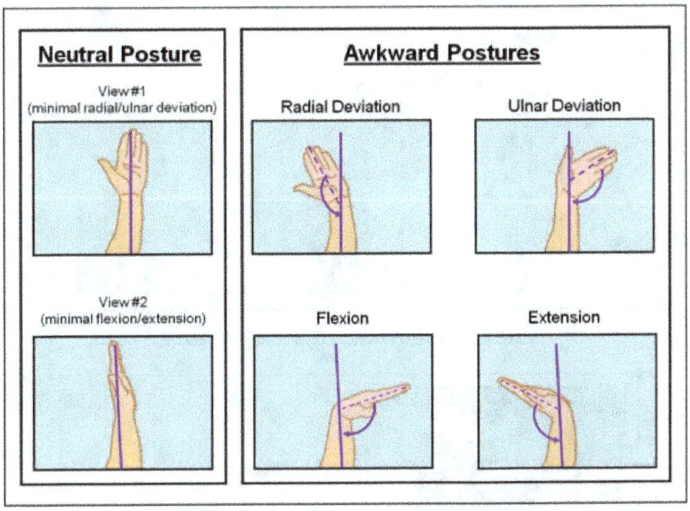

Neutral and awkward wrist postures.

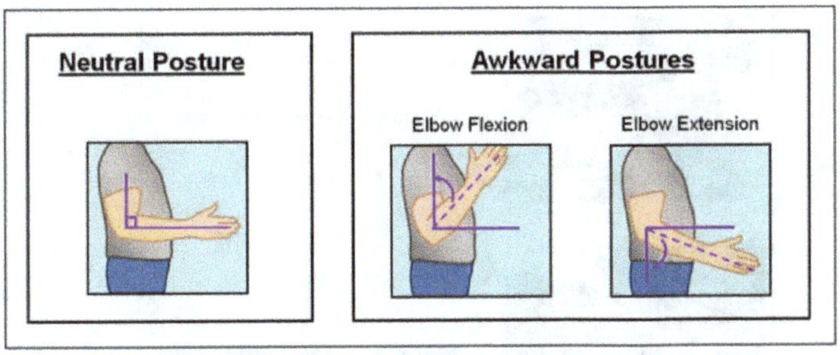

Neutral and awkward elbow postures.

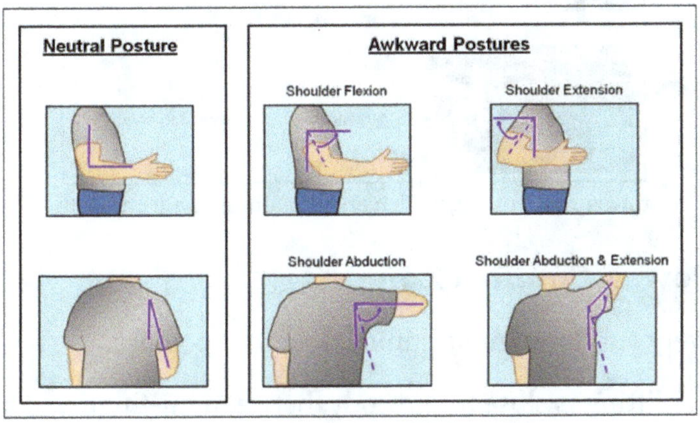

Neutral and awkward shoulder postures.

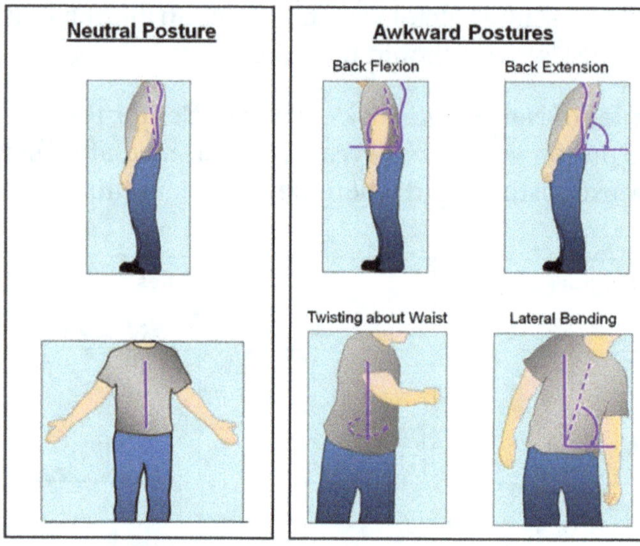

Neutral and awkward back postures.

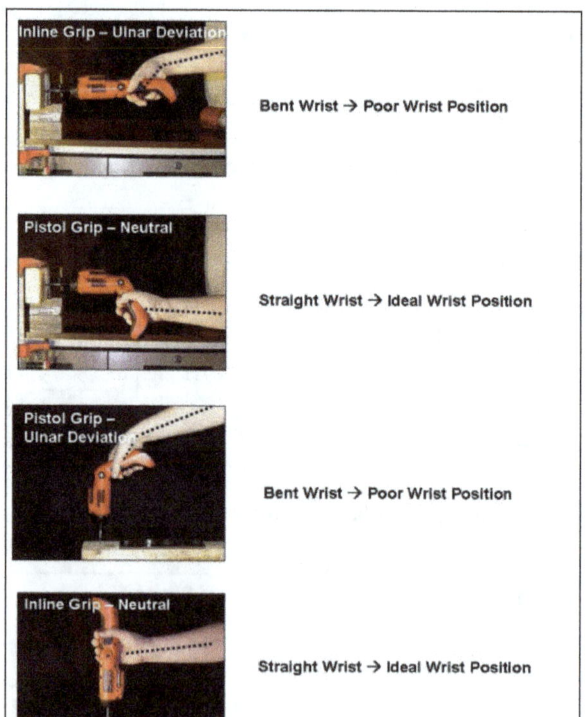

Pistol grip vs. inline grip drivers to maintain neutral posture.

Work in the Power/Comfort Zone

This principle is very similar to maintaining a neutral posture.

The power zone for lifting is close to the body, between mi-thigh and mid-chest height. This zone is where the arms and back can lift the most with the least amount of effort.

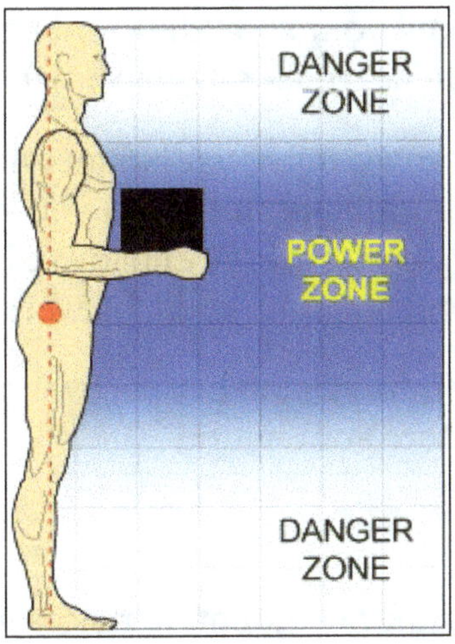

This can also be called the "hand shake zone" or "comfort zone." The principle here is that if you can "shake hands with your work", you are minimizing excessive reach and maintaining a neutral posture.

Working from the power/comfort/handshake zone ensures that you are working from proper heights and reaches, which reduces MSD risk factors and allows for more efficient and pain-free work.

Now when you notice workers who are working with extended reaches and at improper heights, you'll know they are outside their comfort zone and risk factors are present.

Allow for Movement and Stretching

The musculoskeletal system is often referred to as the human body's movement system, and it is designed to move.

Working for long periods of time in a static position will cause your body to fatigue. This is what is known as static load.

For example:

- Raise your hands over your head for the next 30 minutes.
- Remain standing in the same position for the next 8 hours.
- Write with a pencil for 60 minutes straight.

If you do those things, you will experience static load. The first few seconds or minutes don't seem too bad, but the cumulative effect of holding these seemingly stress-free positions over time will cause fatigue and discomfort.

Now, what is the first thing you will naturally do once you when you are finished with these tasks?

You will stretch: You'll stretch out your shoulders and back. You'll stretch out your legs and maybe do some squats. You'll stretch out your fingers and wrist.

Stretching reduces fatigue, improves muscular balance and posture and improves muscle coordination. Everyone is an athlete in life, so you need to prepare your body for work by warming up to improve performance and lower injury risk. A warm-up stretching regimen is a great way to prepare your body for work.

It is also beneficial to take periodic stretch breaks over the course of your work day to get your blood moving and restore your energy.

Reduce Excessive Force

Excessive force is one of the primary ergonomic risk factors. Many work tasks require high force loads on the human body. Muscle effort increases in response to high force requirements which increases fatigue and risk of an MSD.

There are numerous conditions that affect force, but the idea is to recognize when a job or task requires excessive force and then find ways to reduce that force.

Eliminating excessive force requirements will reduce worker fatigue and the risk of MSD formation in most workers. Using mechanical assists, counter balance systems, adjustable height lift tables and workstations, powered equipment and ergonomic tools will reduce work effort and muscle exertions.

Reduce Excessive Motions

Repetitive motion is another one of the primary ergonomic risk factors. Many work tasks and cycles are repetitive in nature, and are frequently controlled by hourly or daily production targets and work processes. High task repetition, when combined with other risks factors such high force and awkward postures, can contribute to the formation of MSD. A job is considered highly repetitive if the cycle time is 30 seconds or less.

Excessive or unnecessary motions should be reduced if at all possible. In situations where this is not possible, it is important to eliminate excessive force requirements and awkward postures.

Other control methods to consider are Job enlargement, job rotation and counteractive stretch breaks.

Minimize Contact Stress

Contact stress results from continuous contact or rubbing between hard or sharp objects/surfaces and sensitive body tissue, such as soft tissue of the fingers, palms, thighs and feet. This contact creates localized pressure for a small area of the body, which can inhibit blood, nerve function, or movement of tendons and muscles.

Examples of contact stress include resting wrists on the sharp edge of a desk or workstation while performing tasks, pressing of tool handles into the palms, especially when they cannot be put down, tasks that require hand hammering, and sitting without adequate space for the knees.

Reduce Excessive Vibration

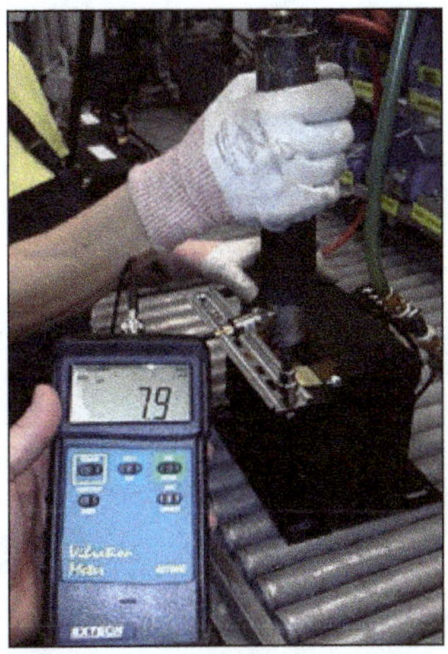

Multiple studies have shown that regular and frequent exposure to vibration can lead to permanent adverse health effects, which are most likely to occur when contact with a vibrating tool or work process is a regular and significant part of a person's job.

Hand-arm vibration can cause a range of conditions collectively known as hand-arm vibration syndrome (HAVS), as well as specific diseases such as white finger or Raynaud's syndrome, carpel tunnel syndrome and tendinitis. Vibration syndrome has adverse circulatory and neural effects in the fingers. The signs and symptoms include numbness, pain, and blanching (turning pale and ashen).

Provide Adequate Lighting

Poor lighting is a common problem in the workplace that can affect a worker's comfort level and performance. Too much or too little light makes work difficult.

Dimly lit work areas and glare can cause eye fatigue and headaches and improperly lit areas put workers at greater risk for all types of injuries.

Providing workers with adjustable task lighting is often a simple solution to lighting problems. At a computer workstation, take steps to control screen glare, and make sure that the monitor is not placed in front of a window or a bright background.

References

- What-is-ergonomics: ergonomics.com.au, Retrieved 20 July, 2020

- What-is-human-factors, humanfactorshiyuwang: sites.tufts.edu, Retrieved 08 March, 2020
- What-is-macroergonomics: ergonomicsblog.uk, Retrieved 14 August, 2020
- Fundamental-ergonomic-principles: ergo-plus.com, Retrieved 10 May, 2020
- Macroergonomics: Theory, methods and applications. Mahwah, NJ: Lawrence Erlbaum Associates; 2002. pp. 24–44

2

Physical Ergonomics

Physical ergonomics deals with the physical activities that are related to human anatomical, physiological, anthropometric, and biomechanical characteristics. Some of the equipment used under it are ergonomic keyboard, datahand, velotype, microwriter, frogPad, etc. This chapter has been carefully written to provide an easy understanding of physical ergonomics.

Physical ergonomics deals with the physical load on the human body when performing activities like work, sports, jobs at home or dealing with products. With regard to the exposure to physical loads and its potential effects on the human body, the presented framework is helpful.

Ergonomics (or human factors) is the scientific discipline concerned with the understanding of the interactions among humans and other elements of a system, and the profession that applies theoretical principles, data and methods to design in order to optimize human well-being and overall system performance (definition International Ergonomics Association (IEA). Within this discipline or profession, physical ergonomics is regarded as one of the domains of specialization, beside organizational ergonomics, and cognitive ergonomics.

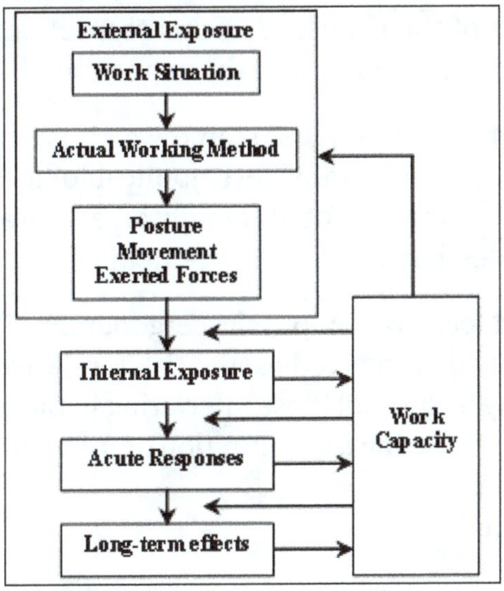

The exposure to physical loads and irs short term and long term effects.

Within the discipline of ergonomics, physical ergonomics is regarded as one of the domains of specialisation, beside organisational ergonomics and cognitive ergonomics. Although the primary focus can be on any one of these, interventions should pay attention to all three aspects and their interactions.

Physical ergonomics deals with the physical load on the human body. With regard to the exposure to physical loads and its potential effects on the human body, the presented framework is helpful. This framework distinguishes external and internal exposures. The human at work is (externally) exposed to a work situation (work demands, working environment) and working methods (the work activities to be performed). These result in the adoption of specific human body postures and the execution of movements, as well as some external forces on the human body. Furthermore, the exposure to posture, movement and force leads to the exposure to internal forces on body structures and to elevated levels of energy expenditure (i.e. internal exposure). Mechanical and physiological responses occur in the short term (i.e. acute responses). Musculoskeletal disorders are among the potential longer term effects that follow acute responses. Musculoskeletal disorders are among the potential longer term effects that follow acute responses. The responses and depend also on the individual worker's capacities (including body dimensions, physical fitness, condition).

Next to health protection, ergonomics focuses on system performance. In today's ergonomics it is obvious that the aims for health protection and enhanced system performance can very well be achieved together.

Risk Assessment

Risk assessment and prevention of risks are among the main issues in physical ergonomics. Risk assessment is about the assessment of the risks for developing a specific type of musculoskeletal disorders associated with the exposure to a specific type physical load. Relevant aspects of the exposure in this respect are: the level or intensity of the exposure duration and the frequency of the exposure.

Of course, risk assessment is only the first step towards good working conditions. The assessment needs to be evaluated and, where applicable, in following steps, improvements developed, tested and implemented. Finally an end evaluation should prove that the enhanced situation indeed meets the requirements.

Prevention is another main focus within physical ergonomics. It entails the definition and implementation of measures that may reduce the risk for developing musculoskeletal disorders. These measures may include all those interfering in the work situation and working methods that potentially decrease the level, duration or frequency of the external exposure.

Types of Physical Load

Framework Directive 89/391 offers a long list of hazards and risks that may occur in occupational settings. Here we address the four major types of physical load, in perspective of prevalence of risks in the contemporary:

- Heavy work.
- Repetitive work.
- Static work.
- Sedentary work.

For each of these, we systematically address the potential risks, the risk assessment methods, and preventive measures.

Heavy Work

Scope and Prevalence

Heavy work includes the type of work that is characterized by high external forces on the body. These may result from:

- Lifting of heavy loads.
- Carrying of heavy loads.
- Pushing of loads.
- Pulling of loads.

Despite the increased mechanization and automation in many sectors of industry, the proportion of workers exposed to heavy work has remained relatively stable over the past decennia. In the Netherlands the percentage of workers exposed to heavy work is about 20%. Across Europe, carrying or moving heavy loads is part of the work of 25-40% of the workers (Eurofound, data can be found for each country. In industrially developing countries that percentage may be much higher. Sectors with high incidences of heavy work are: nursing, construction, metal, agriculture, transport and logistics.

Risk

There is strong evidence that the frequent lifting of heavy loads is related to the occurrence of lower back pain. Many epidemiological studies have investigated this relationship. Estimates for the relative risk associated with occupational lifting and lower back injury ranges from 1.3 to 4.2. It was also established that the risk of developing injury increases with the frequency of lifting.

However, there is no evidence that the frequent pushing and pulling of loads is related to the occurrence of lower back pain. Some studies suggest a relationship of pulling/pushing with shoulder complains, but the number of these studies is quite limited.

Risk Assessment Method

The risk associated with the lifting of loads depends on several factors, among others the weight of the load, the vertical travel distance, the horizontal distance between the load and the body, and the frequency of lifting. These risk factors are addressed in the so-called NIOSH equation which can be considered as the most complete and applied risk assessment method for lifting. The method is relatively simple to use, but one needs to follow the manual carefully (CDC website).

The primary product of the NIOSH lifting equation is the Recommended Weight Limit (RWL), which defines the maximum acceptable weight (load) that nearly all healthy employees could lift over the course of an 8 hour shift, without increasing the risk of musculoskeletal disorders (MSD) to the lower back. In the NIOSH equation:

RWL (kg) = 23 x HM x VM x DM x AM x FM x CM, where 23 reflects the number of kgs considered to be safe in ideal lifting conditions, and HM up to CM represent the multipliers M associated with the following risk factors:

- H = Horizontal location of the object relative to the body.
- V = Vertical location of the object relative to the floor.
- D = Distance the object is moved vertically.
- A = Asymmetry angle or twisting requirement.
- F = Frequency and duration of lifting activity.
- C = Coupling or quality of the workers grip on the object.

Another method for risk assessment is the KIM method. This method not only addresses lifting, but also holding, carrying, pushing and pulling. The method was developed by the Federal Institute for Occupational Safety and Health (BAuA) and Committee of the Laender for Occupational Safety and Health (LASI).

Prevention

The NIOSH calculation allows identification of the factor(s) that are the most promising for intervention. As loads are usually not easy to change, in many cases workplace improvements are the best option. Reducing the horizontal distance is important, and can be attained by both workplace design and good work instruction.

Repetitive Work

Scope and Prevalence

Repetitive work is the type of work that involves repetitive movements of the arms and hands. This type of work is prevalent in many occupations, like assembly, packing, computer work, hair dressing, etc. For the Dutch population of workers it has been established that 35% are exposed to 'repetitive movements of the arms and hands'.

Computer work is a specific form of repetitive work involving repetitive movements mainly of the hands and fingers. Obviously, the prevalence of this type of work has increased dramatically over the past decennia. In many countries about 40% of the employees work almost all the time with computers.

Risk

The type of musculoskeletal disorders associated with repetitive work mainly concern neck, shoulder, elbow and wrist complaints. Several terms are used to group this type of disorder, for instance Repetive Strain Injury or Cumulative Trauma Disorder or Complaints or Arms, neck and Shoulders (CANS).

Epidemiological evidence for the association between repetitive work and repetitive strain injury has been provided: relative risks ratios have been estimated in a range from 2,3 to 8,8.

Typical computer work with keyboard and mouse is characterized by a combination of small repetitive movements of fingers, precise hand operations and static muscles in the neck-shoulder region. It has been reported that the task duration is a main determinant of risk in this kind of work. The risk of developing health complaints particularly increases at a task duration above 6 hours per day. Other extra risk factors are:

- Too little recovery time (minimum 5 minutes per hour).
- No option to take micro breaks (minimum 20 seconds every 10 minutes).
- No individual control of work pace.
- Mental work strain.

Risk Assessment Method

The OCRA method can be used for the assessment of the risk of repetitive movements of elbows, wrists and hands in cases where:

- One or both upper extremities move in cycles of less than 30 seconds.
- These or similar cycles are performed for more than 50% of the working time.
- The cycles are frequent and are identical or similar in nature.

As with the NIOSH formula, the OCRA method calculates the risk with the Recommended Technical Actions, the maximum permissible number of actions per minute:

RTA = 30 x Pf x Rf x Af x Ff x (Rc x Dc) where the risk factors are:

- Constant of Frequency" of technical actions per min = 30.
- Posture (Pf).
- Repetition (Rf).
- Additional factors (Af): Cold, vibrations, noise, gloves.
- Force (Ff).
- Recovery options (Rc).
- Duration (Dc).
- The OCRA index = real number of movements/RTA and is judged according to the following traffic light model: Green <2,2 no risk Orange 2,3 – 3,5 low risk Red >3,5 risk, action must be taken.

Prevention

The OCRA calculation allows identification of the most promising factor(s) for intervention.

Static Work

Static work is the type of work that involves prolonged standing and prolonged postures of the back, neck and arms.

Prolonged Standing

Prolonged standing (more than 4 hours a day) without regular intermittent walking is prevalent in many occupational sectors like healthcare, catering, retail and security. The type of musculoskeletal disorders associated with prolonged standing mainly concern chronic venous insufficiency and musculoskeletal pain of the lower back and feet.

Prolonged Postures

As for repetitive work, prolonged postures (holding times longer than 4 seconds) are prevalent in many occupations like assembly, packing, computer work, hair dressing, etc. Exposure and risk are much the same as for repetitive work, and the risk assessment methods for upper body movements and postures are similar.

Sedentary Work

Scope and Prevalence

Many workers perform their work seated for prolonged periods. In the Netherlands the mean worker sits 5,8 hours per day at work plus 3,5 hours in private life. Jobs with high incidence of sedentary work are: office work, security (control rooms), transport (drivers), services, and cashier work.

Risk

Sedentary work is related to overweight, lack of physical activity and poor and prolonged postures. In addition to MSDs, it has been linked to CVD, digestive cancers, reproductive disorders and reduced mental health.

Prevention

A good workplace design and frequent changes in postures are required in order to prevent strains. Some desks allow alternate sitting and standing, and if one does not have such a desk, one should walk regularly. As a minimum it is advised to move semi-intensively during 30 minutes per day. Mini breaks will contribute to the reduction of overloads. Walking during lunch breaks is an option for office workers. The newest designs in ergonomic seating allow for more dynamic seating, with postural changes. However, even the best furniture cannot overcome the strains on the body from excessive periods of sitting. Good instruction on how to use adjustable furniture is also important.

DVORAK KEYBOARD LAYOUT

Dvorak is a keyboard layout for English patented in 1936 by August Dvorak and his brother-in-law, William Dealey as a faster and more ergonomic alternative to the QWERTY layout (the *de facto* standard keyboard layout). Dvorak proponents claim that it requires less finger motion and as a result reduces errors, increases typing speed, reduces repetitive strain injuries, or is simply more comfortable than QWERTY.

Although Dvorak has failed to replace QWERTY, most major modern operating systems (such as Windows, macOS, Linux, Android, Chrome OS, and BSD) allow a user to switch to the Dvorak layout. iOS does not provide a system-wide, touchscreen Dvorak keyboard, although third-party software is capable of adding the layout to iOS, and the layout can be chosen for use with any hardware keyboard, regardless of printed layout.

Several modifications were designed by the team directed by Dvorak or by ANSI. These variations have been collectively or individually termed the Dvorak Simplified Keyboard, the American Simplified Keyboard or simply the Simplified Keyboard, but they all have come to be known commonly as the Dvorak keyboard or Dvorak layout.

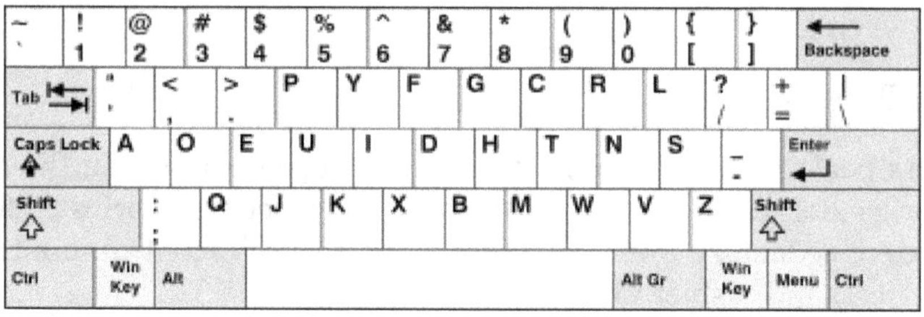

The modern Dvorak layout.

Dvorak was designed with the belief that it would significantly increase typing speeds with respect to the QWERTY layout by alleviating some of its perceived shortcomings, such as:

- Many common letter combinations require awkward finger motions.
- Some common letter combinations are typed with the same finger (e.g. "ed" and "de").
- Many common letter combinations require a finger to jump over the home row.
- Many common letter combinations are typed with one hand while the other sits idle (e.g. was, were).
- Most typing is done with the left hand, which for most people is not the dominant hand.
- About 16% of typing is done on the lower row, 52% on the top row and only 32% on the home row.

August Dvorak studied letter frequencies and the physiology of the hand and created a new layout to alleviate the above problems, based on the following principles:

- Letters should be typed by alternating between hands (which makes typing more rhythmic, increases speed, reduces error, and reduces fatigue). On a Dvorak keyboard, vowels and the most used symbol characters are on the left (with the vowels on the home row), while the most used consonants are on the right.
- For maximum speed and efficiency, the most common letters and bigrams should be typed on the home row, where the fingers rest, and under the strongest fingers (Thus, about 70% of letter keyboard strokes on Dvorak are done on the home row and only 22% and 8% on the top and bottom rows respectively).
- The least common letters should be on the bottom row which is the hardest row to reach.
- The right hand should do more of the typing because most people are right-handed.

- Digraphs should not be typed with adjacent fingers.
- Stroking should generally move from the edges of the board to the middle. An observation of this principle is that, for many people, when tapping fingers on a table, it is easier going from little finger to index than vice versa. This motion on a keyboard is called *inboard stroke flow.*

The Dvorak layout is intended for the English language. For other European languages, letter frequencies, letter sequences, and bigrams differ from those of English. Also, many languages have letters that do not occur in English. For non-English use, these differences lessen the alleged advantages of the original Dvorak keyboard. However, the Dvorak principles have been applied to the design of keyboards for other languages, though the primary keyboards used by most countries are based on the QWERTY design.

The layout was completed in 1932 and granted U.S. Patent 2,040,248 in 1936. The American National Standards Institute (ANSI) designated the Dvorak keyboard as an alternative standard keyboard layout in 1982, "Alternate Keyboard Arrangement for Alphanumeric Machines". The original ANSI Dvorak layout was available as a factory-supplied option on the original IBM Selectric typewriter.

August Dvorak was an educational psychologist and professor of education at the University of Washington Seattle. Touch typing had come into wide use by that time, and Dvorak became interested in the layout while serving as an advisor to Gertrude Ford, who was writing her master's thesis on typing errors. He quickly concluded that the QWERTY layout needed to be replaced. Dvorak was joined by his brother-in-law William Dealey, a professor of education at the then North Texas State Teacher's College in Denton, Texas.

Dvorak and Dealey's objective was to scientifically design a keyboard to decrease typing errors, speed up typing, and lessen typist fatigue. They engaged in extensive research while designing their keyboard layout. In 1914 and 1915, Dealey attended seminars on the science of motion and later reviewed slow-motion films of typists with Dvorak. Dvorak and Dealey meticulously studied the English language, researching the most used letters and letter combinations. They also studied the physiology of the hand. The result in 1932 was the Dvorak Simplified Keyboard.

In 1893, George Blickensderfer had developed a keyboard layout for the Blickensderfer typewriter model 5 that used the letters DHIATENSOR for the home row. Blickensderfer had determined that 85% of English words contained these letters. The Dvorak keyboard uses the same letters in its home row, apart from replacing R with U, and even keeps the consonants in the same order, but moves the vowels to the left: AOEUIDHTNS.

In 1933, Dvorak started entering typists trained on his keyboard into the International Commercial Schools Contest, which were typing contests sponsored by typewriter manufacturers consisting of professional and amateur contests. The professional contests had typists sponsored by typewriter companies to advertise their machines.

QWERTY typists became disconcerted by the rapid-fire clacking of the Dvorak typists, and asked for separate seating.

In the 1930s, the Tacoma, Washington, school district ran an experimental program in typing designed by Dvorak to determine whether to hold Dvorak layout classes. The experiment put 2,700 highschool students through Dvorak typing classes and found that students learned Dvorak in one-third the time it took to learn QWERTY. When a new school board was elected, however, it chose to terminate the Dvorak classes. During World War II, while in the Navy, Dvorak conducted experiments which he claimed showed that typists could be retrained to Dvorak in a mere 10 days, though he discarded at least two previous studies which were conducted and whose results are unknown.

With such great apparent gains, interest in the Dvorak keyboard layout increased by the early 1950s. Numerous businesses and government organizations began to consider retraining their typists on Dvorak keyboards. In this environment, the General Services Administration commissioned Earle Strong to determine whether the switch from QWERTY to Dvorak should be made. After retraining a selection of typists from QWERTY to Dvorak, once the Dvorak group had regained their previous typing speed (which took 100 hours of training, more than was claimed in Dvorak's Navy test), Strong took a second group of QWERTY typists chosen for equal ability to the Dvorak group and retrained them in QWERTY in order to improve their speed at the same time the Dvorak typists were training.

The carefully controlled study failed to show any benefit to the Dvorak keyboard layout in typing or training speed. Strong recommended speed training with QWERTY rather than switching keyboards, and attributed the previous apparent benefits of Dvorak to improper experimental design and outright bias on the part of Dvorak, who had designed and directed the previous studies. However, Strong had a personal grudge against Dvorak and had made public statements before his study opposing new keyboard designs. After this study, interest in the Dvorak keyboard waned. Later experiments have shown that many keyboard designs, including some alphabetical ones, allow very similar typing speeds to QWERTY and Dvorak when typists have been trained for them, suggesting that Dvorak's careful design principles may have had little effect because keyboard layout is only a small part of the complicated physical activity of typing.

The work of Dvorak paved the way for other optimized keyboard layouts for English such as Colemak, but also for other languages such as the German Neo and the French BÉPO.

Original Dvorak Layout

Over the decades, symbol keys were shifted around the keyboard resulting in variations of the Dvorak design. In 1982, the American National Standards Institute (ANSI) implemented a standard for the Dvorak layout known as ANSI X4.22-1983. This standard gave the Dvorak layout official recognition as an alternative to the QWERTY keyboard.

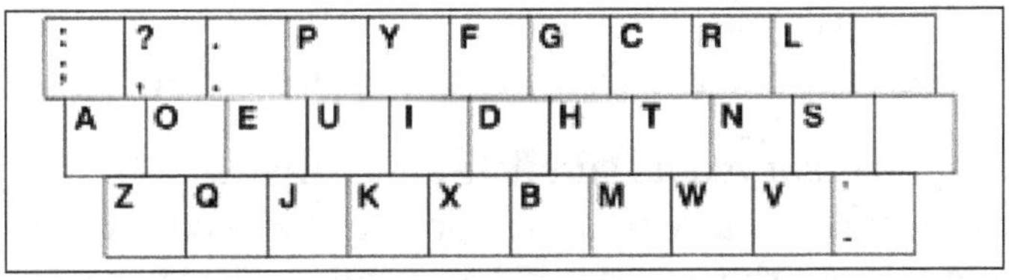

The typewriter keyboard layout that Dvorak & Dealey patented.

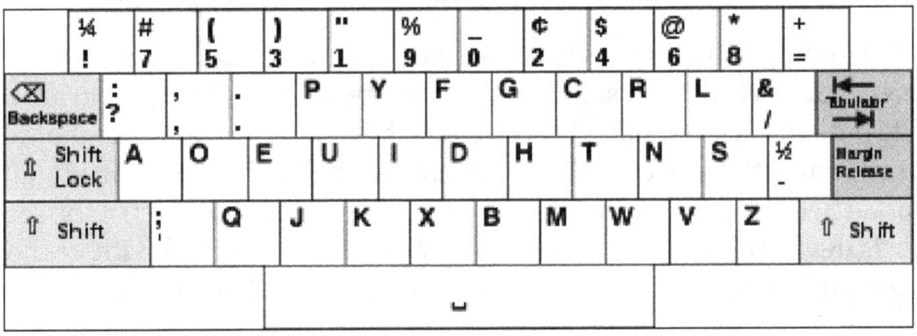

The Dvorak typewriter keyboard layout that was publicly promulgated.

The layout standardized by the ANSI differs from the original or "classic" layout devised and promulgated by Dvorak. Indeed, the layout promulgated publicly by Dvorak differed slightly from the layout for which Dvorak & Dealey applied for a patent in 1932- most notably in the placement of Z. Today's keyboards have more keys than the original typewriter did, and other significant differences existed:

- The numeric keys of the classic Dvorak layout are ordered: 7 5 3 1 9 0 2 4 6 8 (used today by the Programmer Dvorak layout).
- In the classic Dvorak layout, the question mark key [?] is in the leftmost position of the upper row, while the slash key [/] is in the rightmost position of the upper row.
- For the classic Dvorak layout, the following symbols share keys (the second symbol being printed when the SHIFT key is pressed):
    - Colon [:] and question mark [?].
    - Ampersand [&] and slash [/].

Modern U.S. Dvorak layouts almost always place semicolon and colon together on a single key, and slash and question mark together on a single key. Thus, if the keycaps of a modern keyboard are rearranged so that the unshifted symbol characters match the classic Dvorak layout then the result is the ANSI Dvorak layout.

Availability in Operating Systems

Dvorak is included with all major operating systems (such as Windows, macOS, Linux and BSD). Since the introduction of iOS 8 in 2014, Apple iPhone and iPad users have been able to install third party keyboards on their touchscreen devices which allow for alternative keyboard layouts such as Dvorak on a system wide basis.

Although some word processors could simulate alternative keyboard layouts by software, this was application specific; if more than one program was commonly used (e.g., a word processor and a spreadsheet), the user could be forced to switch layouts depending on the application. Occasionally, stickers were provided to place over the keys for these layouts.

However, IBM-compatible PCs used an active, "smart" keyboard. Striking a key generated a key "code", which was sent to the computer. Thus, changing to an alternative keyboard layout was accomplished most easily by simply buying a keyboard with the new layout. Because the key codes were generated by the keyboard itself, all software would respond accordingly. In the mid to late 1980s, a small industry for replacement PC keyboards developed; although most of these were concerned with keyboard "feel" and programmable macros, there were several with alternative layouts, such as Dvorak.

Amiga

Amiga operating systems from the 1986 version 1.2 onward allow the user to modify the keyboard layout by using the setmap command line utility with "usa2" as an argument, or later in 3.x systems by opening the keyboard input preference widget and selecting "Dvorak". Amiga systems versions 1.2 and 1.3 came with the Dvorak keymap on the Workbench disk. Versions 2.x came with the keymaps available on the "Extras" disk. In 3.0 and 3.1 systems, the keymaps were on the "Storage" disk. By copying the respective keymap to the Workbench disk or installing the system to a hard drive, Dvorak was usable for Workbench application programs.

Microsoft Windows

Versions of Microsoft Windows including Windows 95, Windows NT 3.51 and later have shipped with U.S. Dvorak layout capability. Free updates to use the layout on earlier Windows versions are available for download from Microsoft.

Earlier versions, such as DOS 6.2/Windows 3.1, included four keyboard layouts: QWERTY, two-handed Dvorak, right-hand Dvorak, and left-hand Dvorak.

In May 2004, Microsoft published an improved version of its Keyboard Layout Creator (MSKLC version 1.3 – current version is 1.4) that allows anyone to easily create any keyboard layout desired, thus allowing the creation and installation of any international Dvorak keyboard layout such as Dvorak Type II (for German), Svorak (for Swedish) etc.

Another advantage of the Microsoft Keyboard Layout Creator with respect to third-party programs for installing an international Dvorak layout is that it allows creation of a keyboard layout that automatically switches to standard (QWERTY) after pressing the two hotkeys (SHIFT and CTRL).

Unix-based Systems

Many operating systems based on UNIX, including OpenBSD, FreeBSD, NetBSD, OpenSolaris, Plan 9, and most Linux distributions, can be configured to use the U.S. Dvorak layout and a handful of variants. Furthermore, all current Unix-like systems with X.Org and appropriate keymaps installed (and virtually all systems meant for desktop use include them) are able to use any QWERTY-labeled keyboard as a Dvorak one without any problems or additional configuration. This eliminates the burden of producing additional keymaps for every variant of QWERTY provided. Runtime layout switching is also possible.

Chrome OS

Chrome OS and Chromium OS offer Dvorak, and there are three different ways to switch the keyboard to the Dvorak layout. Chrome OS includes the US Dvorak and UK Dvorak layouts.

Apple Computers

Apple ad Dvorak advocates since the company's early (pre-IPO) days. Several engineers devised hardware and software to remap the keyboard, which were used inside the company and even sold commercially.

Apple II

The Apple IIe had a keyboard ROM that translated keystrokes into characters. The ROM contained both QWERTY and Dvorak layouts, but the QWERTY layout was enabled by default. A modification could be made by pulling out the ROM, bending up four pins, soldering a resistor between two pins, soldering two others to a pair of wires connected to a DIP switch, which was installed in a pre-existing hole in the back of the machine, then plugging the modified ROM back in its socket. The "hack" was reversible and did no damage. By flipping the switch, the user could switch from one layout to the other. This modification was entirely unofficial but was inadvertently demonstrated at the 1984 Comdex show, in Las Vegas, by an Apple employee whose mission was to demonstrate Apple Logo II. The employee had become accustomed to the Dvorak layout and brought the necessary parts to the show, installed them in a demo machine, then did his Logo demo. Viewers, curious that he always reached behind the machine before and after allowing other people to type, asked him about the modification. He spent as much time explaining the Dvorak keyboard as explaining Logo.

Apple brought new interest to the Dvorak layout with the Apple IIc, which had a mechanical switch above the keyboard whereby the user could switch back and forth between the QWERTY and Dvorak: this was the most official version of the IIe Dvorak mod. The IIc Dvorak layout was even mentioned by 1984 advertisements, which stated that the world's fastest typist, Barbara Blackburn, had set a record on an Apple IIc with the Dvorak layout.

Dvorak was also selectable using the built-in control panel applet on the Apple IIGS.

Apple III

The Apple III used a keyboard-layout file loaded from a floppy disk: the standard system-software package included QWERTY and Dvorak layout files. Changing layouts required restarting the machine.

Apple Lisa

The Apple Lisa did not offer the Dvorak keyboard mapping, though it was purportedly available through undocumented interfaces.

Mac OS

iBook with alpha and punctuation keys manually rearranged to the Dvorak layout.

During its early days, the Macintosh could be converted to the Dvorak layout by making changes to the "System" file: this was not easily reversible and required restarting the machine. This modification was unofficial, but it was comparable to many other user modifications and customizations that Mac users made. Using the "resource editor", ResEdit, users could create keyboard layouts, icons, and other useful items. A few years later, a third-party developer offered a utility program called MacKeymeleon, which put a menu on the menu bar that allowed on-the-fly switching of keyboard layouts. Eventually, Apple Macintosh engineers built the functionality of this utility into the standard system software, along with a few layouts: QWERTY, Dvorak, French (AZERTY), and other foreign-language layouts.

2010 Apple Wireless Keyboard in Dvorak Layout.

Since about 1998, beginning with Mac OS 8.6, Apple has included the Dvorak layout. It can be activated with the Keyboard Control Panel and selecting "Dvorak". The setting is applied once the Control Panel is closed out. Apple also includes a Dvorak variant they call "Dvorak – Qwerty ⌘". With this layout, the keyboard temporarily becomes QWERTY when the Command (⌘/Apple) key is held down. By keeping familiar keyboard shortcuts like "close" or "copy" on the same keys as ordinary QWERTY, this lets some people use their well-practiced muscle memory and may make the transition easier. Mac OS and subsequently Mac OS X allow additional "on-the-fly" switching between layouts: a menu-bar icon (by default, a national flag that matches the current language, a 'DV' represents Dvorak and a 'DQ' represents Dvorak – Qwerty ⌘) brings up a drop-down menu, allowing the user to choose the desired layout. Subsequent keystrokes will reflect the choice, which can be reversed the same way.

Mac OS X 10.5 "Leopard" and later offer a keyboard identifier program which asks users to press a few keys on their keyboards. Dvorak, QWERTY and many national variations of those designs are available. If multiple keyboards are connected to the same Mac computer, they can be configured to different layouts and use simultaneously. However should the computer shut down (lack of battery, etc.) the computer will revert to QWERTY for reboot, regardless of what layout the Admin was using.

Mobile Phones and PDAs

A number of mobile phones today are built with either full QWERTY keyboards or software implementations of them on a touch screen. Sometimes the keyboard layout can be changed by means of a freeware third-party utility, such as Hacker's Keyboard for Android, AE Keyboard Mapper for Windows Mobile, or KeybLayout for Symbian OS.

The RIM BlackBerry lines offer only QWERTY and its localized variants AZERTY and QWERTZ. Apple's iOS 8.0 and later has the option to install onscreen keyboards from the App Store, which includes several free and paid Dvorak layouts. iOS 4.0 and later supports external Dvorak keyboards. Google's Android OS touchscreen keyboard can use Dvorak and other nonstandard layouts natively as of version 4.1.

Comparison of the QWERTY and Dvorak Layouts

Keyboard Strokes

Touch typing requires typists to rest their fingers in the home row (QWERTY row starting with "ASDF"). The more strokes there are in the home row, the less movement the fingers must do, thus allowing a typist to type faster, more accurately, and with less strain to the hand and fingers.

The majority of the Dvorak layout's key strokes (70%) are done in the home row, claimed to be the easiest row to type because the fingers rest there. Additionally, the

Dvorak layout requires the fewest strokes on the bottom row (the most difficult row to type). By contrast, QWERTY requires typists to move their fingers to the top row for a majority of strokes and has only 32% of the strokes done in the home row.

Because the Dvorak layout concentrates the vast majority of key strokes to the home row, the Dvorak layout uses about 63% of the finger motion required by QWERTY, which is claimed to make the keyboard more ergonomic. In fact, it has been estimated that during a typical 8-hour day a typist's fingers will travel 25 kilometers (16 mi) on a QWERTY keyboard and only 1.6 kilometers (1 mi) on a Dvorak keyboard. Because the Dvorak layout requires less finger motion from the typist compared to QWERTY, some users with repetitive strain injuries have reported that switching from QWERTY to Dvorak alleviated or even eliminated their repetitive strain injuries; however, no scientific study has been conducted verifying this.

The typing loads between hands differs for each of the keyboard layouts. On QWERTY keyboards, 56% of the typing strokes are done by the left hand. As the right hand is dominant for the majority of people, the Dvorak keyboard puts the more often used keys on the right hand side, thereby having 56% of the typing strokes done by the right hand.

Awkward Strokes

Awkward strokes are undesirable because they slow down typing, increase typing errors, and increase finger strain. Hurdling is an awkward stroke requiring a single finger to jump directly from one row, over the home row to another row (e.g., typing "minimum" [which often comes out as "minimun" or "mimimum"] on the QWERTY keyboard). In the English language, there are about 1,200 words that require a hurdle on the QWERTY layout. In contrast, there are only a few words requiring a hurdle on the Dvorak layout.

Hand Alternation and Finger Repetition

Alternating hands while typing is a desirable trait because while one hand is typing a letter, the other hand can get in position to type the next letter. Thus, a typist may fall into a steady rhythm and type quickly. On the other hand, when a string of letters is done with the same hand, the chances of stuttering are increased and a rhythm can be broken, thus decreasing speed and increasing errors and fatigue. Likewise, using the same finger to type consecutive letters is also to be avoided. The QWERTY layout has more than 3,000 words that are typed on the left hand alone and about 300 words that are typed on the right hand alone (the aforementioned word "minimum" is a right-hand-only word). In contrast, with the Dvorak layout, only a few words are typed using only the left hand and even fewer use the right hand alone. This is because most syllables require at least one vowel, and, in a Dvorak layout, all the vowels (and "y") fall on the left side of the keyboard.

Standard Keyboard

QWERTY enjoys advantages with respect to Dvorak due to the fact that it is the de facto standard keyboard:

- Keyboard shortcuts in most major operating systems, including Windows, are designed for QWERTY users, and can be awkward for some Dvorak users, such as Ctrl-C (Copy) and Ctrl-V (Paste). However, Apple computers have a "Dvorak – Qwerty ⌘" setting, which temporarily changes the keyboard mapping to QWERTY when the command (⌘) key is held, and Windows users can replicate this setting using AutoHotkey scripts.
- Some public computers (such as in libraries) will not allow users to change the keyboard to the Dvorak layout.
- Some standardized exams will not allow test takers to use the Dvorak layout (e.g. Graduate Record Examination).
- Support for Dvorak in games, especially those that make use of "WASD" - an ergonomic inverted-T shape using QWERTY but spread out across the keyboard in Dvorak - for in-game movement vary. Some games will automatically detect the keyboard is in Dvorak and adjust keys to the Dvorak equivalent ",AOE" while others allow the same effect with some manual tweaking; games with hard-coded keybinds and do not allow changing the keys away from WASD becomes practically impossible to play under Dvorak.
- People who can touch type with a QWERTY keyboard will be less productive with alternative layouts until they retrain themselves, even if these are closer to the optimum.
- Not all people use keyboard fingerings as specified in touch-typing manuals due to either preference or anatomical difference. This can change the relative efficiency on alternative layouts.

Variants

One-handed Versions

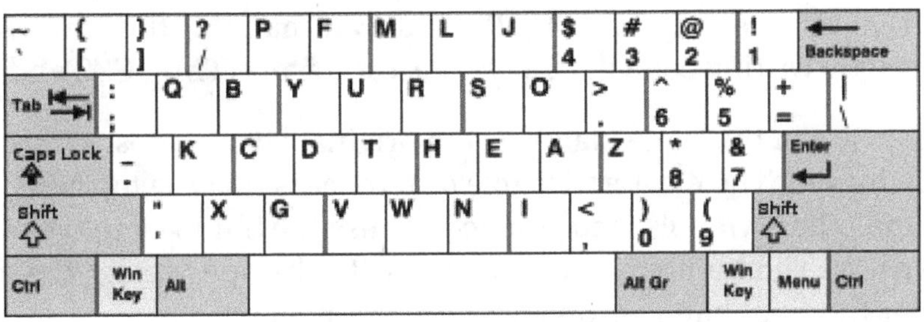

Left-handed Dvorak layout.

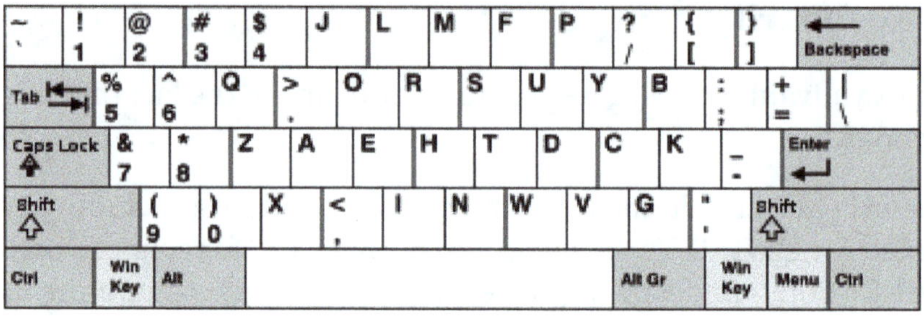

Right-handed Dvorak layout.

In the 1960s, Dvorak designed left- and right-handed Dvorak layouts for touch-typing with only one hand. He tried to minimize the need to move the hand from side to side (lateral travel), as well as to minimize finger movement. Each layout has the hand resting near the center of the keyboard, rather than on one side.

Because the layouts require less hand movement than layouts designed for two hands, they can be more accessible to single-handed users. The layouts are also used by people with full use of two hands, who prefer having one hand free while they type with the other.

The left-handed Dvorak and right-handed Dvorak keyboard layouts are mostly each other's mirror image, with the exception of some punctuation keys, some of the less-used letters, and the 'wide keys' (Enter, Shift, etc.). Dvorak arranged the parentheses ")(" on his left-handed keyboard, but some keyboards place them in the typical "()" reading order.

Programmer Dvorak

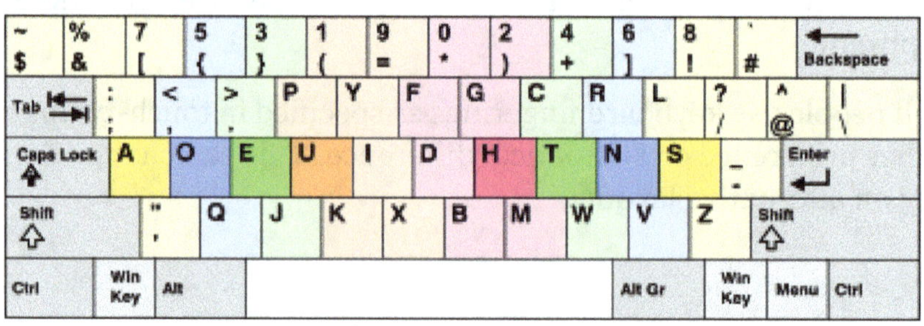

The Programmer Dvorak layout.

Programmer Dvorak was developed by Roland Kaufmann in the early 2000's and is designed for people writing code in C, Java, Pascal, Lisp, HTML, CSS and XML.

While the letters are in the same places as the original layout, most symbols and numbers have been moved. The most noticeable difference is that the top row contains various brackets and other symbols, and you need to use the Shift key to type the numbers, like on typewriters. The numbers are arranged with the odds under the left hand and the evens under the right hand, as on Dvorak's original layout.

It comes preinstalled on Linux and installers are also available for macOS and Windows.

PHYSICAL ERGONOMIC EQUIPMENTS

Ergonomic Keyboard

An ergonomic keyboard is a computer keyboard designed with ergonomic considerations to minimize muscle strain and a host of related problems. Typically such keyboards for two-handed typists are constructed in a V shape, to allow right and left hands to type at a slight angle more natural to the human form.

An ergonomic keyboard.

A "Truly Ergonomic Keyboard" fixed-split keyboard.

Apple Adjustable Keyboard is an adjustable split keyboard.

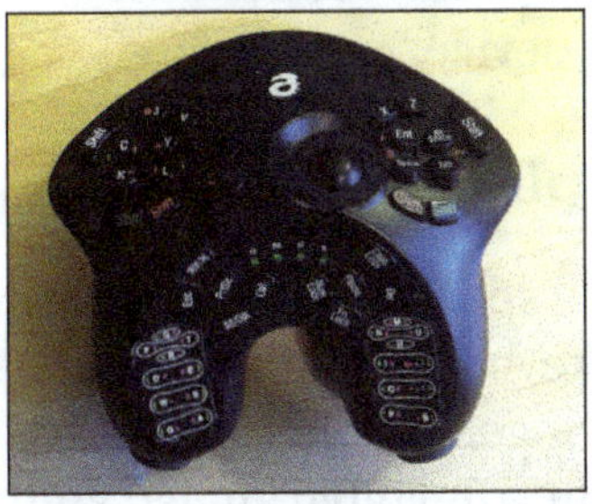

An "AlphaGrip" Handheld Keyboard.

Split Keyboard

A "fixed-split keyboard" is a single board, with the keys separated into two or three groups, allowing the user to type at a different angle than the typical straight keyboard.

An "adjustable split keyboard" has the keyboard split into several independent pieces, so the angle between them can be easily changed.

Contoured Keyboard

A further development of the split concept are contoured keyboards like the 1977

Maltron or the newer Kinesis Advantage line, which place the keys into two depressions set approximately at shoulder width, with function keys set between the key groups for use with the thumbs. In this configuration, very little movement of arms and wrists is required.

Maltron Keyboard with Malt Layout.

Handheld Keyboards

Handheld ergonomic keyboards are designed to be held like a game controller, and can be used as such, instead of laid out flat on top of a table surface. They allow the user the ability to move around a room or to lean back on a chair while also being able to type in front or away from the computer. Some variations of handheld ergonomic keyboards also include a trackball mouse that allow mouse movement and typing included in one handheld device.

Angle Split Keyboard

The angled split keyboard (sometimes referred to as a Klockenburg keyboard) is similar to a split keyboard, but the middle is tented up so that the index fingers are higher than the little fingers while typing. Key Ovation makes the Goldtouch ergonomic keyboard which is an adjustable angled split keyboard.

Other Ergonomic Keyboards

Other ergonomic keyboards have fixed, vertically aligned keys, so the user types with their hands perpendicular to the ground, thumbs-up. Still others allow a range of rotation and elevations. A few ergonomic keyboards do not have the typical one key per letter, such as a keyer or a keyless ergonomic keyboard. DataHand eliminates the need for any wrist motion or finger extension.

Considerations

It is widely claimed that an ergonomic keyboard may reduce muscle strain and reduce risk of carpal tunnel syndrome or other kinds of repetitive strain injury. With respect to "split" keyboards, quality studies that demonstrate injury reductions are lacking, with the exception of physically split keyboards which have "sharply angled keyboard faces". There is evidence, however, that such keyboards are not well-tolerated.

Narrow studies examining hand position at rest neglects many other possible factors. For example, one should be aware that the effect of "ergonomic" keyboards is to change the musculoskeletal region exposed to risk, instead of eliminating hazardous postures.

Chorded Keyboard

A keyset or chorded keyboard (also called a chorded keyset, *chord keyboard* or *chording keyboard*) is a computer input device that allows the user to enter characters or commands formed by pressing several keys together, like playing a "chord" on a piano. The large number of combinations available from a small number of keys allows text or commands to be entered with one hand, leaving the other hand free. A secondary advantage is that it can be built into a device (such as a pocket-sized computer or a bicycle handlebar) that is too small to contain a normal-sized keyboard.

A chorded keyboard minus the board, typically designed to be used while held in the hand, is called a keyer. Douglas Engelbart introduced the chorded keyset as a computer interface in 1968 at what is often called "The Mother of All Demos".

A Microwriter MW4.

The earliest known chord keyboard was part of the "five-needle" telegraph operator station, designed by Wheatstone and Cooke in 1836, in which any two of the five needles could point left or right to indicate letters on a grid. It was designed to be used by untrained operators (who would determine which keys to press by looking at the grid), and was not used where trained telegraph operators were available.

The first widespread use of a chord keyboard was in the stenotype machine used by court reporters, which was invented in 1868 and is still in use. The output of the stenotype was originally a phonetic code that had to be transcribed later (usually by the same operator who produced the original output), rather than arbitrary text—automatic conversion software is now commonplace.

In 1874, the five-bit Baudot telegraph code and a matching 5-key chord keyboard was designed to be used with the operator forming the codes manually. The code is optimized for speed and low wear: chords were chosen so that the most common characters used the simplest chords. But telegraph operators were already using typewriters with QWERTY keyboards to "copy" received messages, and at the time it made more sense to build a typewriter that could generate the codes automatically, rather than making them learn to use a new input device.

Some early keypunch machines used a keyboard with 12 labeled keys to punch the correct holes in paper cards. The numbers 0 through 9 were represented by one punch; 26 letters were represented by combinations of two punches, and symbols were represented by combinations of two or three punches.

A braille keyboard.

Braille (a writing system for the blind) uses either 6 or 8 tactile 'points' from which all letters and numbers are formed. When Louis Braille invented it, it was produced with a needle holing successively all needed points in a cardboard sheet. In 1892, Frank Haven Hall, superintendent of the Illinois Institute for the Education of the Blind, created the Hall Braille Writer, which was like a typewriter with 6 keys, one for each dot in a braille cell. The Perkins Brailler, first manufactured in 1951, uses a 6-key chord keyboard (plus a spacebar) to produce braille output, and has been very successful as a mass market affordable product. Braille, like Baudot, uses a number symbol and a shift symbol, which may be repeated for shift lock, to fit numbers and upper case into the 63 codes that 6 bits offer.

After World War II, with the arrival of electronics for reading chords and looking in tables of "codes", the postal sorting offices started to research chordic solutions to be able to employ people other than trained and expensive typists. In 1954, an important concept was discovered: chordic production is easier to master when the production is done at the release of the keys instead of when they are pressed.

Researchers at IBM investigated chord keyboards for both typewriters and computer data entry as early as 1959, with the idea that it might be faster than touch-typing if some chords were used to enter whole words or parts of words. A 1975 design by IBM Fellow Nat Rochester had 14 keys that were dimpled on the edges as well as the top, so one finger could press two adjacent keys for additional combinations. Their results were inconclusive, but research continued until at least 1978.

Doug Engelbart began experimenting with keysets to use with the mouse in the mid 1960s. In a famous 1968 demonstration, Engelbart introduced a computer human interface that included the QWERTY keyboard, a three button mouse, and a five key keyset. Engelbart used the keyset with his left hand and the mouse with his right to type text and enter commands. The mouse buttons marked selections and confirmed or aborted commands.

Users in Engelbart's Augmentation Research Center at SRI became proficient with the mouse and keyset. In the 1970s the funding Engelbart's group received from the Advanced Research Projects Agency (ARPA) was cut and many key members of Engelbart's team went to work for Xerox PARC where they continued to experiment with the mouse and keyset. Keychord sets were used at Xerox PARC in the early 1980s, along with mice, GUIs, on the Xerox Star and Alto workstations. A one button version of the mouse was incorporated into the Apple Macintosh but Steve Jobs decided against incorporating the chorded keyset.

In the early 1980s, Philips Research labs at Redhill, Surrey did a brief study into small, cheap keyboards for entering text on a telephone. One solution used a grid of hexagonal keys with symbols inscribed into dimples in the keys that were either in the center of a key, across the boundary of two keys, or at the joining of three keys. Pressing down on one of the dimples would cause either one, two or three of the hexagonal buttons to be depressed at the same time, forming a chord that would be unique to that symbol. With this arrangement, a nine button keyboard with three rows of three hexagonal buttons could be fitted onto a telephone and could produce up to 33 different symbols. By choosing widely separated keys, one could employ one dimple as a 'shift' key to allow both letters and numbers to be produced. With eleven keys in a 3/4/4 arrangement, 43 symbols could be arranged allowing for lowercase text, numbers and a modest number of punctuation symbols to be represented along with a 'shift' function for accessing uppercase letters. While this had the advantage of being usable by untrained users via 'hunt and peck' typing and requiring one less key switch than a conventional 12 button keypad, it had the disadvantage that some symbols required three times as much force to depress them as others which made it hard to achieve any speed with the device. That solution is still alive and proposed by Fastap and Unitap among others, and a commercial phone has been produced and promoted in Canada during 2006.

Principles of Operation

Each key is mapped to a number and then can be mapped to a corresponding letter or command. By pressing two or more keys together the user can generate many combinations. In Engelbart's original mapping, he used five keys: 1, 2, 4, 8, and 16. The keys were mapped as follows: a = 1, b = 2, c = 3, d = 4, and so on. If the user pressed keys 1 + 2 = 3 simultaneously, and then released the keys, the letter "c" appeared. Unlike pressing a chord on a piano, the chord is recognized only after all the keys or mouse buttons are released. Since Engelbart introduced the keyset, several different designs have been developed based on similar concepts.

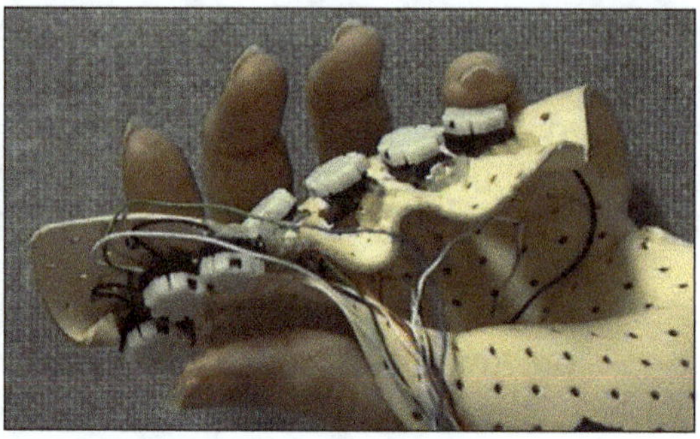

An ergonomic chorded keyboard without the board is known as a keyer.

As a crude example, each finger might control one key which corresponds to one bit in a byte, so that using seven keys and seven fingers, one could enter any character in the ASCII set—if the user could remember the binary codes. Due to the small number of keys required, chording is easily adapted from a desktop to mobile environment.

Practical devices generally use simpler chords for common characters (*e.g.,* Baudot), or may have ways to make it easier to remember the chords (*e.g.,* Microwriter), but the same principles apply. These portable devices first became popular with the wearable computer movement in the 1980s.

Thad Starner from Georgia Institute of Technology and others published numerous studies showing that two handed chorded text entry was faster and yielded fewer errors than on a QWERTY keyboard. Currently stenotype machines hold the record for fastest word entry. Many stenotype users can reach 300 words per minute. However, stenographers typically train for three years before reaching professional levels of speed and accuracy.

Standards

Historically, the baudot and braille keyboards were standardized to some extent, but they are unable to replicate the full character set of a modern keyboard. Braille comes closest, as it has been extended to eight bits.

The only proposed modern standard, GKOS (or Global Keyboard Open Standard) can support most characters and functions found on a computer keyboard but has had little commercial development. There is, however, a GKOS keyboard application available for iPhone since May 8, 2010, for Android since October 3, 2010 and for MeeGo Harmattan since October 27, 2011.

Open-source Designs

Four open source keyer/keyset designs are available:

- The pickey, a PS/2 device based on the PIC microcontroller.
- The spiffchorder, a USB device based on the Atmel AVR family of microcontrollers.

- The FeatherChorder, a BLE chorder based on the Adafruit Feather, an all in one board incorporating an Arduino-compatible microcontroller.
- The GKOS keypad driver for Linux as well as the Gkos library for the Atmel/ Arduino open source board.

A 104-key USB keyboard adapted into a chording keyboard. All phonetic keystrokes may be accomplished by one and two-key chords of the home keys on the top row.

Plover is a free, open-source, cross-platform program intended to bring realtime stenographic technology not just to stenographers, but also to hobbyists using anything from professional Stenotype machines to low-cost NKRO gaming keyboards. It is available for GNU/Linux, Microsoft Windows, and Apple Mac macOS.

Joy2chord is a chorded keyboard driver for GNU/Linux. With a configuration file, any joystick or gamepad can be turned into a chorded keyboard. These design philosophies was decided on to lower the cost of building devices, and in turn lower the entry barrier to becoming familiar with chorded keyboards. Macro keys and multiple modes are also easily implemented with a user space driver.

Commercial Devices

One minimal chordic keyboard example is Edgar Matias' Half-Qwerty keyboard described in patent US 5288158 circa 1992 that produces the letters of the missing half when the user simultaneously presses the space bar along with the mirror key. INTERCHI '93 published a study by Matias, MacKenzie and Buxton showing that people who have already learned to touch-type can quickly recover 50 to 70% of their two-handed typing speed. The loss contributes to the speed discussion above. It is implemented on two popular mobile phones, each provided with software disambiguation, which allows users to avoid using the space-bar.

"Multiambic" keyers for use with wearable computers were invented in Canada in the 1970s. Multiambic keyers are similar to chording keyboards but without the board, in that the keys are grouped in a cluster for being handheld, rather than for sitting on a flat surface.

Chording keyboards are also used as portable but two handed input devices for the visually impaired (either combined with a refreshable braille display or vocal synthesis). Such keyboards use a minimum of seven keys, where each key corresponds to an individual braille point, except one key which is used as a spacebar. In some applications, the spacebar is used to produce additional chords which enable the user to issue editing commands, such as moving the cursor, or deleting words. Note that the number of points used in braille computing is not 6, but 8, as this allows the user, among other things, to distinguish between small and capital letters, as well as identify the position of the cursor. As a result, most newer chorded keyboards for braille input include at least nine keys.

Touch screen chordic keyboards are available to smartphone users as an optional way of entering text. As the number of keys is low the button areas can be made bigger and easier to hit on the small screen. The most common letters do not necessarily require chording as is the case with the GKOS keyboard optimised layouts (Android app) where the twelve most frequent characters only require single keys.

The WriteHander, a 12-key chord keyboard from NewO Company, appeared in 1978 issues of ROM Magazine, an early microcomputer applications magazine.

Another early commercial model was the six-button Microwriter, designed by Cy Endfield and Chris Rainey, and first sold in 1980. Microwriting is the system of chord keying and is based on a set of mnemonics. It was designed only for right-handed use.

In 1982 the Octima 8 keys cord keyboard was presented by Ergoplic Kebords Ltd an Israeli Startup that was founded by Israeli researcher with intensive experience in Man Machine Interface design. The keyboard had 8 keys one for each finger and additional 3 keys that enabled the production of numbers, punctuations and control functions. The keyboard was fully compatible with the IBM PC & AT keyboards and had an Apple IIe version as well. Its key combinations were based on a mnemonic system that enabled fast and easy touch type learning. Within a few hours the user could achieve a typing speed similar to hand writing speed. The unique design also gave a relief from hand stress (Carpal Tunnel Syndrome) and allowed longer typing sessions than traditional keyoards. It was multi-lingual supporting English, German, French and Hebrew.

The BAT is a 7-key hand-sized device from Infogrip, and has been sold since 1985. It provides one key for each finger and three for the thumb. It is proposed for the hand which does not hold the mouse, in an exact continuation of Engelbart's vision.

Modern

Modern examples of chorded keyboards include TipTapSpeech (using Engelbart's original mapping), the GKOS keyboard, the FrogPad, the In10did method, the EkaPad, TextFaster and HotTyper. Some of them are intended for tiny tablet computers and wireless mobile terminals, many of them are additionally available as apps on Apple's iOS devices.

CyKey

Chris Rainey, the co-inventor of Microwriter, re-introduced Microwriting for PC and

Palm PDAs with a standalone miniature chording keyboard called CyKey which caters to both left and right-handed users, being 9-keys. CyKey is named after the Microwriter chord system's co-inventor Cy Endfield, who died in 1995 but the name also reflects its intuitive nature.

SiWriter

The SiWriter is an app for the iPad and iPhone which uses a close variant of the microwriter chording system developed by Cy Enfield. It is available via the Apple app store. The system is let down by the lack of haptic feedback - you can't tell if your fingers are in the right place without looking, but you get better with practice. The finger pad positions are adjustable to fit your hand size. It also works for left handed users and has a live speech output facility that could be helpful for people with speech impairments.

GKOS and ComboKey

The GKOS is a 6-key keyboard with a different signs and commands allocation of the 63 different chords in order to provide all PC keyboard functions and to make entering letters and numbers lighter by having to press fewer keys simultaneously. The *6 physical keys* are intended to be on the back of the device and to be operated with the six free fingers of two hands holding the device. Another option is to have *virtual GKOS keys* positioned towards the sides of a touch sensitive screen. This GKOS for thumbs has additional keys to enable all combos by only one keypress per hand. GKOS iPhone, Android phone/tablet and MeeGo Harmattan applications use this principle.

Later, GKOS has been further developed under name ComboKey to better suit the touch screens of smartphones. There is an Android keyboard application ComboKey Plus enabling e.g. one-hand typing.

EkaPad

The EkaPad is a 12-key chorded keyboard operated with the four fingers of one hand. It is supported on the thumb. With the 9 main keys, (operated by the index, middle, and ring fingers), 2 prefix keys and one delete key, the EkaPad can produce all the inputs of a standard QWERTY keyboard with one, two, and a few three finger chords. For some characters one or two prefix chords are required. 9 main keys (3×3 matrix) can produce a total of 511 chords. With each of the three fingers limited to its own row, 229 chords are possible with 3 fingers. EkaPad uses 66 of these accessible chords. One and two finger chords produce about 85% of American English; with an additional prefix chord about 97%. In addition, the EkaPad can store 100 text strings and 100 keyboard shortcuts. Like many other chorded keyboards, it can be used with one hand.

EkaPads are no longer manufactured at this writing.

FrogPad

The FrogPad is a 20-key chorded keyboard about the size of a numeric keypad that can be used with one hand, and is optimized by character frequency. 85% of average keystrokes in English text can be typed without chording, and chords are limited to 2 fingers.

Decatxt

The Decatxt keyboard uses the IN10DID 10 key chording method, and is currently on Amazon. It is a wireless one-handed chord keyboard that places two keys under each finger in order to utilize one hand for typing. Typically only two fingers are needed for any operations. Each key is essentially a shift key so that with ten keys, there are ten single keystrokes and dozens of two and three key combinations. The alphabet is produced with a single press for ten letters or by shifting with either thumb for sixteen more. Changing modes, such as number lock, can make other input such as numbers, provided with a single keystroke. This avoids complex chords while providing enough keystrokes for efficient typing and allows for some unique implementations such as typing with gloves or on a steering wheel. A video game controller called the X-SKIN, using this system, was expected to be commercially available by 2010to help make Morphs popular on console systems and ease entry of common data such as a username and password, but the USB device was never made commercially available. The IN10DID chording system can be applied in single hand configurations, two handed or with one key at a time if desired. Claimed advantages of the IN10DID method are the diversity of devices, limited motion and simple chords.

Twiddler

The Twiddler is a fully featured 16-key keyboard (plus mouse) designed to fit in the palm of one hand. It was originally introduced in the early 1990s by Handykey and is currently being produced by Tek Gear. It is popular among wearable computer researchers and hobbyists due to its ease of use, large community of users, and active support by the manufacturer. Every single and multi-key chord on the Twiddler can be customized by the end user. The Twiddler comes standard with an "A, B, C, D" chord set, with TabSpace and other chord sets available. Chords are not limited to single keystrokes - multiple keystrokes can be sent with a single chord press. An example of this is an email address or address block can be typed by pressing just one chord. The efficiency gained by using multi-character chords have novice Twiddler users typing at 47 WPM while experts can burst up to 130 WPM.

ASETNIOP

ASETNIOP is a virtual keyboard based on chords that appeared in 2012. The alphabet uses the 8 keys of the home row as ASET and NIOP (the eight most common letters in the English language), plus 18 chorded combinations. The layout also makes a less-cluttered 10-button keypad for tablet computers, touchscreens, touchpads, and can be used in wired gloves.

DataHand

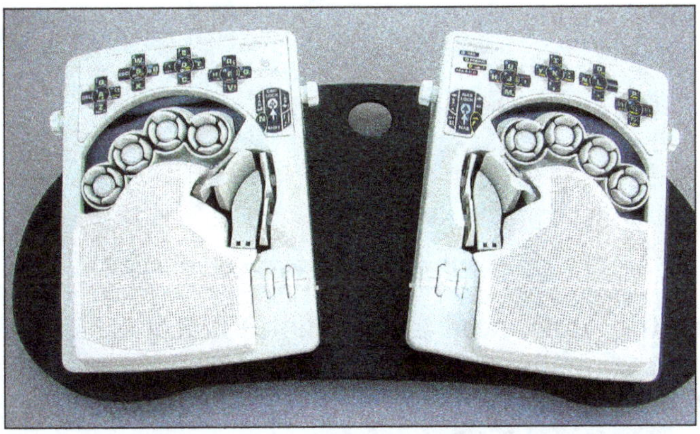

Overhead view of DataHand units that provide full computer keyboard and mouse functionality.

The DataHand keyboard was introduced in 1995 by DataHand Systems, Inc. It was invented by Dale J. Retter and was produced by Industrial Innovations as early as 1992. The keyboard consists of two completely separate "keyboards", one for the left hand and one for the right, that are molded to rest the user's hands on. This allows the user to place each hand wherever it is most comfortable to them. Each finger activates five buttons, the four compass directions as well as down. The thumbs also have five buttons, one inside and two outside as well as up and down. The button modules in which the fingers rest are adjustable to best fit the user's hands—each side can be independently moved up and down, towards the palm or farther away.

This ergonomic layout allows for all typing to occur without any wrist motion, as well as without any finger extension. The keyboard layout is initially similar to a QWERTY keyboard, but the middle two columns of keys (i.e. H,Y,G.) have been delegated to sideways finger movements, and all of the keys outside of the main three rows are accessed through two additional modes, including a mode for mousing. There are three primary modes all together: letters, number and symbols, and function/mouse mode. Some practice is required. However, eventual typing speedups are possible.

Also of note is the button design—instead of being spring-loaded, the buttons are held in place with magnets and are activated using optical sensors. This was done in order to dramatically reduce the finger workload while optimizing tactile feedback.

After the initial prototype was released in 1995, DataHand has released the Professional and Professional II with new bodies. The Professional II also has extended programming capabilities over the Professional, being able to record macros of keystrokes for convenient use.

The right-hand of a Professional II keyboard.

DataHand Systems, Inc. announced in early 2008 that it was ceasing to market and sell its keyboards. The company web site states that due to supplier issues, the company will not sell the DataHand keyboard "until a new manufacturer can be identified". However, the company plans a final, limited production run to satisfy existing customers. In January 2009, the company's website started taking orders for a "limited number of new DataHand Pro II units".

BAT Keyboard

BAT Keyboard is a one-handed, compact input device that replicates all the functions of a full-size keyboard, but with greater efficiency and convenience. The BAT is easy to learn and use. Letters, numbers, commands and macros are simple key combinations, "chords," that you can master in no time. Best of all the BAT's unique ergonomic design reduces hand strain and fatigue for greater comfort and productivity. The BAT is the ultimate typing solution for persons with physical or visual impairments and is proven to increase productivity when used with graphic or desktop publishing software.

Best uses for the Bat Keyboard

- The BAT Personal Keyboard has applicability in any computing environment, especially those using the keyboard with a mouse or other input device. The keyboard is the perfect solution for computer aided drafting, desktop publishing, graphics design and other uses such as accounting, telemarketing, or customer service. It is excellent in applications requiring only one hand. The current trend in ergonomic keyboards (splitting and separating the QWERTY keyboard) makes the BAT keyboard even more compelling for single-handed use.
- It is light weight and compact, takes little desk space and can easily be transported. Take the BAT keyboard with you as your personal keyboard. Use it with your laptop as a remote keyboard. It is convenient and flexible. Use the BAT

keyboard in any comfortable typing position, including the arm of your chair or your lap. Use it alone, in pairs, and with other input devices, such as a traditional keyboard, a mouse or a design tablet.

- The BAT Personal Keyboard was developed over ten years of research by an internationally renowned human factors expert. Both the chord set and the physical design of keyboard are the results of that research. Each BAT keyboard is capable of entering all characters and functions of a traditional keyboard (plus many more) with only seven keys. Data is entered by "chording": pressing a key or combination of keys simultaneously. Chords are easy to learn in about an hour. Moderate proficiency is gained in less than 10 hours, much less than with traditional keyboards. Most people achieve 30-50 wpm. Actual learning performance varies with individuals.

Using the Bat Keyboard for CAD

The BAT Personal Keyboard, developed by Infogrip, Inc., has gained a large following of devoted fans in the world of Computer Aided Drafting. This revolutionary ergonomic keyboard allows full keyboard entry with one hand while the other is using a pointing device; greatly reducing hand and finger movement as well as permitting the user to keep their eyes focused on the monitor.

The BAT Keyboard compresses all the functions of a traditional keyboard into a seven-key unit the size of a hand. With one key for each finger and three color-coded keys for the thumb, users press key combinations, "chords" to type on the BAT.

CAD users typically have very little desk top space, forcing them to crowd multiple items into a small area. The BAT Keyboard's innovative compact design (only one-third the size of a standard keyboard) frees up valuable work space. Additionally, the BAT eliminates both the need to look away from the screen and the travel needed when moving from a mouse or digitizer to a traditional keyboard, thus enhancing the users productivity. While also reducing hand and arm movement providing a more healthy ergonomic work environment.

Joe Kovalski of Accurate Design in Ventura, California uses the BAT Keyboard for CAD applications and finds it indispensable. "I keep one hand on the mouse and one hand on the BAT (Keyboard), I've memorized the keystrokes for the commands I use a lot, and it's a lot faster than looking for those letters on a traditional keyboard."

David Satchell a plant engineer with a computer manufacturing company in Austin, Texas quickly took to the BAT and loves it. "I thought it would be difficult to learn, but I found it to be easier than learning to use a regular keyboard. All your fingers stay in the same place." Satchell said he had "always been uncomfortable at a regular keyboard," and finds that using the BAT Keyboard in conjunction with a mouse helps him work faster in Auto-CAD.

The BAT Keyboard is available for both PC compatible and Macintosh computers as well as having an option of left- or right-hand. (The left-hand model is the most popular.) The PC compatible is a "plug and play" keyboard, no driver is required. The Macintosh model plugs into the ADB port and comes with a software driver.

Other Features Include

- Flexibility: Can be used alone, in pairs, with a traditional keyboard and with a mouse, digitizer or other pointing device.
- Ergonomic design: Reduces strain and fatigue commonly associated with prolonged use of traditional keyboards and keyboard/input device travel.
- Both PC and Macintosh models can be daisy-chained with another BAT Keyboard and a traditional keyboard. All can be used simultaneously.
- Portability: Just 16 ounces and the size of a hand. The PC model comes with a lithium battery allowing the user to download macros to the BAT giving them the power of customized macros where ever they go.

Bat Keyboard and Disabilities

The BAT Personal Keyboard is a fully functioning keyboard for one hand. It's innovative, compact design is ideal for individuals with physical or visual impairments. The keyboard's small size allows user's to easily port the BAT from home to work or school as well as place the keyboard in the most comfortable position to meet their needs.

An input system called "chording" is used to type on the BAT. Similar to Braille combinations of keys are pressed simultaneously. The BAT has seven keys, four for the fingers and three for the thumb. The center thumb key is used in combination with the four finger keys to type "space" and "a" through "z". The two outer thumb keys are used for special keys like "Alt", "Shift" and cursor movement. "Sticky" or "latching" keys are used to enter multiple key sequences, i.e. Alt F to open a file.

The BAT is a keyboard, it is not a mouse. However, all cursor movements can be achieved and with Windows '95 and System 7 for Macintosh users can turn the keypad into a mouse. If a pointing device is desired, most users mount a portable Glidepoint touchpad (available from Infogrip) just above the thumb keys or place a trackball or mouse on the low side of the BAT, thereby minimizing hand movement.

Users can do anything on the BAT keyboard that they would with an extended keyboard and more.

Types of Users

- Physical Disabilities.

- Amputation of a hand or arm.
- Congenital absence or malformation of a hand or arm.
- Physical injury or nerve damage to a hand or arm.
- Limited range of motion from a physical injury.
- Congenital condition.
- Head injury resulting in hemiplegia (paralysis on one side only).
- Cerebral Palsy.
- Muscular Sclerosis.
- Stroke.
- Visually Impaired.
- Total Blindness.

Physical Disabilities

The BAT is an excellent keyboard for people who have good use of only one hand or limited range of motion. Users need to have fairly good control of finger movements on the functional hand; however, the BAT keyboard is forgiving and key action can easily be adjusted to meet an individual's needs.

There is conclusive evidence that the lateral movements required to type on an extended keyboard causes Repetitive Stress Injuries in two handed users. Typing one handed on an extended keyboard is not only slow, it can increase the physical stress put on the hand, wrist and arm. One handed keyboard layouts only minimally cut down the distance needed to travel; the user still has to access 101 individual keys. The key distance the one hand user has to travel on an extended keyboard is double or triple what a two hand user has to cover.

The BAT is a third of the size of an extended keyboard. There is no key distance to travel on the BAT because all of the keys are under the fingers. The physical design is superior for one handed users; the keys are a light tension spring, the keyboard is naturally sloped and has a built in hand rest to encourage proper hand placement and is so small and light weight that it can be placed in the most comfortable and healthy position for the user.

Highlights

- Ability to access the entire extended keyboard with only one hand.
- Very little hand and arm movement required to type.

- Ergonomically designed to position the hand in the most comfortable position.
- Easy to use:
    - IBM Compatible: Just plug and play, easily connected through the keyboard port, no driver required.
    - Macintosh Compatible: Connects through the ADB port and requires a small software driver (98k) be installed.
        - Daisy chainable: Both IBM and Macintosh compatible versions allow for an extended keyboard to be plugged directly into the BAT and used simultaneously allowing other users to access the computer.
        - Compact and light weight: The small size allows for easy placement in any position; i.e. desk top, lap, or mounted on a wheel chair.
- Easy to learn: The learning curve has been shown to be shorter than that of the QWERTY (extended) keyboard. The chord design was based on research which considered a frequency of use character index, the biomechanical action required to chord, and the cognitive process required remembering the chord combination.
- Learning time: Within only a couple of hours of training users are familiar with the idea or feeling of what it is like to chord and have the letters, numbers and basic punctuation memorized. After only 20 to 30 hours users are up to speed, typing anywhere from 301 to 50 words per minute.

Ergonomics of Typing

Many people ask about the ergonomics of typing and if the BAT Personal Keyboard reduces Carpal Tunnel Syndrome.

Cumulative trauma disorders (CTD's) can be described as additive tissue damage accumulating over time. These are referred to as repetitive strain injuries, overuse syndrome, regional musculoskeletal disorders, or other names. Symptoms may surface over time in varying degrees, from mild discomfort to acute pain. CTD's occur in situations where people perform repetitive manual tasks and are subjected to shock, vibration, and strain. Examples may include the use of hand tools, loading and unloading factory machinery, picking and placing operations, and most recently, operating computer keyboards and mice.

Cumulative traumas, as they relate to typing on keyboards, originate from shocks and strains. It is important to note that each of these is very small. CTD's are the accumulation of these shocks over many hours of typing per day, 5 days per week, 50 weeks per year, and so on. Shock is the vibration or impact that the finger feels as it pushes a key. Examples include the shock the finger feels when it first contacts the key, the shock produced by a tactile feed-back "click" in the key, and the shock the finger feels when a key bottoms on its stroke. The shock varies with how hard an individual types. "Heavy handed" typists create more shock than individuals with a light touch, as the key impact and key bottoming is greater.

Strains result from finger exertion and the reaching and stretching of the fingers. The force of exertion is determined by the spring rate of the keys. Keys that have stiffer springs are harder to push, and therefore create greater finger exertion. The reach and stretch of the fingers to the various key positions are called "trajectories". It is believed that trajectories may contribute to the strain of the tendons of the hand and the Median nerve.

The carpal tunnel is a canal in the wrist that contains the median nerve and the hand tendons. Carpal Tunnel Syndrome is the symptom of pain, numbness, and tingling felt in the wrist, fingers, and arm caused by excessive repetitive motion of the tendons within the carpal tunnel, causing irritation, then swelling, then pressure on the median nerve. To alleviate this condition, considerable emphasis has been placed by experts on the correct posture of the forearm, wrist and hand when typing. This includes work station and keyboard design.

Constrained posture is believed to contribute to RSI. Work station design plays a key role in reducing the risk by correcting posture. This includes properly equipping and adjusting chairs, desk heights, lighting and glare, and accessories such as document holders and wrist rests for the individual user. The workstation, when properly adjusted, should produce a posture where the arms and hands extend naturally from the torso and are not rotated (pronation) or turned (ulnar deviation) beyond certain limits. The traditional keyboard design does not fit well within these guidelines. It requires the hands to be placed flat (pronation) and close together. Placing the hands close together causes the typist to turn the hands outward (ulnar deviation). A better solution is a keyboard that allows the hands to be separated at a comfortable width and with the hands at a more natural angle with the thumbs elevated.

There are widely argued opinions about the contributing factors of these disorders, but the most widely accepted related to keyboard use include:

- Pronation: The inward rotation of the forearm and hand from a vertical/thumbs up orientation.
- Ulnar Deviation: The turning of the hand out of horizontal alignment with the forearm (i.e. the bending of the wrist toward the pinkie).
- Wrist Support: Proper wrist support is important for two reasons: a) to remove the weight of the arm from the shoulders; and b) to provide proper height of the wrist to the key-tops for proper hand posture.
- Positioning: The hands should be comfortably apart to relieve wrist extension and elbows should be bent at 90°.

- Frequency of Use: Disorders are cumulative. The less one uses each finger, the better.
- Key effort: Light key pressures cause less strain, impact shock and fatigue over time, but can contribute to key "bottoming".
- Tactile click: The tactile click preferred by most typists is considered a poor choice in that the click produces small shock waves up the fingers to the tendons in the hand.
- Trajectories: The directed reach the fingers perform to type the upper, lower, left, and right keys for each finger.
- Resting Periods: Rest periods and task variety can reduce the risks of CTD's. Warm- up and periodic exercises of the neck, shoulders, wrists and hands are also recommended.
- Constrained Posture:
    - It can be corrected by an adjusted workstation. ANSI Standard HFS-100 provides comprehensive list of recommendations.
    - The BAT Personal Keyboard addresses most of these issues. Pronation is improved by the 15° inclined typing surface. Ulnar deviation is eliminated by rotating the BAT to a proper angle for typing. The built-in wrist pad comfortably supports the arm to relax the shoulders and to provide proper finger posture when typing. Hand positioning is accomplished by moving the BAT in or out from the center of your body.
    - The BAT keyboard uses specially designed springs and non-tactile keys in the keyboard. This produces a low impact, light touch for long term use. The BAT keyboard only has seven keys and uses a typing technique called chording; combinations of keys are pressed simultaneously. This method minimizes finger and hand movement, reducing hand, wrist and arm strain.
    - Resting periods and workstation are the responsibility of the individual and are not addressable by keyboard design. Infogrip recommends regular typing breaks, a properly equipped and adjusted workstation and stretching exercises before, during, and after typing. (Suggested exercises are readily available at your local ergonomic office furniture supplier.) Switching to the BAT Keyboard may extend comfortable working sessions and reduce the risk of cumulative trauma disorders.

Velotype

Velotype is the old trademark for a type of keyboard for typing text known as a syllabic chord keyboard, an invention of the Dutchmen Nico Berkelmans and Marius den Outer. The current tradename is Veyboard. Veyboard is a Dutch company.

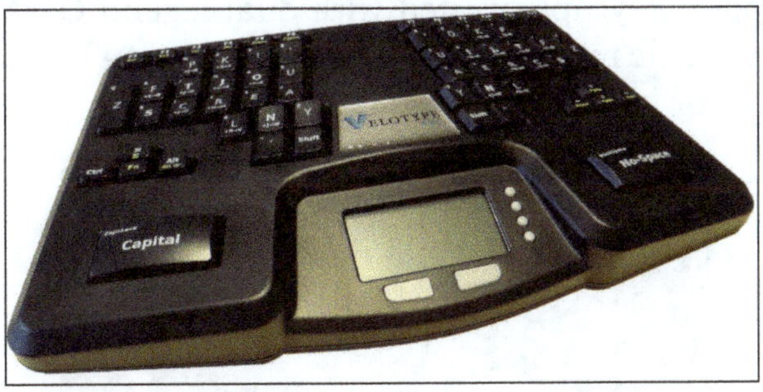

The Velotype.

Contrary to traditional QWERTY type keyboards, on which a typist usually presses one key at a time to create one character at a time, a Veyboard requires the user to press several keys simultaneously, producing syllables rather than letters.

A practiced "veyboarder" can produce more text than on a traditional keyboard, as much as 200 words per minute, double the rate of a fast traditional typist. Because of this, Veyboards are often used for live applications, such as subtitling for television and for the hearing impaired.

The keyboard is an orthographic chord keyboard, very different from phonetic chord keyboards used for verbatim transcription, like the stenotype. Such chorded phonetic keyboards, such as those manufactured by Stenograph, produce an intermediate shorthand format in which a combination of phonetics- and spelling-based strokes are translated by software to produce the output. Orthographic keyboards, on the other hand, allow the operator to rely on more traditional spelling in shaping the output, hence the term "orthographic" as opposed to "phonetic".

Stenographic keyboards are generally more difficult to learn than the Veyboard, but trained stenotype operators can go faster, even upwards of 300 words per minute. However, if unusual words appear, a typist using a stenotype slows down, while the Velotypist can continue with the same speed, which can go up to 200 words per minute.

The Velotype-pro contains software that allows the user to create their own abbreviations and short forms in addition to those pre-built into the machine.

Kinesis (Keyboard)

The Kinesis line of ergonomic computer keyboards is an alternative to the traditional keyboard design. Most widely known among these are the contoured Advantage line, which feature recessed keys in two bucket-like hollows which allow the fingers to reach keys with less effort as well as a central array of modifiers such as enter, alt, backspace, control, etc. where they can be pressed with the thumbs. All Kinesis keyboards (except the Essential) support the capability to re-map individual keys. Recent models also come with the ability to switch between the Dvorak layout with the press of a special key combination, though keycaps printed with dual-legend QWERTY/Dvorak letters are included only on specific models. Moreover, the keys are laid out in perfect vertical rows to avoid the need for lateral movements during typing.

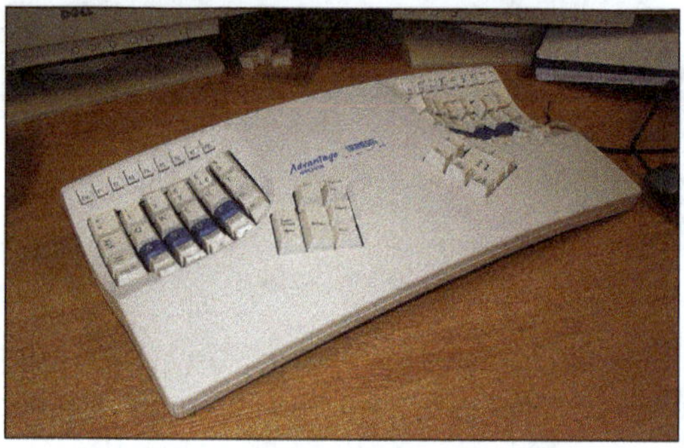

The Kinesis Advantage keyboard.

The top row of keys, including the escape key and function keys, are small soft-touch keys with membrane dome switches. The remaining keys are standard size and each has its own Cherry MX brown key switch, providing a tactile feel, but no click. A piezo buzzer provides optional key click.

Uses

The Kinesis line of keyboards are marketed to those who type throughout the workday, and thus perceive a higher risk for such injuries as RSI. The Kinesis was first used among computer programmers, who continue to be the primary market for the devices.

Kinesis Contoured Advantage Pro employed in conjunction with tiling window manager xmonad.

Microsoft Ergonomic Keyboards

Since 1994, Microsoft has designed and sold a variety of ergonomic keyboards for computers. The oldest is the Microsoft Natural Keyboard. The newest are the Sculpt ergonomic keyboard and the Surface Ergonomic Keyboard.

Models

Side view, showing the snap-on front riser which generates negative slope, front-to-back.

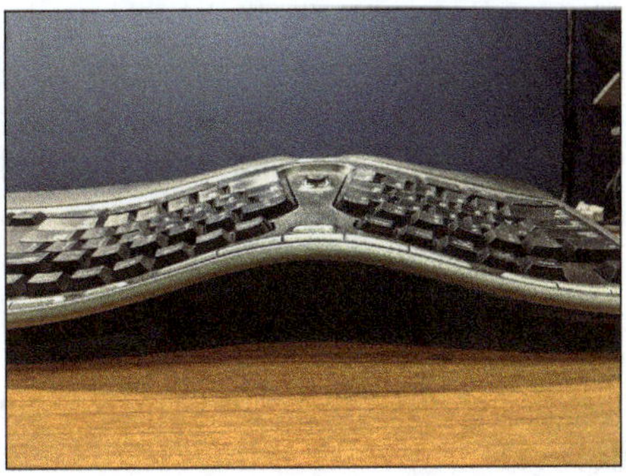

Top view, showing the tent or gable angle between the two alphanumeric halves.

The Microsoft Natural Ergonomic Keyboard 4000, like other keyboards in the Microsoft ergonomic keyboard line, includes fixed slope and tent/gable angle adjustments to distinguish them from the comfort keyboard line, which only incorporate a slant angle change.

In general, ergonomic keyboards are designed to keep the user's arms and wrists in a near-neutral position, which means the slant angle (the lateral rotation angle for the keys in each half relative to the axis of the home row in a conventional keyboard) is approximately 10 to 12.5°, the slope (the angle of the keytop surfaces starting from the front edge closer to the user towards the top of the keyboard, relative to a horizontal plane) is -7.5°, and the tent or gable angle of each half (the angle of the keytops from the center of the keyboard towards its left and right edges, relative to the horizontal desk surface) is 20 to 30°.

Natural Keyboard

Microsoft Natural Keyboard Gen1/V1.

The first generation of the Microsoft ergonomic keyboards, named the *Natural Keyboard*, was released in September 1994, designed for Microsoft Windows 95 and Novell Netware. It was designed for Microsoft by Ziba Design with assistance and manufacturing by Key Tronic. The Microswitch division of Honeywell, which was responsible for that company's keyboards and was acquired by Key Tronic in early 1994, is also credited with design input.

The keyboard uses a fixed-split design, with each half of the alphanumeric section separated, laterally rotated, and tilted upwards and down from the center of the keyboard. This key arrangement was ergonomically designed to prevent carpal tunnel syndrome and other repetitive strain injuries associated with typing for long periods of time. Another innovation was the integrated wrist pad helping to ensure correct posture while sitting at the computer and further reducing strain on the neck, arms and wrists.

This keyboard also introduced three new keys purposed for Microsoft's upcoming operating system: two Windows logo keys (⊞ Win) between the Ctrl and Alt keys on each side, and a ≣ Menu key between the right Windows and Ctrl keys. The three Num Lock/Caps Lock/Scroll Lock status lights are arranged vertically between the two halves of the alphanumeric section.

Although it was not the first ergonomic keyboard, it was the first widely available sub-$100 offering. The keyboard gained popularity quickly, exceeding Microsoft's forecast of 100,000 units sold by the end of 1994. Microsoft soon asked Key Tronic to ramp up production to 100,000 per month in 1995, and the Natural Keyboard sold over 600,000 per month at its peak. Over 3 million units had been sold by February 1998, when its successor, the Natural Keyboard Elite, was introduced.

As with most Microsoft keyboards, software (Microsoft IntelliType) is bundled with the keyboard for both Mac OS X and Windows, allowing users to customize the function keys and modify keys fairly extensively.

Natural Keyboard Elite

Microsoft Natural Keyboard Elite.

The Microsoft Natural Keyboard has had several upgrades and refreshes since its introduction. The first of these was the *Natural Keyboard Elite*, introduced in February 1998 at a retail price of US$64.95 (equivalent to $102 in 2019). Like the original Natural Keyboard, the Elite was manufactured by Key Tronic, who also assisted in its development.

The Elite features a nonstandard layout of the six-key navigation/edit key cluster normally found above the cursor keys (Ins/Del, Home/End, and PgUp/PgDn). Another common criticism of the Elite is that the arrow keys' inverted-T layout has been changed into a cross-like layout, with left/right arrows keys side by side and up/down keys bracketing them from above and below, increasing the distance between the vertical keys. Another significant change was the keyboard's adjustable feet. While the original Microsoft Natural Keyboard had feet in the front to generate reverse tilt, the Elite and its successors have their feet in the back. The Natural Keyboard Elite was manufactured in at least two different color schemes; white with black lettering and black with white lettering.

Natural Keyboard Pro

Microsoft Natural Keyboard Pro, circa Q4 1999.

The third iteration was the *Natural Keyboard Pro*, introduced in June 1999 at a retail price of US$74.95 (equivalent to $115). The Natural Keyboard Pro restored the standard inverted-T layout of the cursor keys and six-key nav/edit cluster 2×3 layout, and added a row of program shortcut keys along the top edge of the keyboard (above F1 – F12 and the numeric keypad), including multimedia keys and Power management keys. In versions of Windows prior to Windows Vista, Microsoft's Intellitype software is required to configure the behavior of the shortcut keys. Vista and Windows 7 have the ability to customize shortcut key behavior without additional software when using the "internet keyboard" keyboard layout. Some other modern operating systems, such as FreeBSD and most Linux distributions, have comparable configuration options. The Natural Keyboard Pro also included an internal two-port USB hub, which was commonly used to connect other input devices such as a mouse or trackball, but this was dropped in subsequent iterations.

Natural Multimedia Keyboard

Microsoft Natural Multimedia Keyboard.

In September 2002, Microsoft introduced the redesigned *Natural Multimedia Keyboard* (sometimes styled as *MultiMedia*) at a retail price of US$54.95 (equivalent to

$78). The Natural Multimedia Keyboard reworked the row of multimedia buttons and included the controversial F Lock feature, originally debuted in the Microsoft Office Keyboard. Another common criticism is that although the bunched arrow keys of previous generation has been fixed by returning to the standard inverted T layout, the six-key nav/edit cluster has been changed to a 2x3 vertical layout, with Ins moved to the F-Lock function of PrtScn/SysRq, and Del key expanded to double height. On the Natural Multimedia Keyboard, the status indicator lights for Num lock, Scroll lock, and Caps lock were moved from between the banks of alphanumeric keys to a more traditional location above and to the right of the backspace key. The Natural Multimedia Keyboard was manufactured in at least three different color schemes, including white with blue accents, black with silver accents, and white with black accents.

Wireless Optical Desktop Pro

The *Wireless Optical Desktop Pro* was introduced alongside the Natural MultiMedia Keyboard in September 2002 at a retail price of US$104.95 (equivalent to $149), That Desktop bundle included a wireless version of that keyboard, a wireless optical mouse (sold separately as the *Wireless Optical Mouse blue*), a USB receiver, and an adapter to convert the USB plug to PS/2 for older systems. The finish of the mouse and keyboard were changed to black with silver accents, and the indicator lights (Num Lock/Caps Lock/Scroll Lock) were moved to the receiver rather than the keyboard to conserve power.

Natural Ergonomic Keyboard 4000

Microsoft Natural Ergonomic Keyboard 4000.

In September 2005, Microsoft introduced the *Natural Ergonomic Keyboard 4000* at a retail price of US$64.95 (equivalent to $85). This keyboard provides a significantly changed ergonomic design, including an integrated leatherette wrist rest, noticeably concave key banks, and a removable front stand to generate negative slope, which helps to straighten the wrist and allows the fingers to drop naturally onto the keys. The multimedia keys have again been redesigned, and the six-key nav/edit cluster has been fixed by returning to the standard 3×2 horizontal rectangular layout. The F Lock key now defaults to "on", providing the original function key features rather than the new "enhanced" functions, and retains its setting across reboots. The 4000 has the indicator lights for Caps lock, etc. moved back to between the banks of keys, although they are now below the Space bar, rather than above. The 4000 is also significantly quieter to type on, with less of the distinctive "click clack" noise that is common with older keyboards. The space bar, however, has been reported by several reviewers to be unusually noisy and difficult to depress. The 4000 is available in two variants, Business and Retail. The exact differences are not known, although product descriptions imply that the packaging is different, and prices are often slightly higher for the Business edition.

Natural Ergonomic 7000 Keyboard

Microsoft Natural Wireless Ergonomic Keyboard 7000.

In June 2007, Microsoft introduced the *Natural Wireless Ergonomic Keyboard 7000* as part of the Natural Ergonomic Desktop 7000 bundle, which includes the Natural Wireless Laser Mouse 7000 at a retail price of US$149.95 (equivalent to $185). The biggest difference between the 7000 and 4000 keyboards, aside from wireless functionality, is the position of the status lights (Num Lock, Caps Lock, Scroll Lock, and F Lock). On the Natural Ergonomic 4000, these lights are on the wrist rest, centered vertically under the spacebar. In their place, on the Natural Ergonomic 7000 keyboard, resides a single battery indicator light.

The Microsoft Natural Ergonomic Desktop 7000 comes with a USB wireless dongle that connects both the mouse and the keyboard. The attachment to elevate the front of the keyboard is separate in the box. The Natural Ergonomic Desktop 7000 bundle also comes with batteries, a very brief user guide, a disk containing the Microsoft Intellitype and Intellipoint software, and the Natural Wireless Laser Mouse 7000, which uses the same physical design as the Natural Wireless Laser Mouse 6000 with a different radio frequency.

Sculpt Ergonomic Keyboard

Microsoft introduced the *Sculpt Ergonomic* keyboard in August 2013 as part of the Sculpt Ergonomic Desktop bundle with the Sculpt Ergonomic mouse at a retail price of US$129.95 (equivalent to $143). The keyboard was made available separately in "Business" packaging for US$80.95 (equivalent to $89).

The wireless keyboard uses a scissor-switch mechanism and features a detached number pad. The arrangement of the six-key nav/edit cluster is nonstandard, although the arrow keys are still laid out as an inverted-T. The Sculpt Ergonomic keyboard and mouse connect to the computer wirelessly using a 2.4 GHz radio through a proprietary USB dongle. The receiver and keyboard communicate using 128-bit AES encryption and are permanently paired at the factory. Because of this, the dongle cannot be replaced and must occupy a USB port; this feature has attracted criticism as a Bluetooth connection would free up a USB port and ensure the keyboard could still be used even if the dongle was misplaced. Microsoft state the proprietary wireless connection eliminates any delay in waking the computer. Rather than using feet to elevate the back of the keyboard, the Sculpt Ergonomic keyboard comes with a reverse-tilt riser that snaps on to the bottom front edge of the keyboard using magnets.

During development, the Sculpt keyboard was codenamed "Manta Ray" for its resemblance to the animal.

Surface Ergonomic Keyboard

The Microsoft *Surface Ergonomic* keyboard was announced in October 2016 at a retail price of US$129.95 (equivalent to $138), alongside other accessories for the Surface Studio.

The shape of the Surface Ergonomic keyboard is similar to the Sculpt, but the six-key navigation block returns to the standard two-row, three-column arrangement, and the number pad is integrated into right side of the Surface Ergonomic. The Surface is gray and the wrist pad is covered with Alcantara instead of the gloss black finish and vinyl wrist pad of the Sculpt. The Surface has also dropped the option to add the magnetic front riser for negative slope. In addition, the Surface Ergonomic is connected wirelessly over Bluetooth instead of using a proprietary dongle.

One reviewer noted the typing action of the Surface scissor switches was "more satisfying with improved quality" than the Sculpt. Paul Thurrott criticized the Surface Ergonomic keyboard for dropping the front riser option and the increased width, which extends the reach needed to use the mouse for right-handed users.

Microwriter

The Microwriter is a hand-held portable word-processor with a chording keyboard. First demonstrated in 1978, it was invented by UK-based, US-born film director Cy Endfield and his partner Chris Rainey and was marketed in the early 1980s by Microwriter Ltd, of Mitcham, Surrey, UK. By using a mnemonic alphabet, it was claimed to allow note-taking of up to 8,000 characters at an input rate averaging 1.5 times that of handwriting.

Microwriter MW4

Although there was an earlier unit with an LED display, the MW4 with an LCD was the most common unit.

The 23 cm × 12 cm × 5 cm (9" x 5" x 2") device comprises:

- A six-button chording keyboard.
- A single line LCD.
- An 8 bit CDP1802 microprocessor.
- Complete Word processing software in ROM.
- 16 kilobytes of RAM.
- Rechargeable Nickel-cadmium batteries - sufficient to run the device for 30 hours.
- Various interfaces.

This device is capable of allowing the user to enter and edit several pages of text - and by connecting a printer to the RS-232 serial port connector, documents can be printed without the aid of a separate computer. It was first sold in the UK in most mail-order shops in computing magazines such as YOUR COMPUTER from Spring/Summer 1983 and cost around £400-£500 (equivalent to around £1500).

Keyboard

The keyboard uses one button for each finger and two for the thumb of the user's right hand. The five buttons immediately beneath the fingers are pressed in different combinations to generate all letters. The second thumb button is used to toggle through a range of modes that allow the user to switch case, enter numbers, insert punctuation and even add ASCII control characters, to be used in editing the document being prepared. To type a letter "T", for example, the user would tap the top thumb button to shift to uppercase, then chord a "t" by pressing the index finger and ring finger buttons simultaneously.

The manufacturers claimed that most people could learn to use it in just a couple of hours. With some practice, it is possible to become a faster typist with the Microwriter than with a conventional keyboard, providing that what is being entered is just text. Typing is slowed if a substantial number of special characters have to be entered using the "shifting" mechanism.

Learning the chords for the basic letters and numbers is facilitated by a set of flash-cards that show simple mnemonics for each character.

External Ports

At the top end of the unit is a 25 pin D-type connector providing an RS-232 port, an interface to an audio cassette player for saving and restoring files and a small white on/off button. At the other end is the connector for the battery charger and a 37 pin D-type connector that can be hooked up to an optional external unit to allow the Microwriter to be connected to a television and thus to perform full-screen editing. The serial port can be used to connect the Microwriter directly to a printer, or to allow it to be plugged into a computer to function in place of the conventional keyboard.

Reception

Despite a lack of similar products, the Microwriter was not a success, and ceased production in 1985. Microwriters were sold direct, in the USA the advertised price was $499.00USD which might have been too high for a successful product offering.

A MicroWriter, MicroWriter AgendA, and its modern successor the CyKey.

A cut-down version of the Microwriter, known as the "Quinkey", was sold as a keyboard add-on for the BBC Micro computer connecting via the analogue port. It came with a game that helped the user to learn the chords. There were two versions of the interface software, one optimised for entering BBC BASIC commands, the other for word processing. Later, drivers were created for the Amstrad CPC and PC1512 home computers that worked through the digital joystick ports, and a version for IBM PC's running MS-DOS that used the IBM RS232 port control pins as a digital port for a 2x3 key matrix. These saw limited use.

Microwriter AgendA

The Microwriter AgendA was one of the first PDAs. Released in 1989, it includes a set of small "conventional" keys arranged inside the half circle of a Microwriter chording keyboard with larger keys. It has 32k of storage, pluggable memory modules, a 4-line LCD screen, and advertised excellent build quality and long battery life. It was designed for text-mode note-taking without a conventional desk or keyboard. In 1990 it was awarded the British Design Award.

Interface cables were available for the common serial (RS-232) and parallel (printer) ports of the day. These use a "smart" cable connected to a single I^2C bus on the AgendA.

CyKey

Chris Rainey, the co-inventor of Microwriter, re-introduced Microwriting for PC and

Palm PDAs with a standalone miniature chording keyboard called CyKey. CyKey is named after the Microwriter chord system's co-inventor Cy Endfield.

SiWriter

The SiWriter is an app for the iPad and iPhone which uses a close variant of the microwriter chording system developed by Cy Enfield. It is available via the Apple app store.

The system is let down by the lack of haptic feedback - you can't tell if your fingers are in the right place without looking, but you get better with practice. The finger pad positions are adjustable to fit your hand size. It also works for left handed users and has a live speech output facility that could be helpful for people with speech impairments.

FrogPad

FrogPad is a small chorded keyboard about the size of a numeric keypad that can be used with one hand. It was produced by Frogpad Inc.

The keyboard is optimized by character frequency. 85% of average keystrokes in English text can be typed without chording, and chords are limited to 2 fingers (opposable thumb and one finger). As a result, the FrogPad has many more keys than a GKOS or Microwriter or Baudot keyboard but fewer than a conventional computer keyboard.

A left-handed USB FrogPad.

The original FrogPads on the market at this time were intended to be used with mobile phones, and supported only Bluetooth.

Two attempts to relaunch the Frogpad had been made. The first was made in February 2012 by Frogpad and Linda Marroquin. However, due to funding difficulties this launch was cancelled and the cost of pre-ordered units was refunded to customers in June 2012.

The second relaunch attempt was made by Andrew Taylor of IT consulting firm Satori Tech Solutions and began to advertise in November 2013 and solicit pre-orders in January 2014 for a "prototype" version to be delivered in February and a final production version in April of that year. However, neither version of the keyboards shipped.

On August 14, 2014, Frogpad founder Linda Marroquin stated that the Frogpad license to Satori Tech Solutions has expired, and that she does not know why Mr. Taylor is not responding to consumers who pre-purchased products. Although she is aware of complaints filed against Mr. Taylor at the Texas AG and IC3, her stated intention is "to regain the brand after I get additional funding."

The one-handed FrogPad Mobile Keyboard can replace your current QWERTY keyboard with only 20 keys and a 5.5- by 3.5-inch frame. You can hook it up to a PC, a PDA, or any device with a USB connection. The keyboard's size makes it easy to travel with; each key represents up to seven different characters. You can switch among number, symbol, and CapsLock modes using a series of buttons that line the bottom ridge.

For efficiency, the Spacebar is located near your thumb, and the vowels are wheeled around your index finger. The most commonly used letters are placed around the strongest fingers. But this board takes some time to master. If you do master it, travel will be a snap.

RECOMMENDED WORKING POSTURES

Recommended Working Postures describe body positions that are neutral and comfortable to use. Using postures other than those recommended will generally waste energy and motion as welol as potentially raise the risk of injury. It's also important to change position frequently and stretch between tasks. This improves circulation and lessens fatigue.

Shoulders and Arms

- Keep the shoulders relaxed - not "shrugged-up" or "slumped-down".
- Keep your elbows close to your body.
- Keep work at about elbow height.

Head and Neck

- Avoid situations that require twisting the neck or bending it forward, backward, or to the side.

Hands and Wrists

- Keep the hands straight and in line with the forearms - avoid twisting hands.
- Avoid working with wrists pressed against sharp or hard edges.

Back

- Stand straight: Avoid situations that require bending (forward or backward), leaning to the side, or twisting.
- A sit/stand stool will allow for changes in posture.
- For work performed while sitting, a back rest will help maintain proper posture.

Feet and Legs

- Placing a foot on a footrest or other support will promote comfort.
- Provide toe space to allow workers to stand closer to counters. This can reduce reaching.
- Good quality anti-fatigue mats reduce back and leg fatigue.

References

- Physical-ergonomics: oshwiki.eu, Retrieved 14 April, 2020
- Liebowitz, Stan J.; Margolis, Stephen E. (2001). "The Fable of the Keys". Winners, Losers and Microsoft. Oakland, Calif.: Independent Inst. p. 30. ISBN 978-0-945999-84-3
- Lyons, K.; Plaisted, D.; Starner, T. (2004-10-31). Expert Chording Text Entry on the Twiddler One-Handed Keyboard. Eighth International Symposium on Wearable Computers. Computer. pp. 94–101. CiteSeerX 10.1.1.69.3470. doi:10.1109/ISWC.2004.19. hdl:1853/58. ISBN 978-0-7695-2186-2
- Frogpad-mobile-keyboard, keyboards-34568: in.pcmag.com, Retrieved 06 July, 2020
- Ergonomics-recommended-working-postures, wellness-ergonomics: spineuniverse.com, Retrieved 18 June, 2020
- Marklin, Richard W.; Simoneau, Guy G. (2004). "Design Features of Alternative Computer Keyboards: A Review of Experimental Data". Journal of Orthopaedic & Sports Physical Therapy. 34 (10): 638–649. doi:10.2519/jospt.2004.34.10.638. PMID 15552709

3

Organizational Ergonomics

Organizational ergonomics deals with the optimization and modification of organizational policies, structures and processes. Crew resource management, work design, participatory design, community ergonomics, cooperative work, virtual organizations, telework, etc. are a few of its concepts. This chapter discusses the subject of organizational ergonomics in detail.

Organizational ergonomics is concerned with the optimization of socio-technical systems, including their organizational structures, policies, and processes. Relevant topics include: communication, crew resource management, work design, work systems, design of working times, teamwork, participatory design, community ergonomics, cooperative work, new work programs, virtual organizations, telework, and quality management).

System Ergonomics

Ergonomics (or human factors) is the scientific discipline concerned with the understanding of the interactions among humans and other elements of a system, and the profession that applies theoretical principles, data and methods to design in order to optimize human well-being and overall system performance (definition International Ergonomics Association (IEA). Within this discipline or profession, physical ergonomics is regarded as one of the domains of specialization, beside organizational ergonomics and cognitive ergonomics.

The words system ergonomics implicate that a systematic approach is chosen for the design or redesign of work situations. Step by step the next items are considered after:

Orientation:

- What is the starting point? What is the question in headlines? Who will be involved? Who is the owner? What will be the project structure? Are there limiting conditions?

Analysis:

- System analysis: What is the goal of the activities: what must be performed, both in quantities and in quality?

- Task analysis: Which tasks are required to achieve the goals? In this analysis an analysis of bottlenecks is done as well.

Design:

- Determine a program of requirements.
- Task allocation: Which tasks can best be allocated to technology (machines, ICT), and which to humans? Both have different capacities and limitations. Consider alternatives, and choose the best solution.
- Design of tasks and jobs, including organisational aspects (e.g. level of education, training; teamwork; work schedules; flexible solutions).
- Testing in a virtual environment using simulations (many kinds possible), mock ups, models.
- Design of interfaces between humans and technology, and of communication.
- Adaptation of the designs.

Two major stages can be distinguished: The global design, followed by the detailed design.

Realisation:

- Realisation: Building, implementation. If required training of staff.

Evaluation:

- Evaluation: How well does the system do what it should? If necessary adaptations are considered.

Orientation:

It is essential that the questions of the owner are as specific as can be. Covers the question all the aspects? Will the objective be achieved with these questions? Would there be an alternative? Ergonomists are excellent in questioning and in thinking ahead. Each question of the ergonomists is in fact already a consult. Limiting conditions must get attention; anyway these include budget, timeline available staff.

Analysis:

The goal of the activities and the system must be well defined in specifications for input (raw materials, information, parts) and output (products, texts, task performance e.g. in control rooms). Both quantitative (quantities, numbers, measurable quality) and qualitative aspects (e.g. non-measurable quality, image, growth of experience) need to get attention. The next step is the task analysis. In an existing situation the actual tasks are described into detail. Typical questions begin with 'how' or 'why'. Many a time already the task analysis leads to the questions why, and the insight that things can be done differently. Usually the analysis has four levels, but in complex situations there may be more. The four levels are: goal; sub goal; tasks; manoeuvres. For instance: the goals of a traffic control room are efficient flow of traffic, a sub-goal can be minimizing exhaust gases, observing screens, communication, are examples of tasks, while taking action with traffic signs, blocking lanes are manoeuvres. The inventory of bottlenecks is another part of the analysis. Here one needs to be as specific as possible in order to determine the real bottleneck. E.g. what is the cause of physical work strain? The loads can be too heavy for manual handling by one person. But what is the real cause? Is it that lifting is inefficient as it should be done by two employees, while all other tasks are performed individually (organisational bottleneck). Or is there not enough space to lift together? Principles of solutions can be determined in the analysis. If the bottlenecks are clear, solutions can be pictured. There may be a risk of that a solution is selected to easily. For instance to improve the situation employees will be trained, while by redesigning the task the problems will be solved basically.

Design

Based on the orientation and the analyses, the program requirements can be fixed. These are the specifications that the system must meet, like system performance, costs, and the level of education of staff. Then the task allocation follows, in which tasks are allocated to technology (machines, ICT), or humans. Both have different capacities and limitations, and different costs. Consider what the consequences are for human tasks and jobs: are these complete, not too complex, can these be performed for a whole working day, during a whole working life? Are there alternatives? Is the technology available, or shall it be developed? Do choose the best solution for humans and the system. Then tasks and jobs are designed into detail. Organisational aspects like the required level of education and training. Aspects of teamwork are considered as well as work schedules and flexible solutions. The basic design can be tested in any stage. Simulations can be done at all levels, varying from a discussion using only paper or white board to virtual environments (software, mock ups, and models). If all is expected to work well, the design of interfaces between humans and technology and of communication can be detailed. A new testing phase will follow in order to check if the interfaces work as objected. Adaptation must be done is problems are met. Ergonomists play a consultancy role in the design process, where designers have the lead.

Realisation

In this stage the design is built, installed, and implemented. Staff is trained where necessary. The ergonomist shall be close at hand; during the realisation and in pilots many smaller questions will arise. For example: the project team designed an ergonomics cabin for a new tram; the cabin is relatively large, allowing space for an instructor. In the first pilots it turns out that passengers tend to enter the instructor's space. The drivers are complaining to be distracted by those passengers. The choice is made to place a door as the optimal solution. It is important that such solutions are in line with the basics of the design. Minor changes are carried through as well in this stage.

Participatory Ergonomics

Participatory ergonomics programs seek to maximize the involvement of the workers in this process, based on the simple fact that a worker is an expert on his or her job. The participatory approach to ergonomics relies on actively involving workers in implementing ergonomic knowledge, procedures and changes with the intention of improving working conditions, safety, productivity, quality, morale and comfort. One basis for participatory ergonomics is the fact that many proposed changes are not successfully implemented. Reasons are for instance:

- Workers question why the proposed change will be feasible, as previous changes were obstructed.
- No need for change is felt, no sense of urgency.
- Previous changes had little effect.
- Proposed changes are simplified, for instance because of budget.

By participation of workers they will be involved in all steps of the change process, which provides a sound base for acceptation and successful implementation.

Participatory Process

A participatory process consists of 9 steps:

- Introduction.
- Analysis.
- Generation of ideas.
- Selection of best ideas.
- Detailing.
- Testing.
- Adaptation.
- Implementation.
- Evaluation.

A successful participatory ergonomics program requires initial and continuing resources and support from the top levels of management within the organization. The resources required include:

- Time for the program to develop.
- Time to develop and implement solutions.
- Financial resources to make meaningful changes in the workplace.
- Management support for the individuals on the ergonomics team.
- An appointed group is responsible for the process.
- Let all employees have their input in the inventory of bottlenecks, in the generation of ideas and for the implementation.

Job Design and Task Allocation

Job design aims to specify the contents, methods and relationships of jobs to satisfy the technological and organisational requirements as well as the personal needs of job holders. It meets the needs of both employer and employees. Both individual human characteristics as group characteristics are considered. A good job design is in line with the best option in the Hierarchy of control, as it will basically eliminate risk. Jobs need to be complete, in order to meet human's needs. Key elements are:

- Autonomy: The worker himself has influence on tha way the tasks are performed.
- Feedback: The worker gets information about the individual performance and the system performance, including aspects like client satisfaction.
- Significance of the task within the extend of the whole company or organization.
- Completeness: A position must consist of preparatory tasks, executive functions, and supportive tasks.

Variation in competencies and demands: A task can be best defined as a piece of assigned work expected to be done within a certain time. It is important to strictly and thoroughly identify tasks that need completion. Motivation describes forces within the individual that account for the level, direction, and persistence of effort expended at work. The best jobs are those in which individuals are compelled, excited, and passionate to do their work. Anyway, it is essential to design jobs that motivate employees. Resource allocation occurs when organizations decide to appropriate or allocate certain resources to specific jobs, tasks, or dilemmas facing the organization. Jobs need to be constructed so that efficiency of the worker or department is maximized, while the health, safety and well-being of staff are secured. Organizations need to use the resources and creativity of their employees effectively and efficiently. In job design it is necessary to identify and structure jobs in a way that the company's resources are being efficiently used. Appropriate resource allocation allows large organizations to foster and develop innovation in their workforce. Reward systems also play a role in job design. Reward systems include compensation, bonuses, raises, job security, benefits, and various other methods of reward for employees. An outline or description of reward packages needs to be established while constructing jobs.

Five important job elements that motivate workers and stimulate performance are: skill variety, task identity, task significance, autonomy, and job feedback. Three different psychological states determine how an employee reacts to job characteristics: experienced meaningfulness, experienced responsibility for outcomes, and knowledge of the actual results.

How to Design Jobs?

It starts with questions like:

- What are the task's aims and objectives?
- How will the objective be achieved?
- Where will the task take place?
- When will the task be performed (continuously, night time, day time)?
- Who will perform the task (skills, training, and competence)?
- Why the task is required – overall context of the activity?

The ideal task design will identify key task requirements and allocate the task roles between man and technology to optimise strengths and minimise weaknesses. This balance will also be influenced by the criticality of the task, the level of reliability required and the urgency of recovering from errors or malfunctions. A basic procedure for allocating function is given in ISO 11064-1.

Table: Traditional labour system versus highly involved labour system.

No.	Step	Procedure
1	Mandatory allocation.	For mandatory functions, allocate to machine.
	Allocation to meet safety/regulatory requirements.	For mandatory manual functions, allocate to human.
2	Attempt at preliminary allocation in terms of human traits, abilities and characteristics with a view to ensuring the safety and reliability of the system's performance.	Re-design system to avoid tasks which cannot be carries out satisfactorily by human or machines.
		Allocate functions which cannot be satisfactorily carries out manually to machines.

	Allocation according to performance characteristics.	Allocate functions which cannot be satisfactorily automated to humans.
		Treat as mandatory automatic functions.
		Initially, allocate machine preference and human preference functions to machines & human respectively.
		Initially, leave without preference functions unallocated.
3	Allocation according to cognitive and affective support criteria.	Consider reallocation of preference functions according to cognitive and affective criteria.
	Complementary or flexible allocation from the viewpoint of ergonomics and system efficiency.	Consider complementary or flexible allocation, which gives users the ability to change the allocation.
4	Ascertain feasibility of automation.	Determine whether functions allocated to humans can be implemented effectively using available automation technology.
5	Ascertain feasibility of human performance. Select tasks which are to be supported by operator support systems to assist with signal detection, information acquisition and decision making.	Assess whether functions allocated to humans can be implemented effectively assuring the availability of operator support systems. Determine whether such systems can be implemented using the available level of technology.
6	Evaluate allocation. Determine need for iteration and revision.	Repeat allocation procedure if the proposed allocation of functions is impractical or requires further refinement if there are unacceptable technical information.

Checklist for Jobs

According to the Dutch WEBA system (well-being at work); the following items need to be for healthy jobs and the prevention of work stress:

- Jobs are complete, and do include:
    - Involvement in the planning of work and the order of tasks.
    - Involvement in how the work is performed.
    - End control of own work.
    - Good division of preparatory, performing, supporting and organizing tasks.
    - If working with machines: Adjust, maintain and small repairs.
- Involvement in the solution of problems:
    - Solve problems in own work as far as the competencies allow.
    - Tool box meetings to discuss and solve problems.
    - Direct access to supervisors in case of trouble.

- Cycle work:
    - Less than 50% of the work consists of tasks with a cycle of <90 seconds.
- Degree of difficulty:
    - A good variation in difficult work and routine work.
- Autonomy and variation:
    - Variation of workplaces is feasible.
    - Short breaks are possible during the execution of tasks.
    - Leaving the workplace is possible for short breaks.
    - Workers can influence their work pace.
- Contacts:
    - The help of co-workers can be called in.
    - Communication with co-workers is possible, also when performing tasks.
    - Noise levels do allow verbal communication without raising one's voice.
- Information:
    - Employee is informed about the progress and results of work.

Though the WEBA system is partly based on German, Austrian and American models no other EU countries have similar methods.

Teamwork and Task Rotation

The socio-technical systems approach is designed around the evolution from individual work to work-groups. This approach has the following guiding principles:

- The design of the organization must fit its goals.
- Employees must be actively involved in designing the structure of the organization.
- Control of variances in production or service must be undertaken as close to their source as possible.
- Subsystems must be designed around relatively self-contained and recognizable units of work.
- Support systems must fit in with the design of the organization.
- The design should allow for a high quality working life.

Changes should continue to be made as necessary to meet the changing environmental pressures.

Today teamwork has become mature: groups bear responsibility. The differences between traditional labour systems and highly involved labour systems.

Table: Labour system.

Tradiotional labour system	Higly involved labour system
Jobs and tasks narrow and precisely defined	Jobs and task defined broadly
Task specialism	Task rotation and integration
Direct supervision	Peer supervision (by co-workers
Focuses on individuals	Focuses on teams
Limited responsibility	Team responsibility
Position related pay	Competence based pay

Work Schedules and Shift Work

Though much of the work is yet performed in a five day workweek, several developments, including multinational work, have changed our world to a 7x24 economy. Modern ICT allows many workers to do computer based tasks at any moment. This may allow them to be more flexible in their balance of work and private life. The drawback is that work may never end; e-mails will be pushed to the mobile devices, and many individuals tend to read and answer those at any moment. Real rest remains important to relax from straining work.

Laws on working hours and work schedules have become less strict over the years. Working days preferably do not exceed 9 hours. If longer, a decrease in productivity and an increase of unsafe situations are likely. The same counts for prolonged periods of work without rests. However, taking short breaks during a shift reduces fatigue and sleepiness significantly.

Shift Work

Shift work is common in many sectors. The traditional habit to spare elderly workers from night shifts has become impossible with the aging workforce. An alternative criterion for the age in years could be the number of years in full shift work. Self-scheduling by teams is an option to get more support for a schedule.

Night Shifts

From a health perspective, night shifts are straining. Sleeping disorders and digestion problems decline significantly when workers' nightshifts end. It is recommended to limit the number of unbroken night shifts to three. Starting times have an influence on vigilance, and it is recommended that morning shifts do not start before 7:00 a.m.

TIPS TO IMPROVE THE ERGONOMICS OF WORKSTATIONS

The worksite environment can be a significant factor that may affect the health and wellness of your employees and also their productivity. And ergonomics plays a key role in designing for staff benefits.

Ergonomics deals with the correct body position to help lower the onset of possible strains and injuries. To maximize health and productivity, tweak the ergonomics and positioning of four main office elements:

Chairs

The height and shape of chairs can greatly affect your employees' comfort:

- Choose chairs with seat pans that are titled slightly downward. This design can help relieve any pressure on the spine.
- Provide lumbar support so that when your employees are typing on their computers, there will be enough support on their lower backs to prevent slouching.
- The back of the seats should allow the knees to clear the seat pan's front.
- Correct seat height is achieved when the employees' feet are lying flat on the floor and their hips are of the same level as their knees.

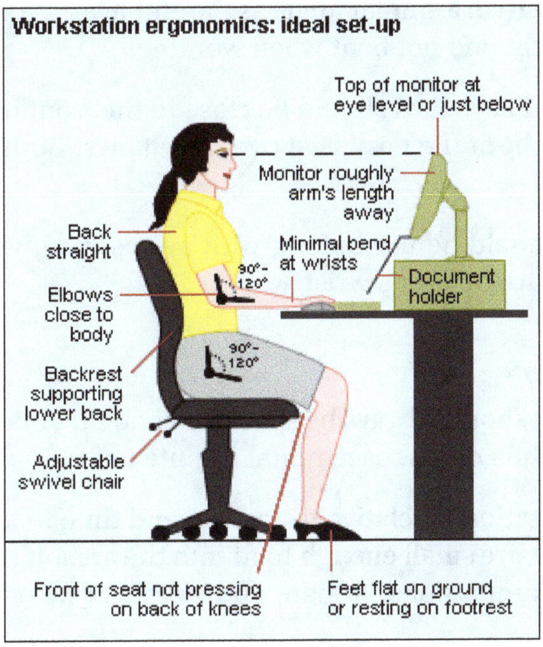

Monitor

Arranging the computer screen to prevent squinting and minimize harmful contrast are two ways to keep employees' eyes protected:

- Eye strain is incurred when there is too much contrast between ambient light or colors and the computer screen. Tweak the monitor display settings and external lighting to minimize contrast.
- Avoid arranging the workstation wherein sources of lights will be pointed towards employees' eyes. That is why the location of windows should be considered when arranging the office.
- Neck strain and eye strain can be prevented or relieved by putting each PC monitors about 20 degrees to 50 degrees below the eye level.
- Position the monitor at a distance suitable to the eye strength of the employee; increase the font sizes on the display to also help relieve any straining that can result from the monitor being too far from the person's eyes.

Keyboards and Mice

Prevent (or avoid) the onset of carpal tunnel syndrome — a common type of inflammation affecting the hands due to improper posture and repetitive actions — with proper placement of keyboards:

- Keyboards should be the same level or height as your employees' elbows.
- Slant the keyboard in a similar angle as the employees' forearms to enable wrists to remain straight and not bent when working.
- Each mouse and keyboard should be close to the front of the desk — or farther away if the height of the desk is above the elbows. Both should be equidistant from the user.
- Every mouse should be used along with a wrist pad, which can help provide proper support to the user's wrist.

Space

Above all, workstations should always be spacious enough. This can be a big challenge, especially these days when office space rental is quite hefty.

If the size of the workstation is relatively small, spend time to look for and buy equipment and furniture that are small enough to fit into the area. If possible, have furniture customized so proper dimensions, design, and sizes can be observed for the sake of office ergonomics.

One way to determine the spaciousness of the office is to see if your employees can easily and quickly roam around. If they can freely and swiftly move within the area despite the presence of furniture and equipment, then, there is enough space. Free movement within the workstation can be a significant factor to ensure productivity and comfort.

MOBILE IT-SUPPORTED WORK – A CHALLENGE FOR OSH AND HUMAN FACTORS

Work in the information society is characterized by a high level of penetration by information and communication technologies (ICT). The corresponding technical artifacts take the form of smartphones, laptops, etc. At the same time, progressive erosion can be observed of the traditional association of work with a particular location. Far-reaching changes like these to the relevant work systems imply corresponding stresses and potential for impairing strain.

Osh and Mobile Work in the Context of the Digitization of the Working World

The digitization of human environments, which has progressed at a breakneck pace since the onset of the third industrial revolution owing to the spread of microelectronics into all areas, has also impacted upon the area of employment. Stationary computer workplaces have been commonplace in administrations and other contexts at least since the late 1970s. Whereas initially the devices used were mere dumb terminals, i.e. input and output devices connected to a central mainframe, PC-based workplaces became widespread in the course of the 1980s. In these networked but decentralized systems, the CPU was made available to individual users, enabling them to complete more complex and less standardized tasks. This made use of the PC as a universal machine attractive for forms of salaried work which had not previously been associated with information technology. Whether in manufacturing and production, administration, teaching, research, or services of all kinds, information technology made inroads into every aspect of vocational activity. Changes in the world of work and the ensuing problems for the occupational safety and health of workers were considered by the parties responsible and suitable measures were taken in the form of field-specific research at research-bodies all over the world. During a phase of comparatively quiet development in the field of IT, the technical performance of the equipment increased considerably; at the same time however, the quality of the associated salaried work and the resulting relevance for occupational safety and health stagnated. Workplaces continued to be stationary. Input devices similar in kind, output devices (especially display screens) underwent substantial ergonomic improvements. The advent of the Internet brought the calm situation of the early 1990s to an abrupt end: PCs rapidly became networked, driven by the economic interest in productivity gains on the one hand and naive proclamations of a "Brave New World" on the other.

More recently, an issue of relevance to occupational safety and health emerged: that of home-based teleworking. It became truly attractive with the advent of networking over the Internet. Even though the actual tasks involve stationary office workplaces in the traditional sense (which are therefore subject in many EU-Ordinances), the spatial distance between the persons carrying out the work nevertheless gives rise to new problems. Communication barriers prevent the potential benefits being exploited to the full; the management of personnel is geared, for want of better alternatives, to pure management by results; the resulting growing disregard for the work context raises the pressure upon the employee. The teleworker is increasingly held responsible for failures and for drops in productivity, if not legally, then at least in the view of the parties involved, who also make this view known. In addition, persistently isolated forms of work also increase the psychosocial stress upon the employee. In consideration of the negative impacts, such workplaces have generally morphed into alternating home-based teleworking.

The technical developments responsible for the sea-change in the human environment and the world of work since the turn of the millennium are due in particular to the interaction between information and communication technology (the smartphone being a classic example) and to the spread of the wireless infrastructure, which is fast becoming ubiquitous. This infrastructure makes familiar facilities such as hotspots and 3G (or successor standards such as LTE/4G) universally available. The concept of always on and always reachable, which has already been embraced wholeheartedly by the young generation of digital natives and is now barely questioned, will be taken to a new level and shape the mentality of whole subsets of society, and will be promoted and exploited by business much more strongly than in the past. Equipped with typical technical products such as laptops, smartphones, etc., the mobile IT-supported worker is a manifestation of the existing technical possibilities in the context of salaried work in all conceivable sectors. A typical workplace is also a more or less networked car as a new mobile office. The relevance of this working group is evident not least when the situation already reached in mobile IT-supported work is compared to that of conventional home-based teleworking.

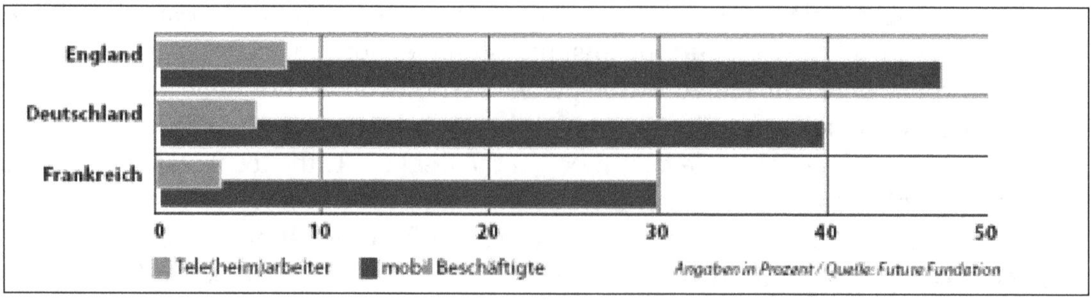

Home-based teleworking vs. mobile employees.

In the performance of their tasks, mobile IT-supported workers face risks from a range of sources, of which there has been only limited awareness to date.

Table: Sources of risks facing IT-supported work.

	Risk/Source of Risk
Technology	Miniaturisation of devices.
	New technologies (e.g. E-paper, wearable computer).
	Poor visual interfaces.
	Repetitive movements.
Work Environment	Excessive noise levels.
	Static and poor posture.
	Cognitive overload.
	Multitude of work-settings.
	Soaring mobility and micro-mobility.
Work Organization	Increasing work load.
	Longer work time.
	Communication barriers.
	Reduced access to information.
	Permanent reachability.
	Difficulties in leadership.
Working Individual	Dual use of devices (work, private).
	Increase autonomy.
	Necessity for self-management.
	Lack of social support.

The identification of these sources of risks is important for a reorganization of the work-spaces. The suspected sources of risk were studied with regard to their actual relevance by the measurement of stresses and strains.

It was shown that mobile workers are often effectively off the radar, are excluded from company support measures, and that their specific needs are not known. Training and other measures which could improve the stress situation, particularly in the area of behavioural prevention, are frequently lacking. The permanent reachability that is made possible by mobile ICT gives rise to a need for arrangements at company-specific arrangements, such as company agreements.

Certain typical and empirical psychosocial, ergonomic and organizational aspects and recommendations are presented below. The recommendations are based essentially upon the quantitative research approach of the Institute for Occupational Safety and Health (IFA), of the DGUV and upon subsequent laboratory studies.

Psychosocial aspects and Organizational Implications: Isolation, Scheduling, Permanent Reachability and Surveillance

The introduction of mobile information and communication technologies has also resulted in changes in the organization of daily work. The possibilities presented by "any place, any time", and the fact that it is at least technically possible for the location of each and every field worker to be determined and for movement profiles to be generated, gives rise to new psychosocial stressors upon the isolated workers during their work. The core aspects and some recommendations are presented below.

Isolation

In many cases, mobile ICT-supported work increases the productivity of the work processes. The mobility has its downside, however. Whereas their co-workers at stationary workplaces often have access to a dense network of social contacts which are conducive not only to social life, but also to the flow of information within a company, mobile employees generally work alone, often with no opportunity for discussion or to meet their colleagues face to face. The isolated situation of the workers concerned has repeatedly been seen to cause difficulties. For example, solutions found to the problems affecting individual workers do not benefit the group as a whole; information on processes of change within the company cannot be discussed within the group; and since they do not happen in the first place, discussions with colleagues do not serve as an outlet for frustration.

Organizations therefore have a vital interest in information being shared. The proverbial chat in the corridor, though often derided, has long served as an intelligent mode of informal communication within companies. The mental well-being of employees is also an essential responsibility of modern occupational safety and health and a cornerstone of any robust organization. Negative impacts can be mitigated by organizational measures. For this purpose, working groups should hold team meetings at least once a month.

Scheduling

Beyond management level, work performed by mobile workers is typically co-ordinated and scheduled with the aid of ICT by a central office or dispatcher who is divorced from the practical work. Target times are defined for the tasks to be carried out, and are used to plan the entire working day. Practical experience shows that these target times are often very optimistic best cases and can be observed only under ideal conditions. They result in the worker being placed under enormous pressure, and often running behind schedule. The pressure is further increased by dissatisfied schedulers and customers, both of which are relying upon the schedule based upon the target time. In order to reduce this mental stress and to improve the satisfaction of all parties involved, it is essential that target times for the tasks be agreed jointly between the mobile service technicians and the planners/schedulers.

Permanent Reachability

The use of mobile ICT results in mobile workers being reachable at all times. On the one hand, this is a blessing: agreements can be reached directly and quickly, and digital information can be transferred at any time through the all-pervading data transmission infrastructure. On the other, it is a curse: the permanent reachability is often treated by the stationary workers (schedulers, managers, etc.) as being synonymous with permanent availability. This leads to frequent disturbances in and interruptions to essential work processes. The consequence is not only stress, but also substantial reductions in productivity. In order for this phenomenon to be addressed pro-actively, company agreements governing the issue have proved to be an effective instrument.

They constitute a collective framework for behaviour which relieves the individual workers from personal, often very difficult decisions. A company agreement may determine the times at which a worker must be reachable, the remuneration for calling on workers outside working hours and when an absent status can/may be activated in order for core tasks to be pursued without interruption. These simple common rules enable the mobile workers to work reliably, productively and with less stress.

Surveillance

It is technically possible for ICT to be used to monitor workers and to generate movement profiles for them. Workers frequently fear this practice and feel spied upon and stressed by the mere theoretical possibility of this happening. Such situations should be governed in a transparent and binding way within companies so as not to provide any basis for such fears. Here too, company agreements and codes of ethics governing have proved effective. They should point up what data are interpreted with the aid of satellite/SIM card technology, and why. Also important is who is able to access the data and where the data is stored.

Ergonomic Aspects

Stationary workplaces offer the great advantage of enabling static environmental conditions to be maintained and controlled. This is of benefit not least for the organization of ergonomic aspects and the facility for their control within companies. By contrast, mobile workers face continually changing environmental conditions that cannot be controlled. The employer's risk assessment is important for mobile tasks in particular. The context of the work remains beyond control; scope is however revealed for influencing the ergonomics of the work equipment and its use in the context of mobility. Selected examples are provided below:

Use of Laptops

Laptops are crucial to the work of most mobile workers. The devices are used to complete a wide range of tasks, from administrative tasks to the reading of plans and sketches. Laptops are the class of equipment offering potentially the best ergonomic compromise, provided certain criteria are observed during their purchase and use:

- Glossy screens vs. anti-glare: Glossy screens have become very popular in recent years. They are however not suitable for commercial use. This is particularly the case when work is performed outdoors. Reflections are distracting, tiring for the eyes, and a source of stress. Commercial users should use exclusively matt, anti-glare screens.

- Display dimensions: Laptops and netbooks must be selected with screen sizes which are suitable both for the tasks to be performed on them and for the mobility requirements. Under no circumstances should the display diagonal be less than 10".
- Luminance: Besides the reflection properties of a display, further quality criteria are relevant to the use of the devices in the field, particularly outdoors. The luminance, measured in candela/m2 (cd/m2), is an important factor. Observations in the field and laboratory tests conducted have led to the conclusion that devices with a luminance of 400 candela/m2 or more are very suitable.

Use of Smartphones

More than virtually any other item of work equipment, smartphones are synonymous with the new mobile, digitized and networked world of work. They combine, in a single device, a range of functions for which multiple items of equipment would have been required only a few years ago. Owing to these properties, they are often the preferred and also the most cost-effective tool. However, as the field observations showed, smartphones are overloaded with tasks for which they are not suitable, particularly for ergonomic reasons. Extended inputting data is possible only under considerable physical strain. Smartphones should therefore be used primarily for verbal communication and for tasks requiring little input and reading.

Mobile IT-supported Work and Vehicles/Driving

Many application scenarios exist, beginning with the use of various types of satellite navigation system through to the integration of laptops. Thousands of workplaces can be found which present no alternative to the use of a road vehicle as a mobile office. In order to make the use of mobile ICT in road vehicles as safe and productive as possible, certain criteria must be observed:

- Mounts (regardless of whether they are for satellite navigation systems, mobile phones or laptops) are considered for the most part under EU law as a load and not as an installation (cf. the classification by DEKRA, TÜV, etc). Where mounts are declared to be loads, they do not automatically require a general operating permit, TÜV certificate or similar in order to be placed on the Single Market. Nor are the manufacturers obliged in this case to conduct crash testing. Their use is classified as the securing of a load, the responsibility for which lies with the driver, or with the employer, who must include the work equipment in his risk assessment. Owing to the unpredictability of critical consequences, only mounts that have been subjected to official product testing should therefore be used.

- Airbags: The ICT device must be installed with consideration for the deployment range of the airbag.
- Obstruction of vision: Some forms of device installation may obstruct the driver's vision and consequently present a very real hazard during driving.
- Distraction: When driving, distractions of any kind constitute a latent hazard. Mobile information and communication technology is of major relevance in this context since phone calls or even audio signals announcing the receipt of any kind of information (SMS, email, etc.) might distract the driver.

Obstruction of vision caused by satellite navigation devices.

Sichtbehinderung = Obstruction of visibility.

nach 15 = At 15 m.

Navigationsgerät = Navigation device.

12 x 8 cm gross = Dimensions 12 x 8 cm.

ca. 60 cm vom Kopf = Approx. 60 cm from the head.

Even a comparatively small VDU device like the satellite navigation device shown produces a blind spot of 2 × 3 m at a viewing distance of 15 m. No devices should therefore be mounted on the windscreen.

Progress of Technology and the Future Impact on Employment

The ongoing development of IT will shape future ways of working with computer-supported collaborative work and will establish new organizational factors. Stationary work will be more and more the exception than the rule. Moreover, the term, stationary work gets a new quality in terms of involvement of the workers presence in the local ambient intelligence: The paradigm of ambient intelligence means to the employee to interact with an autonomously operating environment which must take into account in its work activities. This is especially true for driver jobs and IT integration into vehicles. Via radio frequency identification (RFID) tags the employee becomes recognizable and predictable for the intelligent environment. New stressors and hazards can be expected in this context, because of a loss of control and the increasing dependence on technology, but also because of new cognitive demands of such complex work environments. Virtual environments will be networked to the internet of things (networked objects) soon. As a result the activities of the employees can be represented online (e.g. via wearable transponder which feeds the data in the virtual environment). Accordingly, very sophisticated tracking and monitoring systems will be possible. To consider the authors of the EU Final Report Tender No. VT/2007/0117: "Soon people will be part of a technical system. Peoples roll will change from the acting subject to the object of an automatic process." The briefly shown lines of action in this plot for the labour protection (psychosocial aspects, ergonomics and vehicle integration) will therefore continue to remain highly topical. The occupational safety and health has to accompany these developments in terms of humane work.

PARTICIPATORY DESIGN

Industrial ergonomics programs seek to identify and correct factors that negatively impact the physical health of their workers. Participatory ergonomics programs seek to maximize the involvement of the workers in this process based on the simple fact that a worker is an expert on his or her job. The participatory approach to ergonomics relies on actively involving workers in implementing ergonomic knowledge, procedures and changes with the intention of improving working conditions, safety, productivity, quality, morale and comfort.

Implementing a Participatory Ergonomics Program in the Workplace

In order to determine if an ergonomics team/committee is right for a workplace, five factors need to be considered:

Resources and Support

A successful participatory ergonomics program requires initial and continuing resources and support from the top levels of management within the organization. The resources required include:

- Time for the program to develop.
- Time to develop and implement solutions.
- Financial resources to make meaningful changes in the workplace.
- Management support for the individuals on the ergonomics team.

Ergo Team Formation

The ergonomics committee should be composed of people with the right mix of skills including technical or engineering knowledge, worker knowledge and input from an ergonomics expert. Successful, sustainable participatory ergonomics programs have an individual on the committee who takes on a leadership or "ergonomics champion" role.

Training Needs

Training principles and methods are central to the success of the participatory ergonomics process. Three major aspects of training should be considered early in the process of implementing a participatory ergonomics program. Initial training in ergonomics for committee members should include ergonomics concepts and tools. Training on topics such as meeting and project management may be beneficial, depending on the past experience of committee members with committee work and implementing change. Additionally, it is important for the workforce as a whole to gain an understanding of ergonomics to improve their support for the participatory ergonomics process.

Workplace Organization Factors

The research literature contains limited discussion of the effect of the organization's characteristics (culture) on the success of a participatory ergonomics intervention. The organizational climate and the timing of the introduction of the program can affect the outcome. Integrating the participatory ergonomics program into existing health and safety programs can increase the chances of success.

Involving the Workforce in Ergonomics

The ergonomics committee needs to respond to expectations about the ergonomics program. It is imperative to gain support or "buy in" from the workforce as most will not be directly involved with the ergonomics committee. The ergonomics program needs to be visible within the organization; this can be accomplished by ensuring that there is a focused effort to communicate with the workforce and by involving key stakeholders in all changes that are investigated and implemented.

VIRTUAL ORGANIZATIONS

Driving Forces of Organizational Development

The development of theoretical concepts as 'virtual organization' is related to developing technologies and new organizational practices in a cyclical manner. A model describes quite well driving forces behind various forms of virtual organizations. The driving force may be a new business practice, e.g., a globalised business is not possible with a local organization, a new technology, e.g., mobile and wireless information and communication technology (ICT) creates possibilities to work in any time and place, and even a new strategic thought, e.g., of developing a virtual community.

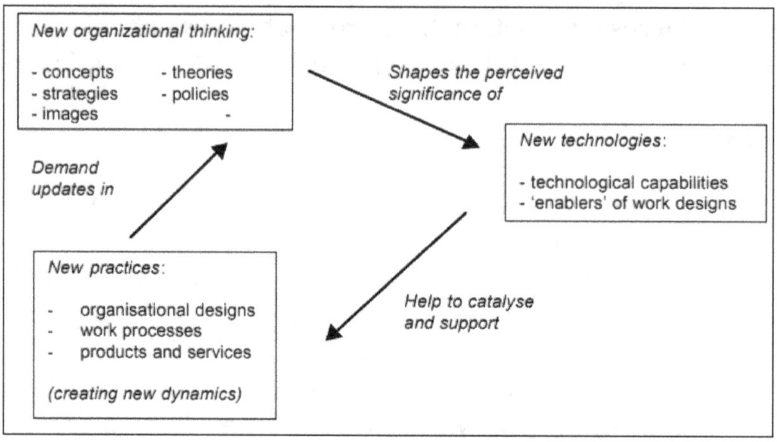

New organizational thinking, technologies and practices.

As is understandable, virtual organizations are needed for several purposes and are justified by several reasons. New products, the globalisation and internalisation of businesses create new kinds of challenges for the management of work processes and practices. The globalisation of economies and businesses increases the number of boundaryless enterprises creating multi-site working in cross-cultural contexts. In order to take full advantage of these changes business must organize itself along radical new lines. For example, small and medium-sized companies are networking to uphold their position in the marketplace. The business environment is turbulent and evolving requiring flexible and fast responses.

At the same time, new information and communication technologies are introduced to facilitate the ongoing change. ICT is often considered to be the main driving force of the societal change into knowledge society. Fast progress of information and communication technologies provides technical bases for the globalisation. The ICT has enabled a decentralization of work. Evolving technologies also create pressures for new organizational structures and job contents. Future mobile and wireless technologies will revolutionize the working life totally by increasing possibilities to work whenever in any place. It is clear that organizations in both the private and public sector have to redesign themselves to utilize fully these new technologies if they are to survive in the dawning spatially and temporally compressed world. Therefore, the number of virtual organizations increases.

Open Systems in Turbulent Fields

The need for work systems' flexibility, adaptability and development seem to be a central justifier for virtual organizational structures. In the traditional socio-technical systems (STS) theory, work systems were considered open systems with respect to their external environment continuously reorganizing their internal sub-systems to achieve a "steady state" at a level where they can still perform their tasks. This indicates that the external environment has a decisive role in work system functioning. Environments, however, differ requiring different adaptation mechanisms. Emery and Trist outlined ideal environmental models into four types:

- A stabile, placid environment, where organizations' response is a simple tactic of attempting to do one's best on a purely local basis.
- A placid, clustered environment, where the new feature of organizational response is the emergence of strategy as distinct from tactics.
- A disturbed-reactive environment, where organizations' response needs an intermediate level of the operation in addition to tactics and strategy.
- 'Turbulent fields', where dynamics arise not simply from the interaction of the component organizations, but also from the field itself.

The dynamics of globalised markets has generated turbulent fields to many work systems. The reality of many organizations consists of a variety of different environments. How to cope with them? Work systems' internal capability, that is, their redundancy, provides principled means to meet external challenges and to be purposive. In the STS theory, 'Redundancy' was considered a princ ipal, intra-system means to cope with external complexity and to achieve flexibility in performing a system's task. This traditional concept may provide a basis to describe and understand flexibility needs and competences also in today's virtual organizations applying new technologies.

Virtual Organizations as Redundant Work Systems

There are two basic ways of building redundancy in organizations. First, redundant parts can be added to the system. Each part is replaceable; as and when one part fails, another takes over. In practice, the redundancy of parts means hiring of new single purpose employees and implementing new single purpose tools and technologies into a work system. Second, redundant functions can be added to the parts, that is, recruit competent employees, tools and technologies. When a multiple purpose part fails, other multiple purpose parts can assume the function.

The traditional STS approach emphasized the redundancy of functions as the main and human-centred manner to increase systems' flexibility capacity by developing individual competencies and by organizing work as group work. Different environments require different forms of an organization. As early as Herbst proposed from organizing viewpoint individual jobs for the stable, placid environment and autonomous groups for the placid, clustered environments. And correspondingly, matrix groups for disturbedreactive environments and network groups for 'turbulent fields'. A network group was described as consisting of members dispersed individually or in small subsets meeting only infrequently for a work session and direct communication.

Adding the possibility of asynchronous working time and the use of ICT result in the definition of a virtual team.

The development of ICT and virtual organizations has questioned the strict division of the two forms of redundancies. Redundant parts, i.e., ICT, have new functional and smart qualities compared to traditional technologies. This has as well raised the question, how technologies enlarge capabilities of employees in virtual working? This topic has come out in discussions on individual and organizational memories and their tools, e.g., learning and knowledge support environments, and mechanisms.

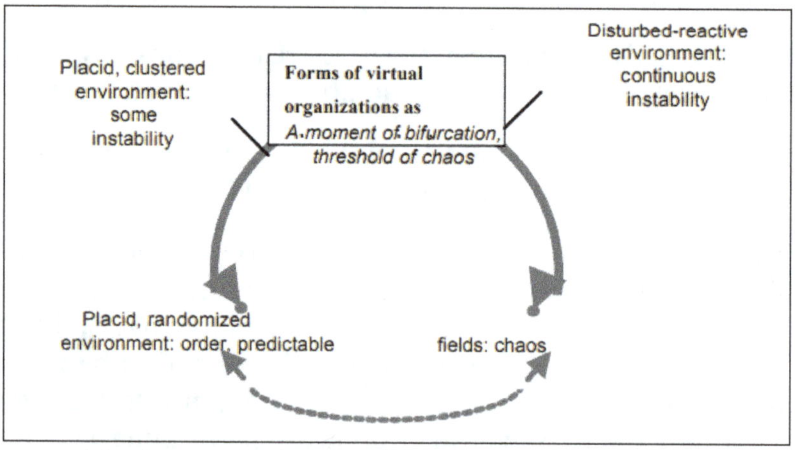

Adaptive organizational mechanisms, e.g., a virtual project, as a regulatory mechanism in various activity environments.

In principle, information and communication technologies provide a large set of tools to enhance communication and knowledge management in virtual organizations. There are tools for knowledge capturing: data analysis and data mining, storing: databases, decision making: decision support systems, performing: electronic performance systems, and transferring knowledge and communication: telephone and teleconference, email and videoconferencing. In addition, there is an increasing number of applicable web tools available including web conferencing and environments that allow shared workplaces and databases.

The concept 'Redundancy' is still relevant and valid when trying to understand and model work systems in various environments. Its content, however, needs to be revised. Instead of two redundancies, we could use three redundancies in increasing the system's flexibility capacity: the redundancies of parts, functions and knowledge. Virtual working needs the integration of the three redundancies as an adaptation mechanism in a turbulent environment. These redundancies are so closely interconnected that you cannot select "either or" but "both and". For example, information and knowledge is so embedded in hardware that it is almost impossible to supply "pure" technology. Employees as well cannot cope with complexity without communicating face-to-face and using different ICT memory tools. In a predictable, placid environment, classical 'Redundancy of Functions' is enough. The more turbulent and chaotic the environment becomes, the more is needed the integration of various redundancies. According to Ashby's law external variety requires internal variety: the integration redundancies of functions are needed the more the degree of environmental turbulences increases.

Dimensions and Types of Virtual Organizations

The background of the concept 'Virtual Organization' dates back to the 80's groupware technologies, and to the resulting discussion on telework, and on visions of virtual corporations. Multi-site, multi-organizational and dynamic organizations began to appear in the 1970s. In the middle of 90's, the first empirical studies were done to understand the nature of virtual organizations and working.

Dimensions of Virtual Organizations

Virtual organizations are often characterized with three dimensions: space (same place – dispersed), time (synchronous – asynchronous) and mode of interaction (face-to-face – electrical). Individual diversity (similar – different) could be the fourth dimension. In a non-virtual organization, employees similar to their cultural and national background are working in a same room, at the same time, and communicating face-to-face.

In virtual organizations, employees work geographically dispersed, often asynchronously and are linked with each other by using various communication technologies. People involved may speak several languages and have diverse cultural, educational and vocational backgrounds. This brings along a strong cultural emphasis. Thus the virtual organization challenges the traditional working here and now, and communicating face-to-face. In order to overcome temp oral, spatial and organizational disablers, ICT is utilized both as means of communication and as a collective memory. In addition, virtual organizations have been described, for example, with the following characterizations: an alliance for a common goal, concentration on knowledge products, temporary nature of an organization (a project), flexibility of working time and place (e.g., telework), diversified and multicultural workforce, mobility of work force, vertical integration, no hierarchy, decentralized, decreased use of offices, etc.

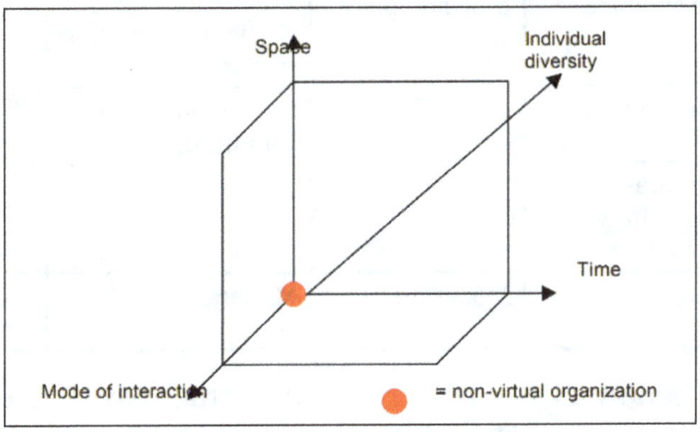

Dimensions of virtual organizations.

- Space: In their review, McDonough et al. note that if team members cannot be collocated they may as well be miles apart, since even a small degree of dispersion among team members will negatively affect the degree of trust and the degree of cooperation between them. Physical proximity is said to reinforce social similarity, shared values, and expectations, and to increase the immediacy of threats from failing to meet commitments. The geographical dispersion also makes communication among team members complex. Cascio considers the lack of physical interaction as the major disadvantages of virtual teams with its associated verbal and non-verbal cues, and the synergies that often accompany face-to-face communication. Thus, we would expect that team members collocated on the same floor would engage in different behaviours than team members in the same building but on different floors, in different parts of the same country, or in different parts of the world.

- Time: For most virtual teams, synchronous interaction, either face-to-face or electrically mediated, is a scarce resource. Work tasks are often realized asynchronously. In global virtual teams, as the distance increases and more time zones are crossed, the possibility to work synchronously decreases. Snow et al. write about R&D team at Texas Instruments, who has turned this type of situation into an advantage by dividing its members among locations in France, California and Japan, and then passing work sequentially so that a 24-hour workday was achieved.

- Mode of interaction: Dispersed working asynchronously emphasizes the meaning of information and communication technologies as communication mode. New mobile technologies provide more and more possibilities to flexible communication in any time and place. Wiesenfeld, Raghuram and Garud compared different communication media with respect to accessibility, formality, shared interpretive context and social context cues.

Table: Comparison of different communication media.

	Face-to-face	Document	Telephone	Electronic Mail
Accessibility/ Synchronicity	Synchronous with respect to time and place	Asynchronous with respect to time and place	Synchronous with respect to time; Asynchronous with respect to place	Asynchronous with respect to time and place
Formality	Dependent upon communicators	Highly formal	Dependent upon communicators	Highly informal
Shared interpretive context	Facilitates creation of interpretive context			Facilitates communication within established interpretive context
Social context cues	Strong	Moderate	Moderate	Weak

Electrical communication as the only mode in virtual working has, however, been strongly questioned from the viewpoint of developing trust. Face-to-face encounters are considered irreplaceable for both building trust and repairing shattered trust. Jarvenpaa and Leidner note that "Paradoxically though, only trust can prevent the geographical and organizational distances of global team members from becoming psychological distances: trust allows people to take part in risky activities that they cannot control or monitor and yet where they may be disappointed by the actions of others." The future will show, to what extent the features of 'virtual presence' can be created and used in virtual working environments.

- Individual diversity: In their review, McDonough et al. also note that cultural diversity impacts team behaviour. Multicultural teams have higher levels of creativity and develop more and better alternatives to a problem than teams with less cultural diversity. Such teams, however, can also have difficulty in developing a task strategy and troubles solving conflicts, creating cohesion and building trust. Different language and culture makes communication among team members complex.

Types of Virtual Organizations

There are different types of virtual organizations. They can be classified by starting from the needs of human interaction and communication. The communication concerning the joint group task organizes people to work together. The main division is made between communities and work organizations. Communities are driven by common interests and informal communication, whereas work organizations by common goals and tasks, and more formal communication. They both can be realized with virtual qualities. This paper deals with virtual work organizations.

There may be informal and formal virtual organizations. The first ones are often called communities instead of formal work organizations. Rheingold defines 'virtual communities' from the viewpoint of Internet as "Social aggregations that emerge from the Net when enough people carry on those public discussions long enough, with sufficient human feeling, to form webs of personal relationships in cyberspace." The definition emphasizes interaction only via information and communication technologies. In communities, people communicate and interact voluntarily, sometimes grouped in small clusters, sometimes acting individually. Communities do have a common interest, but not necessarily a common goal, which characterises work organizations.

Virtual work organizations are divided into networks, companies, teams and dyads. Virtual organizations are essentially network organizations. Typically a company develops its strategy around its core competences and then searches for partners whose expertise and resources complete its own competencies. When the network of partners is spread across large geographical areas, and when relationships change frequently, the organization is considered to be virtual. Virtual organizations are often a group of teams. The activities of large virtual organizations are performed by teams that form among parts of the cooperating organizations. Virtual teams are a kind of "basic cells" of virtual organizations, and, therefore, a significant unit of study.

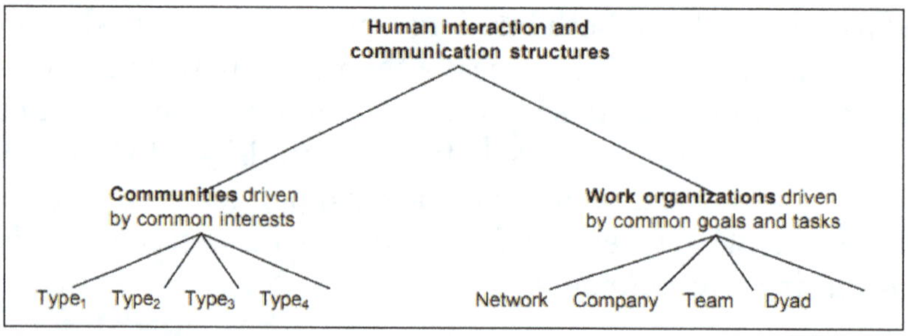

The classification of different forms of human interaction and communication structures.

Snow et al. describe different variants of virtual teams. They describe a distributed team from space and time viewpoints. Distributed teams are composed of people in the same organization who work in different places, either interdependently (e.g., a multi-site product development group), or separately (e.g., branches and local offices). The dimension of organization is also important. There are various cross-organizational teams. Collocated cross-organizational teams comprise people from different organizations who work together in the same place. Distributed cross-organizational teams involve people from different organizations who work in different places. They consider the most extreme type of virtual team one that is cross-organizational and that rarely meets in the course of doing its work. Common forms of virtual teams are task forces and project teams as temporary groups. Such teams are formed specifically to solve a particular problem or to perform a specific task. When the problem is solved or the task completed, the virtual team disappears and team members go back to their normal duties.

Experiences on Virtual Organizations

The material on virtual organizations may roughly be divided into three categories: (1) Material including conceptual descriptions and definitions, (2) empirical studies showing some features of virtual working, and (3) material including managerial implications. The number of empirical studies made on virtual organizations is still limited, although they would be needed to find out critical success factors. Some preliminary conclusions can, however, be made concerning reasons to implement virtual organizations, their advantages and disadvantages.

Advantages

The traditional advantages attributed to virtual organizations include adaptability, flexibility, and the ability to respond quickly to market changes. The following list describes advantages and reasons to implement virtual organizations:

- As companies expand globally, face increasing time compression in product development, and use more foreign based subcontracting labour, virtual teams promise the flexibility, responsiveness, lower costs, and improved resource utilization necessary to meet ever-changing task requirements in highly turbulent and dynamic global business environments.

- The sales division of a large international computer company implemented a mandatory virtual work program. It was initiated both for the cost reduction, i.e., minimizing real estate expenses, and strategic, i.e., encouraging closer contacts with clients and customers, purposes.

- Reduced real estate expenses: IBM saves 40 to 60 per cent per site annually by eliminating offices for all employees except those that truly need them. Increased productivity: internal IBM studies show gains of 15 to 40 per cent. High profits: Hewlett-Packard doubled revenue per salesperson after moving its sales people to virtual workplace arrangements. Improved customer service: Andersen consulting found that its consultants spent 25 per cent more "face time" with customers when they did not have permanent offices.

- Eliminates lack of access to experts. Team can be organized whether or not members are in reasonable proximity to each other. Firms can use outside consultants without incurring expenses for travel, lodging, and downtime. Virtual teams allow firms to expand their potential labour markets, enabling them to hire and retain the best people regardless of their physical location. Employees can accommodate both personal and professional lives. Dynamic team membership allows people to move from one project to another. Employees can be assigned to multiple, concurrent teams. Team communications and work reports are available online to facilitate swift response to the demands of a global market.

- Global teams are needed, because companies move into multinational markets. It is necessary to understand globally distributed customers who locate in different countries, speak different languages, have different sets of cultural beliefs, and who express their preferences in different ways. The needed expertise can be scattered throughout the world.

Disadvantages

Several disadvantages and costs are also mentioned in the material concerning virtual organizations: Such dysfunction as low individual commitment, role overload, role ambiguity, absenteeism, and social loafing may be exaggerated in a virtual context. Customers might perceive a lack of permanency, reliability, and consistency in virtual forms.

- Lack or interaction: There is a tendency for an "in-group" and an "out-group" to develop based on the dominant language. Lack of creative informal interactions. No sense of identity: "It's really difficult to develop 'we' feeling; it's as if whilst we are out of sight we are also out of mind. The team has no real identity. We've never had that from the beginning" ‡ no trust and real commitment to their goal, timetables not held. Who's who: Experienced project workers report frequently that they don't know who the other members of the team are or what they have to offer ‡ in collocated projects, the informal networks have developed. The difficulty of meeting: getting people together is costly. Meetings' agendas tend to be too full ‡ virtual meetings: audio, video and bulletin boards on the e-mail. The impact of time zones: Bitter complaints about the constant invasion into private and family life from telephone calls. It is hard to imagine the situation in other locations. Travelling imposes burdens and stresses.

- Problems with the technology: Hype relating to video conferencing, groupware and other forms of communication technologies has created unrealistic expectations.
- The lack of physical interaction: The meaning of verbal and non-verbal cues in communication.
- The additional cost required to equip a mobile or home worker varies roughly US$3000 to $5000, plus about $1000 in upgrades and supplies every year thereafter.

TELEWORK

Telework can generally be defined as a new way of working, with employees performing work activities which previously were usually carried out at a central work location (office), but which are now carried out remotely from the employer or contractor. Moreover, the work activities require the use of information and communication technology (ICT). At the EU level in 2002, the European social partners signed a Framework agreement on telework. Within the Framework, telework and its scope are defined as: "a form of organising and performing work, using information technology, in the context of an employment contract/relationship, where work, which could also be performed at the employer's premises, is carried out away from those premises on a regular basis. The agreement covers teleworkers. A teleworker is any person carrying out telework as defined above".

Nilles was the first author who used the term 'telecommuting', long before the mobile phone, laptop computers and wireless internet were commonly used in work. However, an exact definition of teleworking, with a clear description of the frequency and average duration of working remotely, is still lacking. There are several different definitions. There is some confusion since teleworking is also referred to as 'telecommuting' or 'remote work' and sometimes even 'distributed work'. Home-working is sometimes also seen as a form of teleworking. These concepts all refer to work arrangements in which employees do not commute to a central place of work, but work at an alternative worksite for any part of their regular or paid hours. There are some differences between the arrangements. Where teleworking refers to all types of technology-assisted work conducted outside of a central work location (office), telecommuting refers to the benefit of reducing travel time from home to the central work location. Distributed work refers to arrangements that allow employees and their tasks to be shared across settings away from a central place of business or organisational location.

What all of these decentralised work arrangements have in common is that they can provide workers with more flexibility and control with regard to where they perform a task. During the industrial revolution employees were bound to their work station in order to be able to perform a certain task. In recent decades, European countries and Western society in general have changed from an industrial based way of working towards a more information based working (especially in service sectors). This, in combination with new technological possibilities, has made it possible for firms to unbind time and tasks from locations. Those who embrace or introduce teleworking, often have high expectations. On the one hand, they aim to increase flexibility and workers' control opportunities on aspects such as working time and place of work in order to create more productive employees with higher job satisfaction. On the other hand, these proponents of telework aim to reduce operating costs by reducing the required number of square meters of office buildings. Besides, telework is promoted as a means to reduce air pollution by decreasing commuter traffic, while also contributing to solving mobility problems.

Prevalence of Teleworking in Europe

Reliable, recent figures on the prevalence of teleworking in the European Union (EU) are scarce. However, in a special module in a survey among enterprises (with 10 persons or more, but without the financial sector) in 31 European countries in 2012, the statistical office of the European Union (Eurostat) incorporated indicators on whether or not an enterprise provides mobile connections to its employees. These indicators may be seen as a relevant proxy indicator on the organisations' policy to allow employees to work remotely, including teleworking. The devices assessed by the indicators, can also be seen as enabling advanced forms of teleworking, i.e. mobile work using portable devices. At least, these proxies can be assumed to correspond with the 'ranking' of countries with regard to telework prevalence. Two of these indicators are presented here. These involve: 1) provision to the persons employed of portable devices that allow a mobile connection to the internet for business use to access the enterprise's email system, and the - even more advanced - indicator 2) enterprises giving portable devices for business use to access and modify documents of the enterprise. The percentages per indicator are shown for the EU27 overall, for each Member State, and for four other European countries.

42% of the enterprises in the EU27 provide their employed persons portable devices that allow a mobile connection to the Internet for business use to access the enterprise's email system. In Finland, even 73% (three out four enterprises) do so, while in the other Nordic countries (Denmark, Norway, Iceland, Sweden) as well as in the Czech Republic, there are also high shares of enterprises providing such e-mail functionality. This involves approximately 60% of the enterprises in these countries. There are only small shares (less than 30%) of enterprises in Bulgaria, Hungary, Greece, Romania and the Former Yugoslav Republic of Macedonia providing persons employed portable devices that allow a mobile connection for such email functionality.

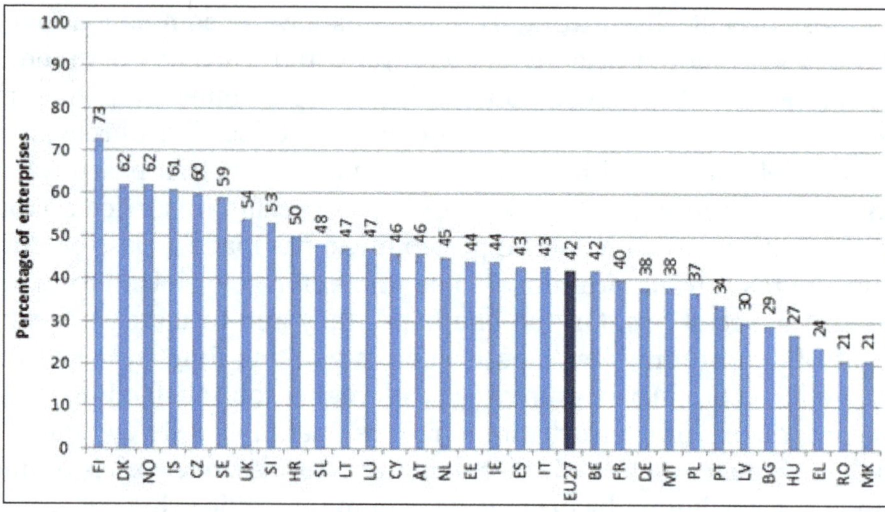

Percentage of enterprises that provide the employed persons with portable devices that allow a mobile connection to the Internet for business use to access the enterprise's email system.

Portable devices with at least 3G technology for accessing the Internet, e.g. via portable computer with modem or via handset using e.g. UMTS but excluding GPRS.

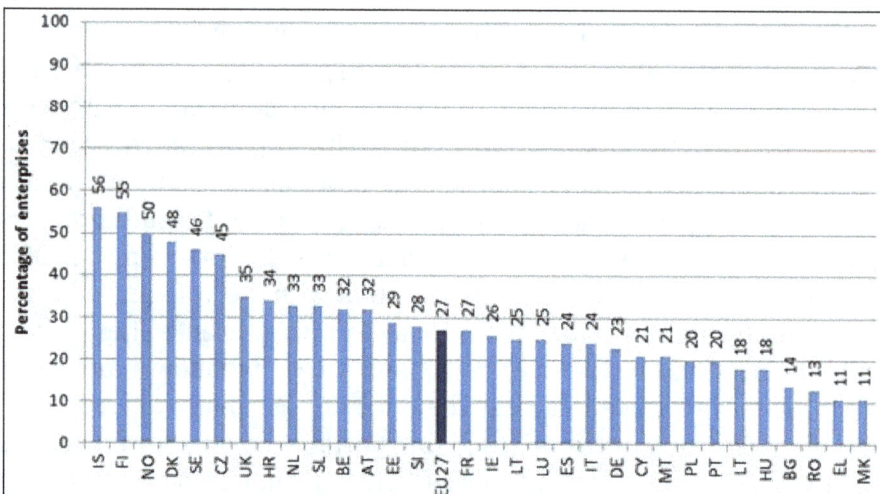

Percentage of enterprises giving employees portable devices for business use in order to access and modify documents of the enterprise.

The percentages in the EU27 and in the individual countries are lower on the second, more advanced, indicator of teleworking. On average, 27% of the EU27 enterprises give portable devices for business use to access and modify documents of the enterprise. The ranking of the countries in this respect is almost similar to the one presented in figure. Iceland and Finland score highest (56% and 55% respectively), followed by Norway, Denmark, Sweden and the Czech Republic (50%; 48%; 46%; 45%), whereas Lithuania, Hungary, Bulgaria, Romania, Greece and the Former Yugoslav Republic of Macedonia rank lowest in this respect. Here, less than 20% of the enterprises give employees portable devices for business use to access and modify documents of the enterprise.

Studies on Characteristics of Teleworkers and their Working Conditions

According to a comparative study including data from the European Working Conditions Survey 2005, in terms of people who telework or work from home, a large number tend to work in the education sector, IT, financial or business and services sectors (e.g., real estate), where access to IT is high.

According to data from the EWCS 2005, professionals were most likely to telework at home using a PC all or almost all of the time (4.4%), followed by legislators, senior officials and managers (3.3%). Professionals were also most likely to telework at home using a PC between one quarter and three quarters of the time (14.6%), followed by legislators, senior officials and managers (12.2%). The types of employees least likely to telework at home using a PC all or almost all of the time were those in elementary occupations (0.4%), followed by plant and machine operators and assemblers (0.5%). The types of employees least likely to telework at home using a PC for between one quarter and three quarters of the time were skilled agriculture and fishery workers (0.7%), followed by plant and machine operators and assemblers (1.7%).

Based on employee surveys, Statistics Netherlands (CBS), for instance, showed that teleworkers were usually highly educated people, were relatively often in a supervisory position and were working long weeks, of more than 40 hours. In a large recent Dutch study, based on four editions of the large-scale National Working Conditions Survey (NWCS) with a representative response of over 22,000 workers per year, teleworkers were relatively often highly educated, men, married or cohabiting with children and living relatively far away from their work, compared to non-teleworkers. Also, teleworkers turned out to be relatively often placed in a supervisory position.

Teleworkers worked more overtime and were (of course) often working with a computer. Regarding their working conditions, teleworkers experienced many degrees of freedom (autonomy) in their work and a lot of task variety. Moreover, they found their managers supportive. However, teleworkers also faced a high workload.

Sectors in which telework is particularly common, are the financial and commercial services, education and the public sector. Sub-sectors that stand out are the ICT sector, of course, followed by the higher education sector. In sectors such as manufacturing, construction, healthcare, transport, catering and agriculture, teleworking is a relatively marginal activity. Such differences, of course, are partly to do with the type of work that is more or less suitable for telework.

Associations between Teleworking, Employee Well-being and Psychosocial Moderators

It is often assumed that employees who have the possibility of teleworking, will experience a greater flexibility in the way they work with colleagues, experience more balance in their personal work situation and increased flexibility in working time. However, working away from the office can also change the contact between colleagues and between employees and firms, which can result in loss of corporate affiliation. At the management level, this causes new challenges for the way managers evaluate performance and supervise employees. The literature also indicates the risks of telework, such as an increase of work-related stress as a result of bad workplace ergonomics in the place where work is carried out, and the loss of work boundaries. To date, little research has been conducted into the effects of teleworking on employees' well-being. There is little understanding on the question whether teleworking constitutes an emerging risk for workers or firms, and under which circumstances. Due to the difference in definitions of teleworking in research studies, making a comparison of results is difficult. For instance, the threshold for telework frequency in which the organisation will identify someone as a teleworker, differs between studies and there are many assumptions about teleworkers and the practice of telework which influences the results.

Working Conditions and Related Health, Well-being and Performance Outcomes

Research showed heterogeneity with regard to where exactly a teleworker is performing work, which makes it impossible to generally address the effect of teleworking on ergonomic and environmental working conditions. The ways in which the teleworker has been given ICT equipment, such as a laptop computer and mobile phone, often remain unknown. This is in line with the research suggestion that the effect of teleworking on productivity and workers' health should not be studied alone, but in interaction with implementation aspects such as proper ICT resources and the role of the manager.

There are, however, some review studies on the effects of telework ('telecommuting') on workers' health, well-being and productivity. These studies found no strong convincing support for an effect of teleworking on productivity. Positive findings were mainly based on self-report measures, with the employees reporting about their own performance. Results that were found, suggest that telecommuting is likely to be more good than bad for individuals. As one large review study concludes, telecommuting had small but mainly beneficial effects on proximal outcomes, such as perceived autonomy and (lower) work–family conflicts. Importantly, telecommuting had no generally detrimental effects on the quality of workplace relationships. Telecommuting was also shown to have beneficial effects on other, more distal outcomes, such as job satisfaction, performance, turnover intent, and role stress. These beneficial consequences appeared to be at least partially mediated by perceived autonomy.

Clear, unambiguous support for the effect of teleworking on health outcomes, such as sickness-absence and well-being, is still lacking. A study, however, showed that telework decreased sickness absence, both among 'average' employees and among employees with a work handicap. In another recent study, access to teleworking predicted higher dedication to the job (being a dimension of work engagement) at follow-up (1 year later).

The working condition 'management by targets/output results' moderated the effects of teleworking on dedication: the combination of access to teleworking and output management was found to have a positive effect. Importantly, when management by output did not coincide with access to teleworking, employees experienced less dedication.

Furthermore, there is some consistent support for the effect of teleworking on job satisfaction. A curvilinear (inverted U) relationship has been reported between the extent of teleworking and job satisfaction. This led to the suggestion that firms should try to find the right balance with respect to extent of telecommuting.

Work-life Balance

For instance, in 2007, a meta-study found that high-intensity telecommuting (more than 2.5 days a week) accentuated telecommuting's beneficial effects on work-family conflict but harmed relationships with coworkers. Telework can be instrumental to reach work-related goals. Generally, it provides employees with more flexibility to perform work roles and more opportunities to adapt working time and location the one's personal situation. Also, time spent on travelling is reduced, which can lower work stress, travel stress and work-life conflict.

Due to new technological possibilities such as mobile phones and fast connectivity to business information, telework has rapidly changed in the last decade (Mobile IT-supported work – a challenge for OSH and human factors). This new way of teleworking may increase family-based interruptions and distraction from work. Teleworkers often experience greater pressure and expectations related to accessibility and availability for work from their employer and also from their colleagues.

Nevertheless, telecommuting did not show straightforward damaging effects on the quality of workplace relationships or perceived career prospects. Researchers suggest that it is of great importance to take into account adoption time, and that the place teleworking is carried out is important. Teleworking programmes are not necessarily 'one size fits all', and firms should differentiate in their job design by looking into the characteristics of their workers and the job tasks that need to be performed.

European Framework Agreement on Telework

At EU level in 2002, the European social partners ETUC (and the liaison committee Eurocadres-CEC), UNICE, UEAPME and CEEP signed a framework agreement on telework. As indicated above, the definition of telework and its scope in the Framework are: "Telework is a form of organising and performing work, using information technology, in the context of an employment contract/ relationship, where work, which could also be performed at the employer's premises, is carried out away from those premises on a regular basis. This agreement covers teleworkers. A teleworker is any person carrying out telework as defined above." The report by the European Social Partners on the 'Implementation of the European Framework Agreement on Telework′ states that the European social partners chose for the first time to implement their European framework agreement by their own means 'in accordance with the national procedures and practices specific to management and labour'. The agreement recalls that teleworkers enjoy the general protection afforded to employees. Hence, the intention was to define a general framework for the use of telework in such a way as to meet the needs of employers and workers. The agreement identifies the key areas requiring adaptation or particular attention when people work away from the employer's premises, for instance data protection, privacy, health and safety, organisation of work, training, etc. At a national level, members of the signatory parties agreed on the instruments and procedures for implementation. They also disseminated, explained and transposed the European text in their national contexts between 2002 and 2006. Relevant OSH themes covered in the Framework include the following:

Voluntary Character

Telework is voluntary for the worker and the employer concerned. Teleworking may be required as part of a worker's initial job description or it may be engaged in as a voluntary arrangement subsequently. In both cases, the employer provides the teleworker with relevant written information in accordance with directive 91/533/EEC, including information on applicable collective agreements, a description of the work to be performed, etc. The specificities of telework normally require additional written information on matters such as the department of the undertaking to which the teleworker is attached, his/her immediate superior or other persons to whom she or he can address questions of professional or personal nature, reporting arrangements, etc.

Employment Status

The passage to telework as such, because it only modifies the way in which work is performed, does not affect the teleworker's employment status. A worker's refusal to opt for telework is not, as such, a reason for terminating the employment relationship or changing the terms and conditions of employment of that worker. If telework is not part of the initial job description, the decision to pass to telework is reversible by individual and collective agreement. The reversibility could imply returning to work at the employer's premises at the worker's or at the employer's request.

Employment Conditions

Regarding employment conditions, teleworkers benefit from the same rights, guaranteed by applicable legislation and collective agreements, as comparable workers at the employer's premises. However, in order to take into account the particularities of telework, specific complementary collective and individual agreements may be necessary.

Privacy

The employer respects the privacy of the teleworker. If any kind of monitoring system is put in place, it needs to be proportionate to the objective and introduced in accordance with Directive 90/270 on visual display units.

Work Equipment

All questions concerning work equipment, liability and costs are clearly defined before starting telework. As a general rule, the employer is responsible for providing, installing and maintaining the equipment necessary for regular telework unless the teleworker uses his/her own equipment.

If telework is performed on a regular basis, the employer compensates for or covers the costs directly caused by the work, in particular those relating to communication. The employer provides the teleworker with an appropriate technical support facility.

Occupational Health and Safety

The employer is responsible for the protection of the occupational health and safety of the teleworker in accordance with Directive 89/391 and relevant daughter directives, national legislation and collective agreements. The employer informs the teleworker of the company's policy on occupational health and safety, in particular requirements on visual display units. The teleworker applies these safety policies correctly.

In order to verify that the applicable health and safety provisions are correctly applied, the employer, workers' representatives and relevant authorities have access to the place where teleworking is being carried out, within the limits of national legislation and collective agreements. If the teleworker is working at home, such access is subject to prior notification and his/her agreement. The teleworker is entitled to request inspection visits.

Organisation of Work

Within the framework of applicable legislation, collective agreements and company rules, the teleworker manages the organisation of his/her working time. The workload and performance standards of the teleworker are equivalent to those of comparable workers at the employers premises. The employer ensures that measures are taken preventing the teleworker from being isolated from the rest of the working community in the company, such as by giving him/her the opportunity to meet with colleagues on a regular basis and access to company information.

Training

Teleworkers have the same access to training and career development opportunities as comparable workers at the employer's premises and are subject to the same appraisal policies as these other workers. Teleworkers receive appropriate training targeted at the technical equipment at their disposal and at the characteristics of this form of work organisation. The teleworker's supervisor and his/her direct colleagues may also need training for this form of work and its management.

Collective Rights

Teleworkers have the same collective rights as workers at the employer's premises. No obstacles are placed in the way of communicating with workers' representatives. The same conditions for participating in and standing for elections to bodies representing workers or providing worker representation apply to them. Teleworkers are included in calculations for determining thresholds for bodies with worker representation in accordance with European and national law, collective agreements or practices. The establishment to which the teleworker will be attached for the purpose of exercising his/her collective rights is specified from the outset. Worker representatives are informed and consulted on the introduction of telework in accordance with European and national legislations, collective agreements and practices.

At a national level, members of the signatory parties agreed on the instruments and procedures for implementation. They also disseminated, explained and transposed the European text in their national contexts between 2002 and 2006. This final joint implementation report describes many initiatives which have enabled the agreement to be implemented in European countries.

WORKING TIME

Working time concerns the hours of the day and the days of the week that work takes place. Most people have standard working hours between 0800 and 1800 on week days. But work also takes place at non-standard hours in the evening, at night and on weekends. Non-standard working times constitute an important part of the economy and society. Work at non-standard hours may have negative effects on the health and well-being of workers because of tiredness and problems of combining work and private life.

Working time is well documented in labour statistics. Mostly the number of working hours and the percentage of part-time contracts is documented. The incidence of non-standard working hours in the European Union (EU) is studied every five years by means of the European Working Conditions Survey (EWCS). An important finding in this survey is that the average length of the European working week is decreasing, which partially related to part-time work is being more popular.

According to the EWCS 2010 nearly 24% of all workers work part time, which is defined as working 34 hours or less. On average 38% of all women work part time, compared to 13% of men. There is a considerable variation in part-time work between European countries. In the Netherlands more than half of all workers work part time, followed by Belgium, Denmark, Ireland and the United Kingdom (UK) where about 30% of workers work part time. Women often work part time to combine work and family care.

In the past 20 years the length of the average working week in the EU-12 (number refers to the number of member states during the first survey year, has fallen from 40.5 hours in 1991 to 36.4 hours in 2010 (37.5 hours in the EU-27 in 2010). Another important fact from this survey is that the standard five-day working week (40 hours between 0800 and 1800 from Monday to Friday) is still the norm for most Europeans workers.

Table: Overview of member states of the EU belonging to the EU-12, EU-15, and EU-27*, and other countries in the EWCS sample of 2010.

Member State		Year of Entry	Group in EWCS
BE	Belgium	1952	EU-12
FR	France	1952	EU-12
DE	Germany	1952	EU-12
IT	Italy	1952	EU-12
LU	Luxembourg	1952	EU-12
NL	Netherlands	1952	EU-12
DK	Denmark	1973	EU-12
IE	Ireland	1973	EU-12
UK	United Kingdom	1973	EU-12
EL	Greece	1981	EU-12
PT	Portugal	1986	EU-12
ES	Spain	1986	EU-12
AT	Austria	1995	EU-15
FI	Finland	1995	EU-15
SE	Sweden	1995	EU-15
CY	Cyprus	2004	EU-27
CZ	Czech Republic	2004	EU-27
EE	Estonia	2004	EU-27
HU	Hungary	2004	EU-27
LV	Latvia	2004	EU-27
LT	Lithuania	2004	EU-27
MT	Malta	2004	EU-27
PL	Poland	2004	EU-27
SL	Slovakia	2004	EU-27
SI	Slovenia	2004	EU-27
BG	Bulgaria	2007	EU-27
RO	Romania	2007	EU-27

Candidate countries in the EWCS sample of 2010	
HR	Croatia
MK	Former Yugoslav Republic of Macedonia
MO	Montenegro (not an official code)
TR	Turkey
Potential candidates in the EWCS sample of 2010	
AL	Albania

XK	Kosovo
Other in the EWCS sample of 2010	
NO	Norway
*In 2000 and 2001 there were two surveys which constituted the 2000 EU-27 sample: the 2000 survey covered EU15, and the 2001 survey covered 12	

Night and Shift Work

In the EWCS night work is defined as work between 0000 and 0600. Shift work may imply night work (night shifts), but also involves shifts in the morning, afternoon, evening, and weekend. The incidence of night work is given, because this is the part of shift work with the highest impact on health. There is no clear geographical pattern in the distribution of night work.

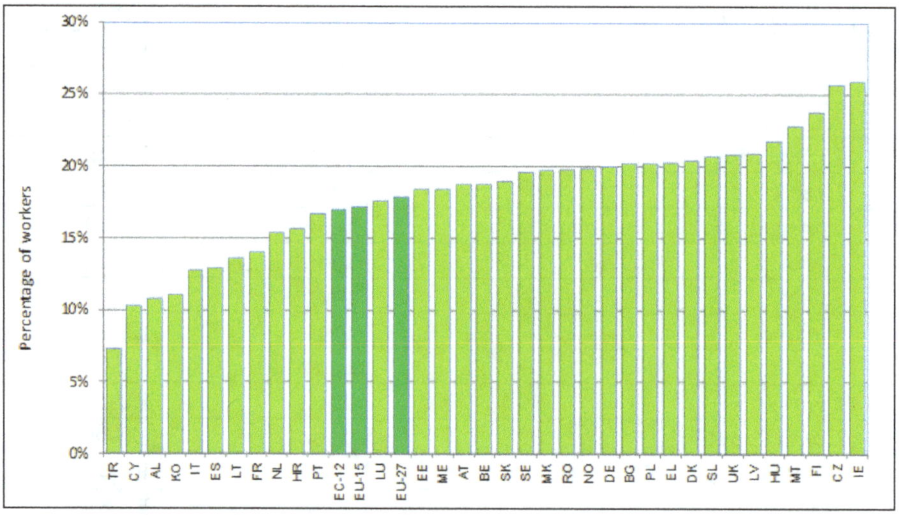

Percentage of workers in 2010 with night work at least one time per month, in the EU-27, and in six other European countries and Turkey.

Night work tends to decline in Europe. In 1995 the EWCS indicated that 20.6% of all workers in the EU-15 worked at least one night per month. In 2010 this declined to 17.2%. In the EU-27 this percentage dropped from 18.7% in 2000 to 17.9% in 2010. Workers of all ages may work at night, but men, self-employed (groups at risk self-employed), and workers in the service sector do so more often than others.

Long Working Hours

The term 'long working hours' may refer to working days that are longer than eight hours and working weeks that are longer than 40 hours, but also to working days longer than 10 or 12 hours or working weeks longer than 48 hours. In Anglo-Saxon and east Asiatic countries, long working days of 12 and more hours occur. In Europe long working hours are often related to overtime and extended working hours in the case of compressed working weeks.

On average about 24% of European workers (EU-27) had a working week that lasted more than 40 hours in 2010. The incidence of long working hours is highest in a number of south-eastern European countries and Turkey.

In 2000 29% of the workers in the EU-27 had a working week that lasted more than 40 hours. The incidence of long working hours is gradually declining in most countries. Men, self-employed groups at risk self-employed, and industrial and high-skilled workers more often have working weeks that exceed 40 hours. Young workers (less than age 30) often have shorter working weeks.

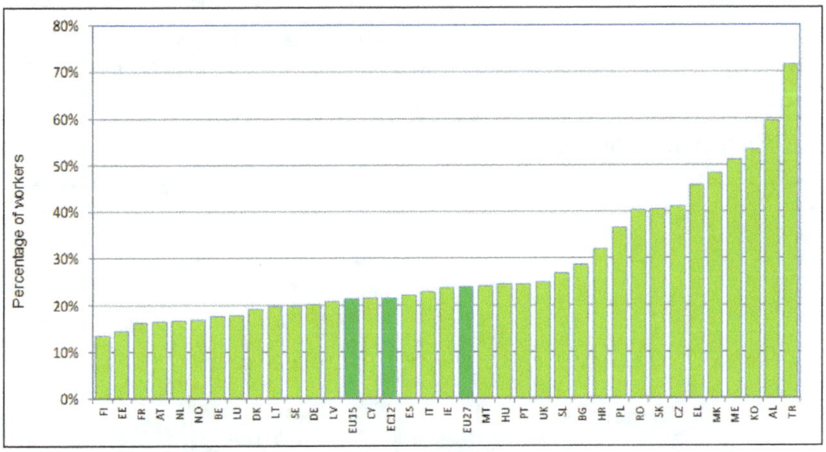

Percentage of workers in 2010 with a usual working week of more than 40 hours in the EU-27, and six other European countries and Turkey.

Weekend Work

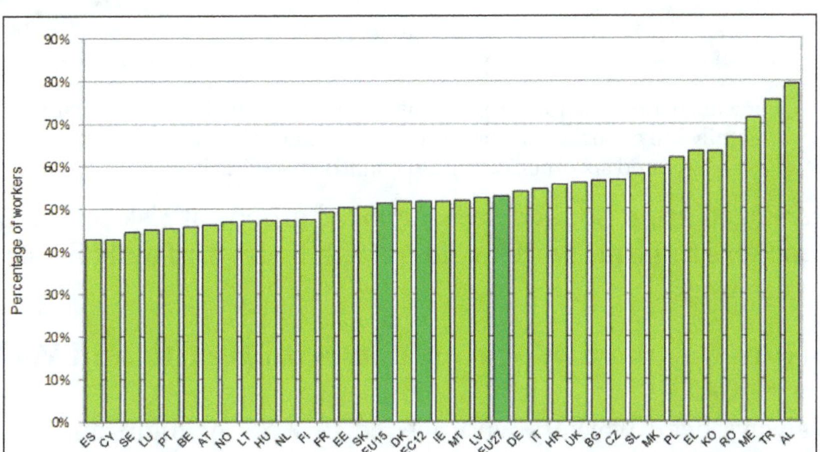

Percentage of workers in 2010 with weekend work at least once a month in the EU-27, and six other European countries and Turkey.

Weekend work implies working Saturdays and Sundays. Weekend work has tended to decrease slightly in Europe. In 2000 about 56% of the working population in the EU-27 worked at least one day per month in a weekend. In 2010 this was 53%. Males, young people, and self-employed groups at risk self-employed work more often at weekends and weekend work is more often found in service-oriented sectors.

In in 2010 in all 34 European countries covered by the EWCS survey, weekend work constitutes an important part of economic activity, but there is a greater occurrence in most south-eastern countries and Turkey.

Work and Private Life

Work at non-standard hours may cause problems with regards to reconciling work and family life. Figure indicates that, on average, 18.5% of European workers reported difficulties in achieving a satisfactory work–life balance in 2010. In 2000 this was 19.6% and in 2005 this was 20.5%. Combining work and private life is less often a problem in north and west European countries.

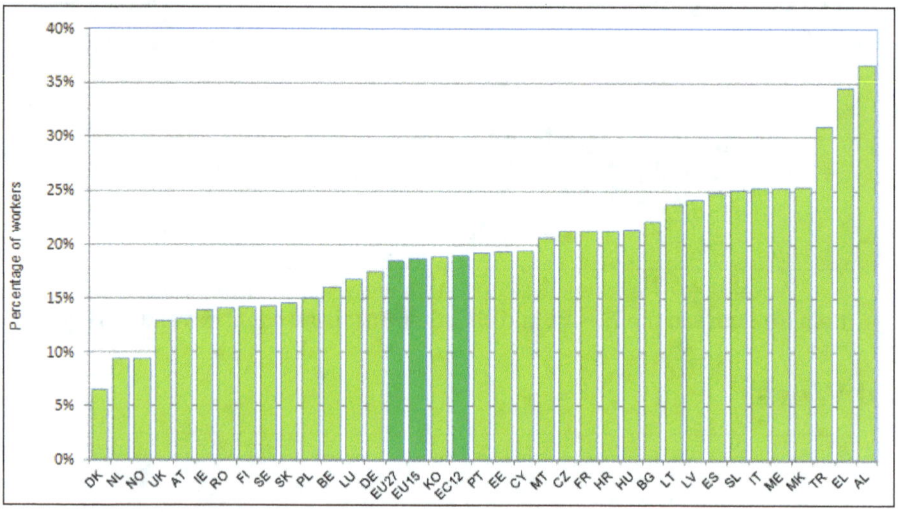

Percentage of workers in 2010 whose working hours do not fit in with family life or social life commitments outside work in the EU-27, and six other European countries and Turkey.

Males, workers aged 30 to 50, and self-employed groups at risk self-employed more often have problems in fitting working hours with hours for family life or social commitments outside work.

Effects of Non-standard Working Times on Health and Well-being

There have always been workers who needed to work at night and at times when most people are free. But in the industrial revolution the invention of the steam engine and the light bulb made it possible to organise massive amounts of workers to work during all 24 hours of the day and seven days of the week. From that time the negative effects of, in particular, night work and long working hours became visible. Nowadays a huge body of research confirms these effects. Only some of these studies can be summarized here.

Night and Shift Work

The negative effect of night work on health is related to the biological clock of human beings, which are set to day activity. Working at night is more exhaustive than working in the daytime. Body functions become less active due to hormonal secretion. Additionally, sleeping in the daytime is less restorative because body functions are set to optimal activity. Most people will not experience serious negative effects after one night of work, but with a higher number of night shifts in succession problems emerge such as: fatigue, mistakes and accidents, and also due to reduced lighting (physical agents; lighting), decreased productivity, and emotional exhaustion and job stress psycho-social risk factors. Also the immune system becomes less effective so that people are more vulnerable to health problems health and well-being and exposure to dangerous substances (occupational exposure limit values) and: risk management tools for dangerous substances. In the long run cancer is related to night work, in particular breast cancer. Night work may also have negative effects on sleep duration, smoking, no exercise and obesity, and on eating habits, leading to gastrointestinal and nutritional problems. In working time legislation the number of consecutive night shifts is often restricted. Knauth and Hornberger reviewed working time literature and proposed a maximum of three consecutive night shifts.

Long Working Hours

In the literature the negative health impact of long working hours is most often confirmed when working days last 10 hours or more and working weeks last 48 hours or more. Long working hours more often are a problem in Anglo-Saxon and eastern-Asiatic countries than in European countries, including the Anglo-Saxon countries. For instance, in Canada, New Zealand, Australia and the United States the average number of working hours per year lies between 1,800 and 1,900; in Thailand, Hong Kong and South Korea it lies between 2,250 hours and 2,500 hours per year; and in Europe it lies below 1,700 hours per year.

In Europe long working hours are related to working overtime (and not in the standard employment contract), the compressed working week, and the self-chosen working times of the self-employed. Long working hours are related to increased tiredness, but also aggravate the effects of exposition to burdening working circumstances ergonomics; physiological fatigue and human errors. Exposition to physically burdening work, for instance, may lead more rapidly to musculoskeletal problems in case of long working hours. The type of work therefore is an influencing factor. Non-exhaustive work and task variation are considered more appropriate for long working days than exhaustive and repetitive work. An opposite problem is that, due to long working hours, the number of hours for sleep decreases, which may also lead to health problems health and well-being because of sleep loss. Long working hours may lead to all kinds of sleep loss and fatigue-related problems, such as accidents safety; accidents and incidents, health problems, and coronary heart disease. Another effect is that long working hours interfere with health-related lifestyle factors, with negative effects on smoking behaviour, no exercise and obesity. In the past century, periods of war in particular caused extremely long working hours. After World War I and II research confirmed the negative effects of long working hours on the production capacity of workers. War products manufactured at the end of extremely long working days often failed to function correctly.

Weekend Work

Weekend work refers to work on Saturdays and Sundays. Night work and long working hours can also take place during the weekends but have the same effect as working on weekdays. Weekend work in the daytime in general has the same effect on health as daytime work during weekdays. What is different is that weekend work has social implications related to family life and other social activities.

Work and Private Life

Work at non-standard times may cause stress and emotional problems. This study shows that employees with weekend work reported more emotional exhaustion, job stress and psychosomatic health problems than employees not involved with weekend work. Employees on non-standard work shifts reported significantly higher overall burnout, emotional exhaustion, job stress and health problems than employees with day work.

These problems may also emerge from the tension of not being able to combine work and private life, or may continue in private life work–life balance. Presser found that working in the evening, at night, in the weekend, and with rotating schedules affects the likelihood of marriages ending in separation or divorce within approximately five years. Nabe-Nielsen and colleagues found that that a misfit between working time preferences and actual work at non-standard times was associated with an increased dissatisfaction with working hours and an increased intention to leave the workplace because of one's working hours. Non-standard working hours can be in particular disruptive for work–life balance when employees are in a precarious employment situation with causal or temporary work, while regular and predictable non-standard working hours and non-extended working hours can contribute to a better work–life balance.

Individual Differences and Individual Choices

Individual choices of employees are often related to career decisions and decisions related to the combination of work and private life. Having a health care job, for instance, often also implies working at night and at the weekend. Family care may be an important factor for working at non-standard times, in particular when the partner has a standard day job and takes over care responsibilities.

Individual differences related to non-standard working times often have weak correlations in research. One reason for the reduced visibility of individual differences is that people differ strongly in physical constitution and health status, which leads to health selection on the labour market. This means that people who dislike or are not able to work during non-standard hours or with long working hours are not likely to apply for these jobs. On the other hand, people tend to leave the job when problems related to non-standard working times or long working hours emerge. Only people with good physical condition and strong motivation are able keep their job with non-standard working times for a long time (healthy worker effect). This is for instance visible in the literature in the often good health conditions of older shift work groups groups at risk ageing workers. Young age is often considered to be related to better shift work tolerance.

Intervention Techniques

Optimal intervention techniques may prevent negative effects of non-standard working times. Four ways of influencing the negative effects of working time are distinguished.

Role of Governments and Social Partners

Governments regulate working time by law. In Europe this is regulated by the EU's Working Time Directive (2003/88/EC) or some other sectoral regulations. Under the EU's Working Time Directive, each member state must ensure that every worker is entitled to:

- A limit to weekly working time, which must not exceed 48 hours on average, including any overtime.
- A minimum daily rest period of 11 consecutive hours in every 24.
- A rest break during working time, if the worker is on duty for longer than six hours.
- A minimum weekly rest period of 24 uninterrupted hours for each seven-day period, which is added to the 11 hours of daily rest.
- Paid annual leave of at least four weeks per year.
- Extra protection in the case of night work (for example, average working hours must not exceed eight hours per 24-hour period; night workers must not perform heavy or dangerous work for longer than eight hours in any 24-hour period; there should be a right to free health assessments and in certain situations, to transfer to day work).

In the 20th century social partners achieved an important role in the negotiation on working time and financial compensation by social agreements OSH in general. Nowadays working time is an important term of employment, directly after salary OSH Management and organisation. In these social negotiations interests may be balanced to prevent negative effects. Trade unions may negotiate better OSH situations and may convince employers to abandon too much night work and overtime, because increased tiredness lowers the production capacity of employees. The salary of employees is increased when working non-regular hours and overtime, but they suffer more because of increased tiredness and a negative work–life balance. Trade unions may be able to prevent too much irregularity and prevent sickness and disability in the long run.

Rostering

Rosters are important tools to regulate non-standard working times. Rostering is necessary when company production times exceed the workday of the employees or when the workflow is irregular. This mostly is the case when the company continues its activity in the evening, at night, and at the weekend. Rosters often involve a rotating sequence where employees alternately work in the morning, afternoon, evening, at night and at the weekend.

There is a huge amount of roster variants. An important distinction is regular versus irregular rosters. In regular rotating rosters the same number of employees is staffed during all hours. Regular rosters are mostly found in industry (for instance: chemical, metal and automotive companies). Irregular rosters are applied when the staffing need varies over the day. They are applied, for instance, in health care facilities where most activity takes place during the day, and less staff is needed in the evening, at night and at the weekend.

Rosters can be constructed in such a way that they reduce the negative effects on health and work–life balance. Knauth and Hornberger give an overview of roster rules from this point of view. Examples of these rules are that the maximum number of consecutive shifts has to be three, that forward rotation (first morning shifts, then evening shifts and then night shifts) is preferred to backward rotation, and that after a night shift there should be at least two days off. The maximum number of consecutive shifts should be 5–7. Bambra and colleagues reviewed 26 shift work interventions and found that three factors are most effective considering health and work-life balance:

- Switching from slow to fast rotation.
- Changing from backward to forward rotation.
- Self-scheduling of shifts.

Self-scheduling or Self-rostering

Most rosters are prearranged by social agreement, but worked out at the organisation level. This gives employees a chance to influence their personal roster by formulating roster preferences. Most companies comply to this and also to informal exchange of shifts among employees, as far as this does not interfere with the interests of the organisation. This practice was recently worked out one step further by allowing employees to 'self-roster'. With self-rostering (also called self-scheduling, prioritised working hours or self-selected working hours), employees may select working hours which fit their personal needs and preferences.

Several studies have been carried out recently that indicate that control over working hours is associated with improved well-being. But also a warning is given, because employees may not change their working hours or choose working hours which do not favour health. Software applications may be used for monitoring, so that shift-workers also improve their health and well-being by planning their own working hours.

Technical and Organisational Solutions

As an alternative to making use of flexible working hours, companies can also consider a number of other organisational measures to meet the fluctuations in production demand (work organisation; Job design; WEI-11-15-5). Examples are: flexible staffing of internal personnel over different work places or functions, hiring external personnel, 'flexible working hours' by giving workers the possibility to decide about the exact time of starting and finishing work, applying logistic solutions such as stockpiling, and reconsidering the production process. However, in a number of cases this is not possible, because production processes require continuous operation or technical investment is too high.

Also, temporary alleviating solutions to improve personnel functioning are possible. Pallessen and colleagues reviewed a number of countermeasures to reduce the negative effects of night work. They found research supporting the positive effects of applying bright light therapy, melatonin administration, naps (small periods of sleep during working time), use of stimulants to improve wakefulness, use of hypnotics to improve daytime sleep, and proper work scheduling. But it is unknown if these effects have long-term consequences. Insufficient studies were found that confirm the effects of proper personnel selection, exercise, and sleepiness-detection devices.

COMPUTER-AIDED ERGONOMICS METHODS IN DESIGN

Computers are being used more frequently to improve the quality of different areas of ergonomics and safety. Computer-Aided production and design technology requires implementation of Computer-Aided Ergonomics methods.

Computer-Aided Ergonomics Methods can be defined as the implementation of information technology in ergonomics and safety methods and the integration of those methods into design, production and decision making. In Lithuania Ergonomics and Ergonomics methods are not developed.

Ergonomics in Design

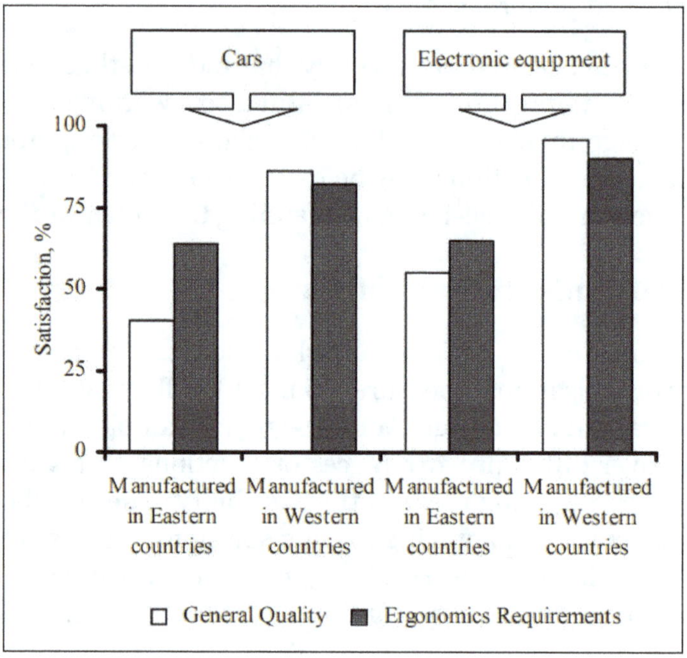

Subjective evaluation of products quality.

Ergonomics helps to make the best use of human and technical resources trough optimizing the application of existing and new technology to the benefit of users and environment. Its applications enhance job satisfaction, productivity and maximize the product or system quality by improving usability.

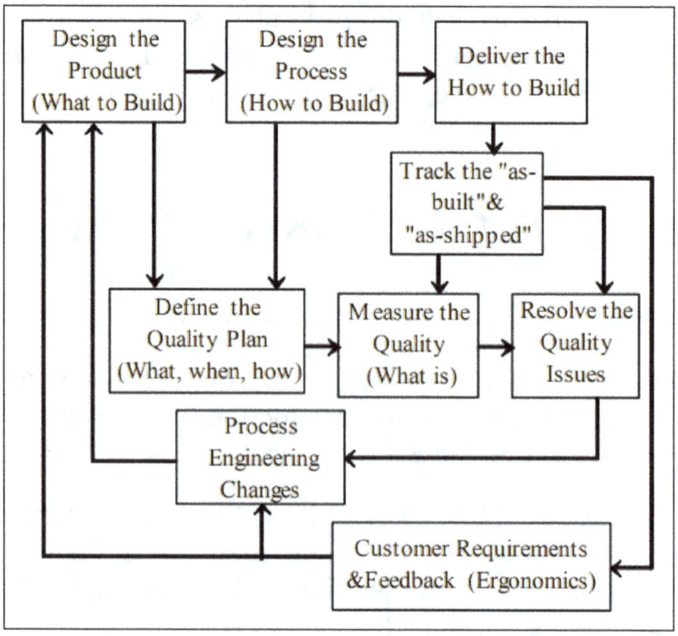

Scheme of product design and production process.

Ergonomics requirements have to be respected in all branches of production, such as mechanical and electronic equipment, machine-tools, work place design. Especially ergonomics methods in design and production process are wanted for Middle- and East-European countries industry, where Human factors/Ergonomics requirements traditionally were not respected. Not consideration in to Human factors/Ergonomics requirements caused low production quality. Peoples evaluation (subjective) of quality and Ergonomics design quality of products manufactured in East-European countries, and in Western countries, where Human factors/Ergonomics requirements are respected (more 300 respondents were tested).

Ergonomics integrates knowledge derived from the human sciences to match jobs, systems, productions and environments to the physical and mental abilities and limitations of people.

Design and production process requires the Feedback realized by Ergonomics. The feedback contains the Ergonomics data from design and engineering change reviews, suggested product and process improvements, and comments about actual situations encountered during production which affect the "What to Build".

Computer-aided Ergonomics and Safety Design

Computer-aided Design (CAD) clearly offers new possibilities to integrate new possibilities to integrate ergonomic knowledge into the design process. A wide variety of ergonomic topics are of relevance to the application of computer-aided design systems concerned with layout design, displays and controls, fields of vision, areas of movement, physical strength and working environment. Computer systems have been developed, for example, to analyze and to improve workplace structures, man-machine systems, production information systems, working methods and operator instructions.

Different approaches to realizing this may be categorized as follows:

- Computer-based checklists for design quality analysis such as the FMS Safety Checklist.
- Computer-supported risk analysis like STARS: A program package for computer-aided safety and reliability analysis.
- Knowledge-based expert systems in ergonomics and safety, like M-LIFTAN, ALIE, and GSA.
- Ergonomic oriented information systems for workplace designers.
- Computer models of man.
- Systems for the measuring of 3-dimensional postures.

- Computer-based tool for evaluation and design of manual materials handling tasks. Ergonomic principles require user-centred design. A user-centred information systems development approach is one in which, through appropriate structures, process and scope, all types of user needs (functional, physical and aspirational) are addressed so that usability (effectiveness, efficiency and satisfaction) is maximized in the end product.

Ergonomics Expert Systems

One simple example of this kind of designer support programs is the FMS (Flexible Manufacturing System) ergonomic and safety checklist. In the FMS ergonomic and safety checklist computer program all the ergonomic and safety requirements for FMS given in the relevant standards are presented and are able to be checked by the designer when the system is under design. Through the use of this program, ergonomics and safety information is integrated in to the design process. The designer is able to document the standards used for the object in question, and is thereafter able to accept liability as required by modern legislation.

A new ergonomic oriented information system, ErgoCop, has been developed for workplace designers. Designers during the design process for assembly workplaces intend ErgoCop for use. The program consists of:

- Information about ergonomic requirements and design principles for different workplaces.
- Cards containing the documents created during the design process for each workplace designed.
- Feedback from workers and safety and health professionals about workplaces in operation.
- Photographs and drawings of workplaces and successful ergonomic solutions.

A library of components (equipment, tools and fittings) used when building workplaces. The ErgoCop program is accessible to the ergonomic and safety personnel so they can add their knowledge to the program and give both their own and workers feedback about the design implemented. Designers can consult the system when they need ergonomic information during designing and take advantage of the solutions used in earlier projects and the feedback given in order to avoid poor solutions and reinforce good ones.

Man Models

Several computer-aided man-models have been developed using different computer programs. The most obvious application of a man model is in the visualization of man-machine interactions and in placing humans in the workplace design.

There are categorized different applications of computer-aided man-models as follows: assessment of fit, maximal reach, clearance, and field of vision.

Assessment of strength demands to predict strength require and lower back load, posture recording and muscle activation.

Man models have been developed to enable the calculation of biomechanical forces and the risks for musculoskeletal injuries or to analyze working postures required, when the planned tasks will be carried out by the forthcoming operator. One example of 3-Dimensional Anthropometric Man-Models is CAD tool RAMSIS widely used to improve the design of cars.

The integration of ergonomic questions in the construction process of workplaces requires the use of adequate construction aids. In the past decades, the templates of percentile types were used. The conventional templates resulted from the measurement of lengths of human body parts of a large number of persons. The data was statistically analyzed by calculation of percentiles.

The basically new idea, which distinguishes the RAMSIS-measuring concept from other systems, is to use the man model itself as a measuring tool. The man is recorded by up to four digital cameras. A frame grabber digitizes the picture signals delivered by the cameras and visualizes them on the screen of the computer. After the 3-dimensional man models has been adapted to the anthropometric measures of the test person, "mathematical photos" of the manare calculated. For the calculation of images the same camera parameters (focal length, camera distance, and camera position) are available as those in case of a real recording with a digital camera. The essential measuring process is affected by an interactive posture adjustment of the man model to the recordings of the test person. RAMSIS program is widely used by car manufactures FIAT, AUDI, BMW, FORD, OPEL, and MERCEDES-BENZ.

Evaluation and Design of Manual Materials Handling Tasks

One of the most important occupational health problems is the high number and severity of chronic or acute back disorders caused by manual materials handling. In 1990 the European Community has issued the directive 90/269/EC on manual materials handling. This Directive requires from the employer the evaluation of the design of manual materials handling tasks with respect to workers health risk. A simple way to introduce the idea of prevention injuries in the industry would be evaluation of the workers' health risk by determining a load limit characteristic of the worker. Several methods have been developed to determine a weight limit for the manual handling of objects. The NIOSH-method (USA) is internationally accepted. In 1991 the NIOSH lifting equations were modified. The ErgonLIFT-computer based tool for evaluation and design of manual material handling tasks uses NIOSH modified equations.

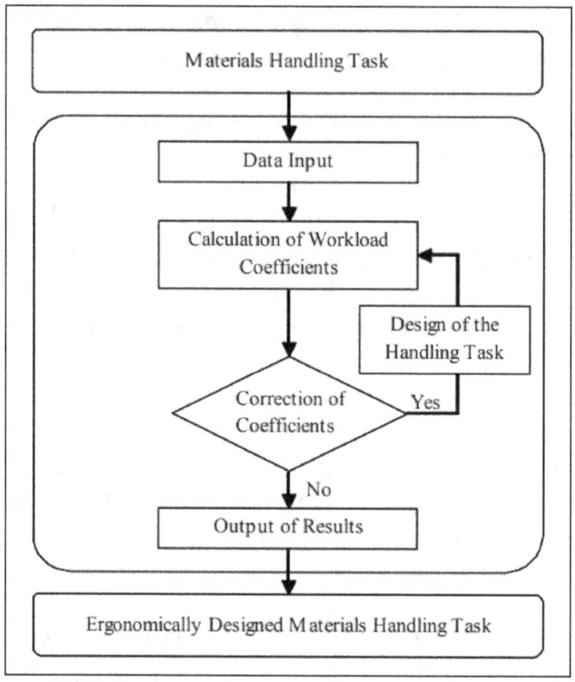

Flow chart of a risk analysis with ErgonLIFT.

A risk analysis of a manual material handling task using ErgonLIFT starts with the input of the task data, and of the individual characteristic of the worker. Ergon LIFT then calculates the described workload coefficients.

The process of the risk analysis and the re-design of the manual materials handling task with ErgonLIFT. With ErgonLIFT the practical user in industry gets an easy-to-use tool enabling him to quantitatively describe the health risk of a worker performing a manual material handling task. If the health risk cannot be characterized as tolerable, ErgonLIFT proposes preventive measures to reduce the risk, and the user is led to an ergonomic re-design of the task.

References

- Approaches-to-work-design: oshwiki.eu, Retrieved 16 July, 2020
- 4-tips-to-improve-the-ergonomics-of-workstations: workdesign.com, Retrieved 14 May, 2020
- Telework: oshwiki.eu, Retrieved 09 March, 2020
- Haines, H.; Wilson, J. R.; Vink, P.; Koningsveld, E. (2002). "Validating a framework for participatory ergonomics (the PEF)". Ergonomics. 45 (4): 309–327. doi:10.1080/00140130210123516. PMID 12028727
- Possibilities of Ergonomic Modelling of Products and Workplaces. Advances in Occupational Ergonomics and Safety 1. – Switzerland – Vol. 2. – P. 566 – 571
- Working-time: oshwiki.eu, Retrieved 10 January, 2020

4

Occupational Safety and Ergonomics

Occupational safety in ergonomics deals with ergonomic hazards and risk assessment, work related musculoskeletal disorders and ergonomics training. Carpal tunnel syndrome, repetitive strain injury, etc. are some of the injuries related to ergonomics. This chapter delves into the subject of occupational safety and ergonomics for a thorough understanding of it.

ERGONOMIC HAZARDS

An ergonomic hazard is a physical factor within the environment that harms the musculoskeletal system. Ergonomic hazards include themes such as repetitive movement, manual handling, workplace/job/task design, uncomfortable workstation height and poor body positioning.

Although ergonomics is a broad field, the main areas of concern for workplaces and employees will often relate to:

- Workstations (sitting and standing).
- Equipment layout and operation.
- Computer systems.
- Noise.
- Lighting.
- Thermal comfort.
- Maintenance tasks performed on plant items.

Ergonomic issues can be associated with a wide range of concerns including the physical design of workstations, workspaces, the working environment, tools, vehicles, computer programs and plant. It can also involve cognitive processes such as those involved with workload, decision making, skilled performance and stress. There are procedures for dealing with all these issues to make sure any difficulties are addressed.

Ergonomic practices address the intersection between people and the made environment. The goal is to design and arrange space, objects, and systems so that the user experiences the safest, most natural, and most efficient movement and body position possible.

An ergonomic hazard is any interaction with the mad world that causes the user discomfort or strain. There are three primary types of ergonomic hazards: objects, environments, and systems that result in poor posture or unnatural, uncomfortable, or awkward movements.

When you're looking for ergonomic hazards in the workplace, consider workstations and desks; all tools, equipment, and machinery workers use to do their jobs; and the physical processes workers perform.

Link between Ergonomic Hazards in the Workplace and Safety

While no employer wants their workers to be uncomfortable, it's important to understand that ergonomics isn't just about comfort; it's directly linked to safety and injury prevention. Poor ergonomics contributes to muscle strain, muscle imbalances, and fatigue.

Many muscle strains result from performing the same motion over and over again. These become repetitive stress injuries, which are some of the most common workplace injuries. Ergonomics alone won't eliminate this type of injury (even if you do a movement correctly, if you do it too often, you're bound to get tired or overuse your muscles and connective tissue). However, proper ergonomics will significantly reduce fatigue and strain.

Several common work activities pose repetitive stress ergonomic hazards. Examples include typing and mousing, which can result in carpal tunnel syndrome.

Other work-related actions that cause repetitive stress injuries include:

- Overhead work.
- Auto mechanical work.
- Driving.
- Stocking shelves.
- Massaging clients.
- Butchering.

Poorly designed or maintained tools and equipment may require workers to perform awkward movements or to contort their body in order to perform a task. Repeated day after day, this causes excessive fatigue and may result in an injury. Fatigue is another of the most common causes of workplace injuries.

How to Prevent Ergonomic Hazards in the Workplace

Now that we are familiar with some examples of ergonomic hazards in the workplace, we can get to the important work of preventing them.

Work Environment

In a perfect world, every workstation and desk would be custom designed for the person who is using it. But this is unrealistic. A better approach is to give your workers the tools and education they need to make sure their work area fits them.

Include ergonomics as a topic to cover in safety moments. Hire an ergonomics expert to give a presentation to your staff and work with employees one on one. Provide workers with the resources they need to change elements of their workspace that are causing problems.

Tools and Machines

Make sure all tools and machines are ergonomically designed. Go through your entire tool and machine inventory and see where you can improve. You may be surprised by how non-ergonomic some traditional designs are, and what better alternatives exist.

- Ergonomic hazards impact employers and workers and their families. Poor workplace design, awkward body mechanics or postures, repetitive movements, and other ergonomic hazards induce or contribute to a staggering number of cumulative trauma disorders.
- Cumulative trauma disorders (CTD) affect hands, wrists, elbows, arms, shoulders, the lower back, and the cervical spine area. Structures involved include tendons, muscles, bones, nerves, and blood vessels. One can plan strategies for abatement by learning to recognize the hazards that contribute to CTD.
- OSHA has published the Ergonomic Program Management Guidelines. OSHA has also given Advance Notice of Proposed Rulemaking for an Ergonomic Standard that will affect all industries.
- A companywide ergonomic assessment should be developed, followed by a well written ergonomic plan. Ergonomic abatement will decrease the costs associated with CTD and ultimately impact the corporate "bottom line."

Occupational Injury

An occupational injury is bodily damage resulting from working. The most common organs involved are the spine, hands, the head, lungs, eyes, skeleton, and skin. Occupational injuries can result from exposure to occupational hazards (physical, chemical, biological, or psychosocial), such as temperature, noise, insect or animal bites, blood-borne pathogens, aerosols, hazardous chemicals, radiation, and occupational burnout.

While many prevention methods are set in place, injuries may still occur due to poor ergonomics, manual handling of heavy loads, misuse or failure of equipment, exposure to general hazards, and inadequate safety training.

It has been estimated that worldwide there are more than 350,000 workplace fatalities and more than 270 million workplace injuries annually. In 2000 there were approximately 2.9 billion workers worldwide. Occupational injuries resulted in the loss of 3.5 years of healthy life for every 1,000 workers. 300,000 of the occupational injuries resulted in a fatality.

The most common occupations associated with these hazards vary throughout the world depending on the major industries in a particular country. Overall, the most hazardous occupations are in farming, fishing, and forestry. In more developed countries, construction and manufacturing occupations are associated with high rates of spine, hand, and wrist injuries.

United States

In the United States in 2012, 4,383 workers died from job injuries, 92% of which were men, and nearly 3 million nonfatal workplace injuries & illness were reported which cost businesses a collective loss of $198.2 billion and 60 million workdays. In 2007, 5,488 workers died from job injuries, 92% of which were men, and 49,000 died from work-related injuries. NIOSH estimates that 4 million workers in the U.S. in 2007 suffered from non-fatal work related injuries or illnesses.

According to data from the National Institute for Occupational Safety and Health (NIOSH) and the Bureau of Labor Statistics, an average of 15 workers die from traumatic injuries each day in the United States, and an additional 200 workers are hospitalized.

In a study in the state of Washington, injured workers were followed for 14 years to determine the long term effects of work injury on employment. The work injuries resulted in an average of 1.06 years of lost productivity for each of the 31,588 allowed claims.

Common Injuries

As in the United Kingdom, slips, trips and falls are common and account for 20-40% of disabling occupational injuries. Often these accidents result in a back injury that can persist to a permanent disability. In the United States, a high risk of back injuries occurs in the health care industry. 25% of reported injuries in health care workers in the state of Pennsylvania are for back pain. Among nurses, the prevalence of lower back pain may be as high as 72% mostly as a result of transferring patients. Some of these injuries can be prevented with the availability of patient lifts, improved worker training, and allocation of more time to perform work procedures. Another common type of injury is carpal tunnel syndrome associated with overuse of the hands and wrists. Studies on a cohort of newly hired workers have thus far identified forceful gripping, repetitive lifting of > 1 kg, and using vibrating power tools as high risk work activities.

Additionally, noise exposure in the workplace can cause hearing loss, which accounted for 14% of reported occupational illnesses in 2007. Many initiatives have been created to prevent this common workplace injury. For example, the Buy Quiet program encourages employers to purchase tools and machines that produce less noise and the Safe-In-Sound Award was created to recognize companies and program that excel in the area of hearing loss prevention.

Accidental injection or needlestick injuries are a common injury that plague agriculture workers and veterinarians. The majority of these injuries are located to the hands or legs, and can result in mild to severe reactions, including possible hospitalization. Due to the wide variety of biologics used in animal agriculture, needlestick injuries can result in bacterial or fungal infections, lacerations, local inflammation, vaccine/antibiotic reactions, amputations, miscarriage, and death. Due to daily human-animal interactions, livestock related injuries are also a prevalent injury of agriculture workers, and are responsible for the majority of nonfatal worker injuries on dairy farms. Additionally, approximately 30 people die of cattle and horse-related deaths in the United States annually.

Employees at Risk

Perhaps the most important personal factor that predisposes to an increased risk is age. In the United States in 1998 17 million workers were over age 55 and by 2018 this population is expected to more than double. Workers in this age group are more likely to suffer from lower back pain that may be worsened by work conditions that normally do not affect a younger worker. Older workers are also more likely by be killed in a construction related fall. They are also at higher risk for injury due to age-related hearing loss, visual impairment, and use of multiple prescription medications that has been linked to higher rates of work injuries. In addition to age, other personal risk factors for injury include obesity particularly its associated risk with back injury, and depression.

Lack of proper education or training can also predispose an individual to an occupational injury. For example, there is limited needlestick injury awareness among agriculture workers, and there is a need for comprehensive programs to prevent needlestick injuries on livestock operations. Proper animal handling techniques and training, or stockmanship, can also decrease the risk of livestock injury. A handler's timing, positioning, speed, direction of movement, and sounds made will affect the behavior of an animal and consequently the safety of the handler. The agriculture industry has begun to focus more on proper education and training, and has made a variety of resources available to producers. For example, organizations like the Upper Midwest Agriculture Safety and Health Center (UMASH) have a variety of informational fact sheets and training videos easily accessible online. Additionally, organizations like Beef Quality Assurance offer stockman ship training seminars and demonstrations.

United Kingdom

In the United Kingdom in 2013/2014, 133 people were killed at work. Of those 133 people, 89 were employed, while 44 were self-employed. In 2013/2014, an estimated 629,000 injuries occurred at work. Of these injuries 629,000 injuries, 203,000 led to more than 3 days absence from work. Of these, over 148,000 resulted in the victim being absent from work for more than 7 days. If you do suffer an occupational injury in the UK, there is workplace injury advice guides online offering support on dealing with this situation.

Dangerous Sectors

- Construction: 42 deaths.
- Agriculture: 27 deaths.
- Waste and Recycling: Four deaths.
- Other: 60 deaths.

Of all the workplace accidents that resulted in death, the most common were falls from height, contact with moving machinery and being struck by a vehicle. These types of accidents resulted in over half of all recorded deaths.

Common Injuries

Slips, trips and falls account for over a third of all injuries that happen at work. Incorrect handling of items was the most common cause of injuries that led to absences from work of more than 7 days. Upper limb injuries represented 47.3% of workplace injuries in 2010-2011, the most common area injured.

In all, over 1,900,000 working days were lost in 2013/2014 due to slips, trips and falls.

Employees at Risk

Unsurprisingly, occupation is the biggest influence on the risk of workplace injuries. Workers new to the job are at a much higher risk of injury than more experienced staff, while shift workers and part-time staff also have a greater risk of being injured at work.

Employer Prosecutions

The Health & Safety Executive (HSE) prosecuted 582 cases in 2013/2014, with at least one conviction secured in 547 cases (94%).

Local authorities prosecuted a total of 92 cases during the same period, with at least one conviction achieved in 89 cases (97%).

A total of 13,790 notices were issued by the HSE and local authorities, with over £16,700,000 issued in fines.

Prevention

There are many methods of preventing or reducing industrial injuries, including anticipation of problems by risk assessment, safety training, control banding, personal protective equipment safety guards, mechanisms on machinery, and safety barriers. In addition, past problems can be analyzed to find their root causes by using a technique called root cause analysis. A 2013 Cochrane review found low-quality evidence showing that inspections, especially focused inspections, can reduce work-related injuries in the long term.

Carpal Tunnel Syndrome

Carpal tunnel syndrome (CTS) is a medical condition due to compression of the median nerve as it travels through the wrist at the carpal tunnel. The main symptoms are pain, numbness and tingling in the thumb, index finger, middle finger and the thumb side of the ring finger. Symptoms typically start gradually and during the night. Pain may extend up the arm. Weak grip strength may occur, and after a long period of time the muscles at the base of the thumb may waste away. In more than half of cases, both sides are affected.

Types of work that are associated include computer work, work with vibrating tools and work that requires a strong grip. Diagnosis is suspected based on signs, symptoms and specific physical tests and may be confirmed with electrodiagnostic tests. If muscle wasting at the base of the thumb is present, the diagnosis is likely.

Being physically active can decrease the risk of developing CTS. Symptoms can be improved by wearing a wrist splint or with corticosteroid injections. Taking NSAIDs or gabapentin does not appear to be useful. Surgery to cut the transverse carpal ligament is effective with better results at a year compared to non-surgical options. Further splinting after surgery is not needed. Evidence does not support magnet therapy.

About 5% of people in the United States have carpal tunnel syndrome. It usually begins in adulthood, and women are more commonly affected than men. Up to 33% of people may improve without specific treatment over approximately a year. Carpal tunnel syndrome was first fully described after World War II.

Signs and Symptoms

People with CTS experience numbness, tingling, or burning sensations in the thumb and fingers, in particular the index and middle fingers and radial half of the ring finger, because these receive their sensory and motor function (muscle control) from the median nerve. Ache and discomfort can possibly be felt more proximally in the forearm or even the upper arm. Less-specific symptoms may include pain in the wrists or hands, loss of grip strength, and loss of manual dexterity.

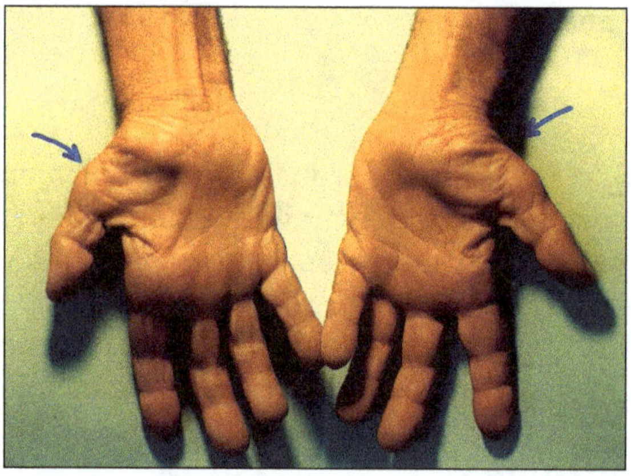

Untreated carpal tunnel syndrome, showing how the muscles at the base of the thumb have wasted away (atrophied).

Some suggest that median nerve symptoms can arise from compression at the level of the thoracic outlet or the area where the median nerve passes between the two heads of the pronator teres in the forearm, although this is debated.

Numbness and paresthesias in the median nerve distribution are the hallmark neuropathic symptoms (NS) of carpal tunnel entrapment syndrome. Weakness and atrophy of the thumb muscles may occur if the condition remains untreated, because the muscles are not receiving sufficient nerve stimulation. Discomfort is usually worse at night and in the morning.

Work Related

The international debate regarding the relationship between CTS and repetitive motion in work is ongoing. The Occupational Safety and Health Administration (OSHA) has adopted rules and regulations regarding cumulative trauma disorders. Occupational risk factors of repetitive tasks, force, posture, and vibration have been cited. The relationship between work and CTS is controversial; in many locations, workers diagnosed with carpal tunnel syndrome are entitled to time off and compensation.

Some speculate that carpal tunnel syndrome is provoked by repetitive movement and manipulating activities and that the exposure can be cumulative. It has also been stated that symptoms are commonly exacerbated by forceful and repetitive use of the hand and wrists in industrial occupations, but it is unclear as to whether this refers to pain (which may not be due to carpal tunnel syndrome) or the more typical numbness symptoms.

A review of available scientific data by the National Institute for Occupational Safety and Health (NIOSH) indicated that job tasks that involve highly repetitive manual acts or specific wrist postures were associated with incidents of CTS, but causation was not established, and the distinction from work-related arm pains that are not carpal tunnel syndrome was not clear. It has been proposed that repetitive use of the arm can affect the biomechanics of the upper limb or cause damage to tissues. It has also been proposed that postural and spinal assessment along with ergonomic assessments should be included in the overall determination of the condition. Addressing these factors has been found to improve comfort in some studies. A 2010 survey by NIOSH showed that 2/3 of the 5 million carpal tunnel cases in the US that year were related to work. Women have more work-related carpal tunnel syndrome than men.

Speculation that CTS is work-related is based on claims such as CTS being found mostly in the working adult population, though evidence is lacking for this. For instance, in one recent representative series of a consecutive experience, most patients were older and not working. Based on the claimed increased incidence in the workplace, arm use is implicated, but the weight of evidence suggests that this is an inherent, genetic, slowly but inevitably progressive idiopathic peripheral mononeuropathy.

Pathophysiology

The carpal tunnel is an anatomical compartment located at the base of the palm. Nine flexor tendons and the median nerve pass through the carpal tunnel that is surrounded on three sides by the carpal bones that form an arch. The median nerve provides feeling or sensation to the thumb, index finger, long finger, and half of the ring finger. At the level of the wrist, the median nerve supplies the muscles at the base of the thumb that allow it to abduct, move away from the other four fingers, as well as move out of the plane of the palm. The carpal tunnel is located at the middle third of the base of the palm, bounded by the bony prominence of the scaphoid tubercle and trapezium at the base of the thumb, and the hamate hook that can be palpated along the axis of the ring finger. From the anatomical position, the carpal tunnel is bordered on the anterior surface by the transverse carpal ligament, also known as the flexor retinaculum.

The flexor retinaculum is a strong, fibrous band that attaches to the pisiform and the hamulus of the hamate. The proximal boundary is the distal wrist skin crease, and the distal boundary is approximated by a line known as Kaplan's cardinal line. This line uses surface landmarks, and is drawn between the apex of the skin fold between the thumb and index finger to the palpated hamate hook. The median nerve can be compressed by a decrease in the size of the canal, an increase in the size of the contents (such as the swelling of lubrication tissue around the flexor tendons), or both. Since the carpal tunnel is bordered by carpal bones on one side and a ligament on the other, when the pressure builds up inside the tunnel, there is nowhere for it to escape and thus it ends up pressing up against and damaging the median nerve. Simply flexing the wrist to 90 degrees will decrease the size of the canal.

Compression of the median nerve as it runs deep to the transverse carpal ligament (TCL) causes atrophy of the thenar eminence, weakness of the flexor pollicis brevis, opponens pollicis, abductor pollicis brevis, as well as sensory loss in the digits supplied by the median nerve. The superficial sensory branch of the median nerve, which provides sensation to the base of the palm, branches proximal to the TCL and travels superficial to it. Thus, this branch spared in carpal tunnel syndrome, and there is no loss of palmar sensation.

Prevention

There is little or no data to support the concept that activity adjustment prevents carpal tunnel syndrome. The evidence for wrist rest is debated. There is also little research supporting that ergonomics is related to CTS. Due to risk factors for hand and wrist dysfunction being multifactorial and very complex it is difficult to assess the true physical factors of CTS.

Biological factors such as genetic predisposition and anthropometric features had significantly stronger causal association with carpal tunnel syndrome than occupational/environmental factors such as repetitive hand use and stressful manual work. This suggests that carpal tunnel syndrome might not be preventable simply by avoiding certain activities or types of work/activities.

Treatment

Generally accepted treatments include: physiotherapy, steroids either orally or injected locally, splinting, and surgical release of the transverse carpal ligament. Limited evidence suggests that gabapentin is no more effective than placebo for CTS treatment. There is insufficient evidence for therapeutic ultrasound, yoga, acupuncture, low level laser therapy, vitamin B6, and exercise. Change in activity may include avoiding activities that worsen symptoms.

The American Academy of Orthopedic Surgeons recommends proceeding conservatively with a course of nonsurgical therapies tried before release surgery is considered. A different treatment should be tried if the current treatment fails to resolve the symptoms within 2 to 7 weeks. Early surgery with carpal tunnel release is indicated where there is evidence of median nerve denervation or a person elects to proceed directly to surgical treatment. Recommendations may differ when carpal tunnel syndrome is found in association with the following conditions: diabetes mellitus, coexistent cervical radiculopathy, hypothyroidism, polyneuropathy, pregnancy, rheumatoid arthritis, and carpal tunnel syndrome in the workplace.

Splints

The importance of wrist braces and splints in the carpal tunnel syndrome therapy is known, but many people are unwilling to use braces. In 1993, The American Academy of Neurology recommend a non-invasive treatment for the CTS at the beginning (except for sensitive or motor deficit or grave report at EMG/ENG): a therapy using splints was indicated for light and moderate pathology. Current recommendations generally don't suggest immobilizing braces, but instead activity modification and non-steroidal anti-inflammatory drugs as initial therapy, followed by more aggressive options or specialist referral if symptoms do not improve.

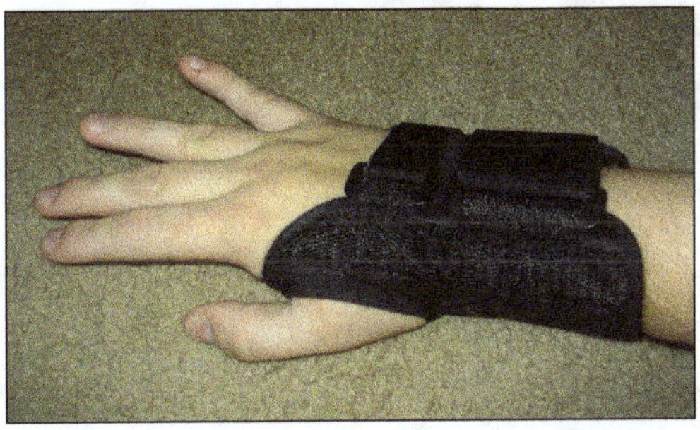

A rigid splint can keep the wrist straight.

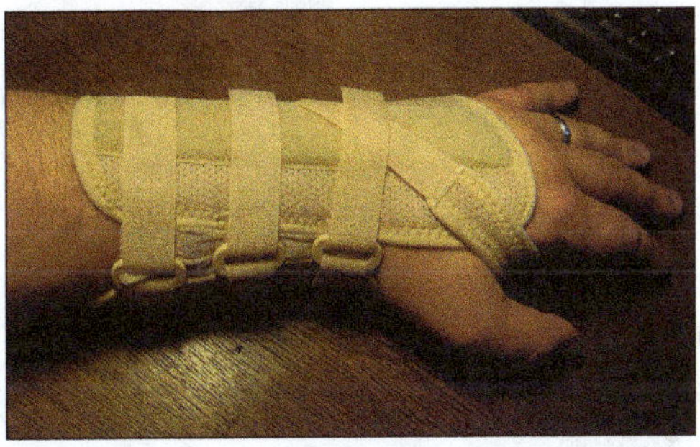

A different type of rigid splint used in carpal tunnel syndrome.

Many health professionals suggest that, for the best results, one should wear braces at night. When possible, braces can be worn during the activity primarily causing stress on the wrists. The brace should not generally be used during the day as wrist activity is needed to keep the wrist from becoming stiff and to prevent muscles from weakening.

Corticosteroids

Corticosteroid injections can be effective for temporary relief from symptoms while a person develops a long-term strategy that fits their lifestyle. This form of treatment is thought to reduce discomfort in those with CTS due to its ability to decrease median nerve swelling. The use of ultrasound while performing the injection is more expensive but leads to faster resolution of CTS symptoms. The injections are done under local anesthesia. This treatment is not appropriate for extended periods, however. In general, local steroid injections are only used until more definitive treatment options can be used. Corticosteroid injections do not appear to be very effective for slowing disease progression.

Surgery

Release of the transverse carpal ligament is known as "carpal tunnel release" surgery.

It is recommended when there is static (constant, not just intermittent) numbness, muscle weakness, or atrophy, and when night-splinting or other conservative interventions no longer control intermittent symptoms. The surgery may be done with local or regional anesthesia with or without sedation, or under general anesthesia. In general, milder cases can be controlled for months to years, but severe cases are unrelenting symptomatically and are likely to result in surgical treatment.

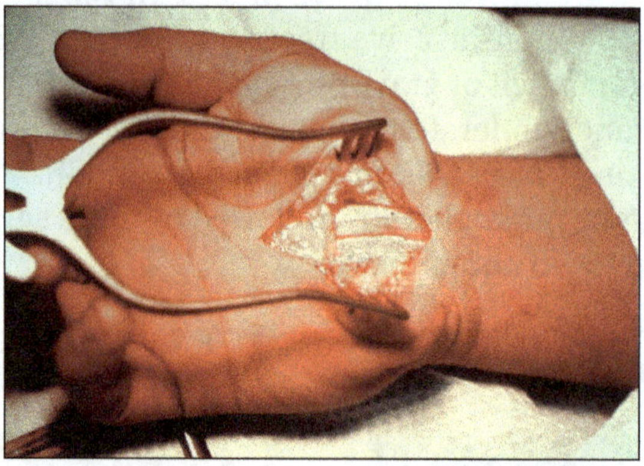

Carpal tunnel syndrome operation.

Surgery is more beneficial in the short term to alleviate symptoms (up to six months) than wearing an orthosis for a minimum of 6 weeks. However, surgery and wearing a brace resulted in similar symptom relief in the long term (12–18 month outcomes).

Physical Therapy

An evidence based guideline produced by the American Academy of Orthopedic Surgeons assigned various grades of recommendation to physical therapy and other nonsurgical treatments. One of the primary issues with physiotherapy is that it attempts to reverse (often) years of pathology inside the carpal tunnel. Practitioners caution that any physiotherapy such as myofascial release may take weeks of persistent application to effectively manage carpal tunnel syndrome.

Again, some claim that pro-active ways to reduce stress on the wrists, which alleviates wrist pain and strain, involve adopting a more ergonomic work and life environment. For example, some have claimed that switching from a QWERTY computer keyboard layout to a more optimised ergonomic layout such as Dvorak was commonly cited as beneficial in early CTS studies; however, some meta-analyses of these studies claim that the evidence that they present is limited.

Tendon and nerve gliding exercises appear to be useful in carpal tunnel syndrome.

Prognosis

Scars from carpal tunnel release surgery. Two different techniques were used. The left scar is 6 weeks old, the right scar is 2 weeks old. Also note the muscular atrophy of the thenar eminence in the left hand, a common sign of advanced CTS.

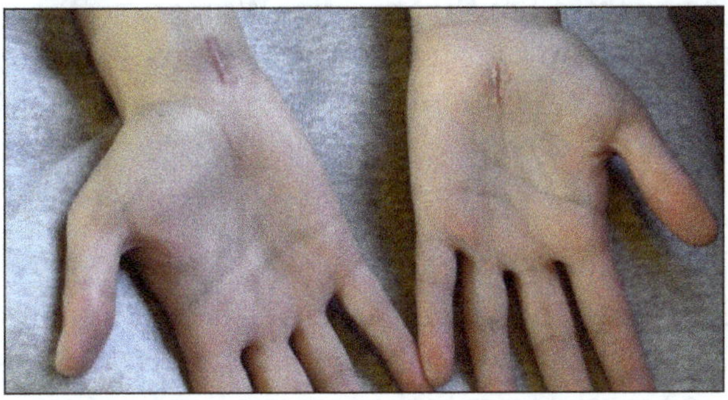

Most people relieved of their carpal tunnel symptoms with conservative or surgical management find minimal residual or "nerve damage". Long-term chronic carpal tunnel syndrome (typically seen in the elderly) can result in permanent "nerve damage", i.e. irreversible numbness, muscle wasting, and weakness. Those that undergo a carpal tunnel release are nearly twice as likely as those not having surgery to develop trigger thumb in the months following the procedure.

While outcomes are generally good, certain factors can contribute to poorer results that have little to do with nerves, anatomy, or surgery type. One study showed that mental status parameters or alcohol use yields much poorer overall results of treatment.

Recurrence of carpal tunnel syndrome after successful surgery is rare.

Epidemiology

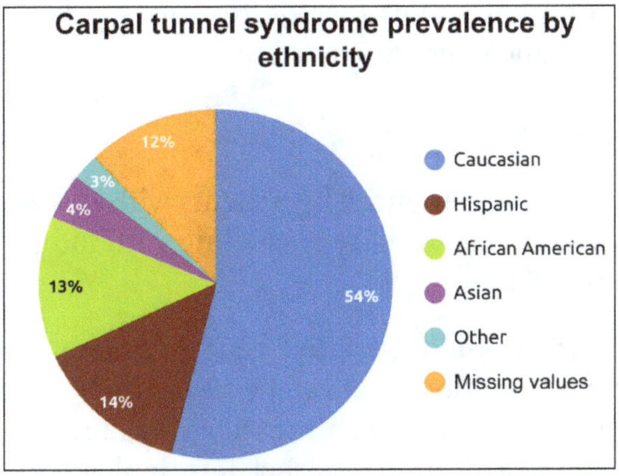

Rates of carpal tunnel syndrome by ethnicity.
CTS is much more common in Caucasians.

Carpal tunnel syndrome is estimated to affect one out of ten people during their lifetime and is the most common nerve compression syndrome. It accounts for about

90% of all nerve compression syndromes. In the U.S., 5% of people have the effects of carpal tunnel syndrome. Caucasians have the highest risk of CTS compared with other races such as non-white South Africans. Women suffer more from CTS than men with a ratio of 3:1 between the ages of 45–60 years. Only 10% of reported cases of CTS are younger than 30 years. Increasing age is a risk factor. CTS is also common in pregnancy.

Occupational

As of 2010, 8% of U.S. workers reported ever having carpal tunnel syndrome and 4% reported carpal tunnel syndrome in the past 12 months. Prevalence rates for carpal tunnel syndrome in the past 12 months were higher among females than among males; among workers aged 45–64 than among those aged 18–44. Overall, 67% of current carpal tunnel syndrome cases among current/recent workers were reportedly attributed to work by health professionals, indicating that the prevalence rate of work-related carpal tunnel syndrome among workers was 2%, and that there were approximately 3.1 million cases of work-related carpal tunnel syndrome among U.S. workers in 2010. Among current carpal tunnel syndrome cases attributed to specific jobs, 24% were attributed to jobs in the manufacturing industry, a proportion 2.5 times higher than the proportion of current/recent workers employed in the manufacturing industry, suggesting that jobs in this industry are associated with an increased risk of work-related carpal tunnel syndrome.

Repetitive Strain Injury

A repetitive strain injury (RSI) is an injury to part of the musculoskeletal or nervous system which is caused by repetitive use, vibrations, compression or long periods in a fixed position. Other common names include repetitive stress disorders, cumulative trauma disorders (CTDs), and overuse syndrome.

Signs and Symptoms

Some examples of symptoms experienced by patients with RSI are aching, pulsing pain, tingling and extremity weakness, initially presenting with intermittent discomfort and then with a higher degree of frequency.

Repetitive strain injury (RSI) and associative trauma orders are umbrella terms used to refer to several discrete conditions that can be associated with repetitive tasks, forceful exertions, vibrations, mechanical compression, sustained or awkward positions, or repetitive eccentric contractions. The exact terminology is controversial, but the terms now used by the United States Department of Labor and the National Institute of Occupational Safety and Health (NIOSH) are musculoskeletal disorders (MSDs) and work-related muscular skeletal disorders (WMDs).

Examples of conditions that may sometimes be attributed to such causes include tendinosis (or less often tendinitis), carpal tunnel syndrome, cubital tunnel syndrome, De Quervain syndrome, thoracic outlet syndrome, intersection syndrome, golfer's elbow (medial epicondylitis), tennis elbow (lateral epicondylitis), trigger finger (so-called stenosing tenosynovitis), radial tunnel syndrome, ulnar tunnel syndrome, and focal dystonia.

A general worldwide increase since the 1970s in RSIs of the arms, hands, neck, and shoulder has been attributed to the widespread use in the workplace of keyboard entry devices, such as typewriters and computers, which require long periods of repetitive motions in a fixed posture. Extreme temperatures have also been reported as risk factor for RSI.

Risk Factors

Occupational Risk Factors

Workers in certain fields are at risk of repetitive strains. Most occupational injuries are musculoskeletal disorders, and many of these are caused by cumulative trauma rather than a single event. Miners and poultry workers, for example, must make repeated motions which can cause tendon, muscular, and skeletal injuries. Jobs that involve repeated motion patterns or prolonged posture within a work cycle, or both, may be repetitive. Young athletes are predisposed to RSIs due to an underdeveloped musculoskeletal system.

Psychosocial Factors

Factors such as personality differences to work-place organization problems. Certain workers may negatively perceive their work organization due to excessive work rate, long work hours, limited job control, and low social support. Previous studies shown elevated urinary catecholamines (stress-related chemicals) in workers with RSI. Pain related to RSI may evolve into chronic pain syndrome particularly for workers who do not have supports from co-workers and supervisors.

Diagnosis

RSIs are assessed using a number of objective clinical measures. These include effort-based tests such as grip and pinch strength, diagnostic tests such as Finkelstein's test for De Quervain's tendinitis, Phalen's Contortion, Tinel's Percussion for carpal tunnel syndrome, and nerve conduction velocity tests that show nerve compression in the wrist. Various imaging techniques can also be used to show nerve compression such as x-ray for the wrist, and MRI for the thoracic outlet and cervico-brachial areas. Utilization of routine imaging is useful in early detection and treatment of overuse injuries in at risk populations, which is important in preventing long term adverse effects.

Treatment

There are no quick fixes for RSI. Early diagnosis is critical to limiting damage. RICE is used as the first treatment for many muscle strains, ligament sprains, or other bruises and injuries. RICE stands for Rest, Ice, Compression, and Elevation. RICE is used immediately after an injury happens and for the first 24 to 48 hours after the injury. These modalities can help reduce the swelling and pain. Commonly prescribed treatments for early-stage RSIs include analgesics, myofeedback, biofeedback, physical therapy, relaxation, and ultrasound therapy. Low-grade RSIs can sometimes resolve themselves if treatments begin shortly after the onset of symptoms. However, some RSIs may require more aggressive intervention including surgery and can persist for years.

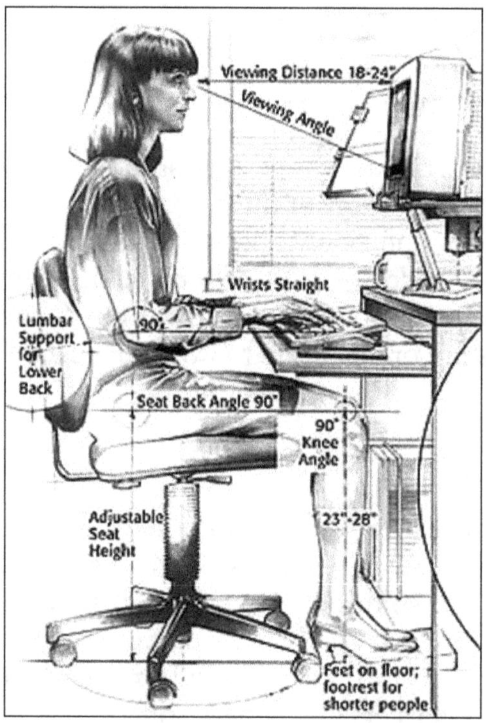

Ergonomics: The science of designing the job, equipment, and workplace.

Although there are no "quick fixes" for RSI, there are effective approaches to its treatment and prevention. One is that of ergonomics, the changing of one's environment (especially workplace equipment) to minimize repetitive strain. Another is specific massage techniques such as trigger point therapy and related techniques such as the Alexander Technique. Licensed massage therapists specializing in RSI, as well as physical therapists and chiropractors, generally provide hands-on therapy, but also expect that the patient supplement and reinforce the office-visit therapy sessions with daily (or several times daily) exercises, self-massage, and stretching as prescribed by the practitioner.

General exercise has been shown to decrease the risk of developing RSI. Doctors sometimes recommend that RSI sufferers engage in specific strengthening exercises, for example to improve sitting posture, reduce excessive kyphosis, and potentially thoracic outlet syndrome. Modifications of posture and arm use (human factors and ergonomics) are often recommended.

Work-related Musculoskeletal Disorders

Work-related musculoskeletal disorders (WMSD) related with repetitive and demanding working conditions continue to represent one of the biggest problems in industrialized countries.

The World Health Organization (WHO), recognizing the impact of 'work-related' musculoskeletal diseases, has characterized WMSD s as multifactorial, indicating that a number of risk factors contribute to and exacerbates these maladies. The presence of these risk factors produced increases in the occurrence of these injuries, thus making WMSD s an international health concern. These types of injuries of the soft tissues are referred to by many names, including WMSD s, repetitive strain injuries (RSI), repetitive motion injuries (RMI), and cumulative trauma disorders (CTDs).

WMSD are diseases related and aggravated by work that can affect the upper limb extremities, the lower back area, and the lower limbs. WMSD can be defined by impairments of bodily structures such as muscles, joints, tendons, ligaments, nerves, bones and the localized blood circulation system, caused or aggravated primarily by work itself or by the work environment.

Besides the physically demanding of the jobs the ageing of the workforce are also a contribution to the widespread of WMSD, since the propensity for developing a WMSD is related more to the difference between the demands of work and the worker's physical work capacity that decreases with age.

Despite the variety of efforts to control WMSD, including engineering design changes, organizational modifications or working training programs, these set of disorders account for a huge amount of human suffering due to worker impairment, often leading to permanent, partial or total disability. WMSD have also heavy economic costs to companies and to healthcare systems. The costs are due to loss of productivity, training of new workers and compensation costs. These costs are felt globally, particularly as organizations begin to develop international partnerships for manufacturing and service roles.

Conclusions derived from the 4th European Working Conditions Survey (conducted in 2005 in 31 countries: EU27 plus Norway, Croatia, Turkey and Switzerland by European Foundation for the Improvement of Living and Working Conditions) state that about 60 million workers reportedly suffer from WMSD in Europe. Therefore, within the EU, backache seems to be the most prevalent work-related health problem, followed by overall fatigue (22.5%) and stress (22.3%). Variability among Member States' self-reported backache levels are high, ranging from a maximum of 47%, in Greece, to a minimum of 10.8%, in the United Kingdom. Self-reported WMSD from the newer Member States tend to be higher: overall fatigue (40.7%) and backache (38.9%).

The same European Foundation according to data from the 5th European Working Conditions Survey, which have collected data during 2010 from around 44,000 workers in 34 European countries (EU27, Norway, Croatia, the former Yugoslav Republic of Macedonia, Turkey, Albania, Montenegro and Kosovo) concluded that European workers remain exposed to physical hazards, which means that many Europeans' jobs still involve physical labour. For instance, 33% of workers carry heavy loads at least a quarter of their working time, while 23% are exposed to vibrations. About half of all workers (46%) work in tiring or painful positions at least a quarter of the time. Also repetitive hand or arm movements are performed by more Europeans than 10 years ago. Women and men are exposed to different physical hazards, due to gender segregation that occurs in many sectors. This report reveals also that, 33% of men, but only 10% of women, are regularly exposed to vibrations, while 42% of men, but 24% of women, carry heavy loads. In contrast, 13% of women, but only 5% of men, lift or move people as part of their work. However, similar proportions of men and women work in tiring positions (48% and 45% respectively), or make repetitive hand and arm movements (64% and 63% respectively).

WMSD are the most common occupational illness in the European Union; however, it would appear that musculoskeletal disorders directly linked to strenuous working conditions are on the decline, while those related to stress and work overload are increasing. Pain in the lower limbs may be as important as pain in the upper limbs, but there is limited research to support pain as a symptom, associated risk factors and broad evidence that has been recognized as specific lower extremity WMSD risk.

Work Related Musculoskeletal Disorders

The recognition that the work may adversely affect health is not new. Musculoskeletal disorders have been diagnosed for many years in the medical field. In the eighteenth century the Italian physician Bernardino Ramazzini, was the first to recognize the relationship between work and certain disorders of the musculoskeletal system due to the performance of sudden and irregular movements and the adoption of awkward postures. In old medical records is also possible to find references to a variety of injuries related to the execution of certain work. In the nineteenth century, Raynauld's phenomenon, also called dead finger or jackhammer disease, was found to be caused by a lack of blood supply and related to repetitive motions. In 1893, Gray gave explanations of inflammations of the extensor tendons of the thumb in their sheaths after performing extreme exercises. Long before the Workers' Compensation Act was passed in Great Britain and CTDs were recognized by the medical community as an insurable diagnosis, workers were victims of the trade they pursued. Since these injuries only manifest themselves after a long period of time, they often went unrecognized.

Some disorders were identified by names related with the professions where they mainly occurred, for instance 'carpenter's elbow', 'seamstress', 'wrist' or 'bricklayer's shoulder', 'washer woman's sprain,' 'gamekeeper's thumb,' 'drummer's palsy,' 'pipe fitter's thumb,' 'reed maker's elbow,' 'pizza cutter's palsy,' and 'flute player's hand'. During and after the 1960s, physiological and biomechanical strains of human tissue, particularly of the tendons and their sheaths, revealed that they were indeed associated to repetitive tasks. As a result, several recommendations have been developed for the design and arrangement of workstations, as well as the use of tools and equipment to ultimately alleviate or reduce WMSDs.

In international literature there is variability in the terminology related to WMSD. Of thing to be noted is that several of these designations are intended to translate the relationship between the disorder and the suspected causal factor or mechanism of injury.

Also the classification of the conditions allows the scientific community to understand how to treat the conditions, as well as provides information that engineers can utilize to design processes and equipment to mitigate the risk factors.

Table: WMSD designation.

Designation	Country
Cervicobrachial Syndrome	Japan, Sweden
Cumulative Trauma Disorder	USA
Occupational Cervicobrachial Disorder	Japan, Sweden
Occupational Overuse Syndrome	Australia
Repetitive Strain Injury	Australia, Canada, Netherlands
Work-Related Neck and Upper Limb Disorders; Work-Related Upper Limb Disorders	United Kingdom
Work-Related Musculoskeletal Disorders	World
Repetitive stress injury; Repetitive motion injuries	-

WMSD Risk Factors

The strong correlation between the incidence of WMSD and the working conditions is well known, particularly the physical risk factors associated with jobs e.g., awkward postures, high repetition, excessive force, static work, cold or vibration. Work intensification and stress and other psychosocial factors also seem to be factors that increasingly contribute to the onset of those disorders.

As referred WHO attributes a multifactorial etiology to WMSD, which means that these disorders appear as consequence of the worker exposure to a number of work related risk factors.

Besides risk factors related to work other risk factors contribute to its development, namely factors intrinsic to the worker and factors unrelated to work. A risk factor is any source or situation with the potential to cause injury or lead to the development of a disease. The variety and complexity of the factors that contribute to the appearance of these disorders explains the difficulties often encountered, to determine the best suited ergonomic intervention to be accomplished in a given workplace, to control them.

Moreover, despite all the available knowledge some uncertainty remains about the level of exposure to risk factors that triggers WMSD. In addition there is significant variability of individual response to the risk factors exposure.

The literature review and epidemiological studies have shown that in the genesis of the WMSD three sets of risk factors can be considered:

- Physical factors: E.g., sustained or awkward postures, repetition of the same movements, forceful exertions, hand-arm vibration, all-body vibration, mechanical compression, and cold.
- Psychosocial factors: E.g., work pace, autonomy, monotony, work/rest cycle, task demands, social support from colleagues and management and job uncertainty.
- Individual factors: E.g., age, gender, professional activities, sport activities, domestic activities, recreational activities, alcohol/tobacco consumption and, previous WMSD.

In order to evaluate the possibility of an employee develop WMSD it is important to include all the relevant activities performed both at work and outside work. Most of the WMSD risk factors can occur both at work and in leisure time activities.

Risk factors act simultaneously in a synergistic effect on a joint or body region. Therefore to manage risk factors it is advisable and important to take into account this interaction rather than focus on a single risk factor. Due to the high individual variability it is impossible to estimate the probability of developing WMSD at individual level. As physicians usually say 'There are no diseases, but patients.'

Physical Factors

A comprehensive review of epidemiological studies was performed to assess the risk factors associated with WMSDs. The review categorized WMSDs by the body part impacted including:

- Neck and neck-shoulder.
- Shoulder.
- Elbow.
- Hand-wrist.
- Back.

The widely accepted physical or task-related risk factors include repetition, force, posture, vibration, temperature extremes, and static posture.

The physical risk factors are a subset of work related risk factors including the environment and biomechanical risk factors, such as posture, force, repetition, direct external pressure (stress per contact), vibration and cold. Another risk factor that affects all risk factors is duration. Since WMSD develop associated with joints, it is necessary that each of these risk factors is controlled for each joints of the human body.

Psychosocial Factors

Psychosocial risk factors are non-biomechanical risk factors related with work. The work-related psychosocial factors are subjective perceptions that workers have of the organizational factors, which are the objective aspects of how the work is organized, is supervised and is carried out. Although organizational and psychosocial factors may be identical, psychosocial factors include the worker emotional perception. Psychosocial risk factors are related with work content (eg, the work load, the task monotony, work control and work clarity), it organizational characteristics (for example, vertical or horizontal organizational structure), interpersonal relationships at work (e.g., relations supervisor-worker) and financial/economic aspects (eg, salary, benefits and equity) and social (e.g., prestige and status in society). Psychosocial factors cannot be seen as risk factors that, by themselves, led to the development of WMSDs. However, in combination with physical risk factors, they can increase the risk of injuries, which has been confirmed by experience. Thus, if the psychological perceptions of the work are negative, there may be negative reactions of physiological and psychological stress. These reactions can lead to physical problems, such as muscle tension. On the other hand, workers may have an inappropriate behaviour at work, such as the use of incorrect working methods, the use of excessive force to perform a task or the omission of the rest periods required to reduce fatigue. Any these conditions can trigger WMSDs.

Individual or Personal Risk Factors

The field of ergonomics does not attempt to screen workers for elimination as potential employees. The recognition of personal risk factors can be useful in providing training, administrative controls, and awareness. Personal or individual risk factors can impact the likelihood for occurrence of a WMSD. These factors vary depending on the study but may include age, gender, smoking, physical activity, strength, anthropometry and previous WMSD, and degenerative joint diseases.

Gender

Women are three times more likely to have CTS than men. Women also deal with strong hormonal changes during pregnancy and menopause that make them more likely to suffer from WMSD, due to increased fluid retention and other physiological conditions. Other reasons for the increased presence of WMSDs in women may be attributed to differences in muscular strength, anthropometry, or hormonal issues. Generally, women are at higher risk of the CTS between the ages of 45 and 54. Then, the risk increases for both men and women as they age. Some studies have found a higher prevalence of some WMSDs in women, but the fact that more women are employed in hand-intensive jobs may account for the greater number of reported work-related MSDs among women. Likewise, reported that men were more likely to have deQuervain's disease than women and attributed this to more frequent use of power hand tools. Whether the gender difference seen with WMSDs in some studies is due to physiological differences or differences in exposure is not fully understood.

To differentiate the effect of work risk factors from potential effects that might be attributable to biological differences, researchers must study jobs that men and women perform relatively equally.

Physical Activity

Studies on physical fitness level as a risk factor for WMSDs have produced mixed results. Physical activity may cause injury. However, the lack of physical activity may increase susceptibility to injury, and after injury, the threshold for further injury is reduced. In construction workers, more frequent leisure time was related to healthy lower backs and severe low-back pain was related to less leisure time activity. On the other hand, some standard treatment regimens have found that musculoskeletal symptoms are often relieved by physical activity. National Institute for Occupational Safety and Health stated that people with high aerobic capacity may be fit for jobs that require high oxygen uptake, but will not necessarily be fit for jobs that require high static and dynamic strengths and vice versa.

Strength

Epidemiologic evidence exists for the relationship between back injury and weak back strength in job tasks. Chaffin & Park found a substantial increase in back injury rates in subjects performing jobs requiring strength that was greater or equal to their isometric strength-test values. The risk was three times greater in weaker subjects. In a second longitudinal study, Chaffin et al. evaluated the risk of back injuries and strength and found the risk to be three times greater in weaker subjects. Other studies have not found the same relationship with physical strength. Two prospective studies of low-back pain reports (or claims) of large populations of blue collar workers failed to demonstrate that stronger workers (defined by isometric lifting strength) are at lower risk for low back pain claims or episodes.

Anthropometry

Weight, height, body mass index (BMI) (a ratio of weight to height squared), and obesity have all been identified in studies as potential risk factors for certain WMSDs, particularly CTS and lumbar disc herniation. Vessey et al. found that the risk for CTS among obese women was double that of slender women. The relationship of CTS and BMI has been suggested to be related to increased fatty tissue within the carpal canal or to increased hydrostatic pressure throughout the carpal canal in obese persons compared with slender persons. Carpal tunnel canal size and wrist size has been suggested as a risk factor for CTS; however, some studies have linked both small and large canal areas to CTS. Studies on anthropometric data are conflicting, but in general indicate that there is no strong correlation between stature, body weight, body build, and low back pain. Obesity seems to play a small but significant role in the occurrence of CTS.

Smoking

Several studies have presented evidence that smoking is associated with low-back pain, sciatica, or intervertebral herniated disc; whereas in others, the relationship was negative found a relationship between smoking and back pain only in those occupations that required physical exertion. In this study, smoking was more clearly related to pain in the extremities than to pain in the neck or the back. Deyo & Bass noted that the prevalence of back pain increased with the number of pack-years of cigarette smoking and with the heaviest smoking level. Several explanations for the relationship have been proposed. One hypothesis is that back pain is caused by coughing from smoking.

Coughing increases the abdominal pressure and intradiscal pressure, thereby producing strain on the spine. Several studies have observed this relationship. Other theories include nicotine-induced diminished blood flow to vulnerable tissues, and smoking-induced diminished mineral content of bone causing microfractures.

Interaction among Risk Factors

All risk factors interact among each other. For example, the stress felt by a worker may be influenced by the physical demands of the task, the psychological reaction to this requirement, or by both. Once the requirement of the task reaches a high value, the worker may have stress reactions and biological and behavioral unsuitable reactions. As these reactions are more frequent and occur over an extended period they cause health problems. These health problems reduce the 'resistance' of individuals to cope with the subsequent demands of work, thus increasing the possibility of occurrence of WMSDs. As mentioned, the duration of exposure to risk factors is one of the parameters that must be taken into account when a risk assessment is performed. For example, the heuristic model dose-response to cumulative risk factors in repetitive manual work, proposed by Tanaka McGlothlin, underlines the role of the duration of the activity in the development of musculoskeletal disorders of the hand/wrist.

It's possible to observe the interaction of the following risk factors: force, repetition and wrist posture with exposure duration. In order to keep workers operating in a safe area an increase in exposure duration should be accompanying with a reduction of the other risk factors.

Repetitive Motion Injury Prevention

Fatigue or tiredness in muscles and joints is your body's way of telling you to change your pattern of working. Doing the same motion over and over or using certain types of positions or grips can cause pain and inflammation. Some of the common inflammations are:

- Tendinitis: Inflammation of the tendons. Can be caused by performing repeated motions incorrectly or in an awkward position.
- Tenosynovitis: A condition in which both the tendon and its covering become inflamed. Can be caused by improper or repetitive bending of the wrist.
- Carpal Tunnel Syndrome: Painful squeezing of the median nerve in the wrist. Causes loss of grip, muscle pain, weakness, and numbness in the thumb and first two fingers. If after an appropriate period of time, test and medication do not work, surgery may be necessary.

Limit Repetitive Motions

The best form of prevention is to limit the time anyone spends doing the same motion over and over, whether it's packing, using a keyboard, using a hand or power tool, etc. To reduce your risks of Cumulative Trauma Disorders, avoid or minimize these physically straining activities:

- Repetitive twisting movements, usually in combination with poor body position.
- Exposure to cold, combined with repetitive motions.
- Excessive standing with no chance to lean, sits, or comfortably repositions body.
- Holding arms with no support.
- Hand operation of vibrating machinery.
- Repetitive physical force using shoulders, arms, legs, and back.
- Repetitive motions using a bent wrist.

It is up to everyone to help identify poor ergonomic practices in the workplace. Managers, supervisors, employees, and health professionals should work as a team to correct existing ergonomic problems. When analyzing a specific job for ergonomic problems, the following points must be considered:

- Weight of objects being handled.

- Body positions.
- Repetitions of certain movements or tasks.
- How workers grip objects.

Engineering Controls is the preferred method of control. This should be accomplished through the following procedures:

- Work Station Design: Work stations should be made easily adjustable and either designed or selected to fit the task, so they are comfortable for the worker using them.
- Design for Work Methods: Work methods should be designed to reduce static, extreme and awkward postures, repetitive motion and excessive force.
- Tool and Handle Design: A variety of sizes should be available to achieve proper fit and reduce ergonomic risk. The appropriate tool will be used to do a specific job.

Work Practices should include a program with key elements such as proper work techniques, employee conditioning, inspections, feedback, and maintenance.

- Proper work techniques include training on the correct lifting procedures and correct use of ergonomicaly designed work stations, fixtures, and tools.
- Employee conditioning should include employees gradually being worked into a full workload as appropriate for their specific job. Employees reassigned to new jobs should also have a break-in training period.
- Inspections shall be conducted periodically to ensure safe operating procedures are being followed.
- Feedback will provide a system for employees to notify supervisors about conditions with potential ergonomic hazards. Employees are instructed to report ergonomicaly related symptoms to their supervisors immediately.
- These would include:
    - Numbing, burning, or tingling in your fingers.
    - Pain in your wrists.
    - Loss of grip or muscle weakness.
    - Fatigue or abnormal tiredness.
    - Pain in your back, legs, feet, neck or shoulders.
- Maintenance should be the preventive program for monitoring mechanical equipment and tools to ensure they are in proper working condition.

Administrative Controls should reduce the duration, frequency, and severity of exposures to ergonomic hazards. Options to be considered:

- Pacing: Reducing the number of repetitions per hour.
- Breaks: Providing short rest periods to relieve fatigue.
- Job rotation: Rotate periodically to a different task involving different movements.

Exercise and Techniques for Prevention

Exercise is an important part of the prevention program. Fit people are less likely to experience physical problems and are more likely to recover quickly when they do.

Body stretch.	Reach up.
Side Bends.	Slow and easy.
Upper body twist.	With hands on hips, twist to the right and then to the left. Repeat 4-6 times.
Shoulder shrugs.	Inhale and bring shoulders to ears. Exhale and allow shoulders to drop.
Finger stretch.	Spread your fingers wide. Hold for 5 seconds, relax. Repeat 3-5 times, alternate hands.
Wrist stretch.	With opposite hand, gently pull your fingers back allowing wrist to bend. Hold for 3 seconds, Switch hands. Repeat 3-5 times.
Thumb stretch.	Extend one hand and with the other hand, gently pull back on your thumb for 3 seconds. Relax. Repeat 3-5 times on each hand.
Finger squeezes.	Make a fist around a firm yet soft ball, and then squeeze towards your palm 5-10 times. Following this exercise, repeat finger stretch.
Shake.	While standing or sitting, drop your arms to your sides. Gently shake out your arms and hands for a few seconds. Relax and repeat 3 times.

Solutions to Control Ergonomic Hazards

Many industries have successfully implemented ergonomic solutions in their facilities as a way to address their workers' MSD injury risks. These interventions have included modifying existing equipment, making changes in work practices and purchasing new tools or other devices to assist in the production process. Making these changes has reduced physical demands, eliminated unnecessary movements, lowered injury rates and their associated workers' compensation costs, and reduced employee turnover. In many cases, work efficiency and productivity have increased as well. Simple, low-cost solutions are often available to solve problems.

To reduce the chance of injury, work tasks should be designed to limit exposure to ergonomic risk factors. Engineering controls are the most desirable, where possible.

Administrative or work practice controls may be appropriate in some cases where engineering controls cannot be implemented or when different procedures are needed after implementation of the new engineering controls. Personal protection solutions have only limited effectiveness when dealing with ergonomic hazards.

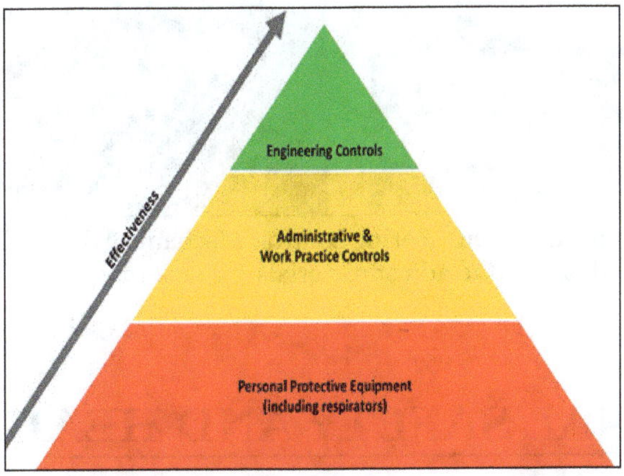

Type of Control	Workplace Examples
Engineering Controls (implement physical change to the workplace, which eliminates/reduces the hazard on the job/task).	• Use a device to lift and reposition heavy objects to limit force exertion. • Reduce the weight of a load to limit force exertion. • Reposition a work table to eliminate a long/excessive reach and enable working in neutral postures. • Use diverging conveyors off a main line so that tasks are less repetitive. • Install diverters on conveyors to direct materials toward the worker to eliminate excessive leaning or reaching. • Redesign tools to enable neutral postures.
Administrative and Work Practice Controls (establish efficient processes or procedures).	• Require that heavy loads are only lifted by two people to limit force exertion. • Establish systems so workers are rotated away from tasks to minimize the duration of continual exertion, repetitive motions, and awkward postures. Design a job rotation system in which employees rotate between jobs that use different muscle groups. • Staff "floaters" to provide periodic breaks between scheduled breaks. • Properly use and maintain pneumatic and power tools.
Personal Protective Equipment (use protection to reduce exposure to ergonomics-related risk factors).	• Use padding to reduce direct contact with hard, sharp, or vibrating surfaces. • Wear good fitting thermal gloves to help with cold conditions while maintaining the ability to grasp items easily.

Example of an engineering control: Mechanical devices that lift and tilt to adjust materials for easier handling.

OCCUPATIONAL SAFETY AND HEALTH

Occupational safety and health (OSH), also commonly referred to as occupational health and safety (OHS), occupational health, or workplace health and safety (WHS), is a multidisciplinary field concerned with the safety, health, and welfare of people at work.

The goal of occupational safety and health programs is to foster a safe and healthy work environment. OSH may also protect co-workers, family members, employers, customers, and many others who might be affected by the workplace environment. In the United States, the term occupational health and safety is referred to as occupational health and occupational and non-occupational safety and includes safety for activities outside of work.

In common-law jurisdictions, employers have a common law duty to take reasonable care of the safety of their employees. Statute law may in addition impose other general duties, introduce specific duties, and create government bodies with powers to regulate workplace safety issues: details of this vary from jurisdiction to jurisdiction.

This painting depicts a woman examining her work on a lathe at a factory in Britain during World War II. Her eyes are not protected. Today, such practice would not be permitted in most industrialized countries that adhere to occupational health and safety standards for workers. In many countries, however, such standards are still either weak or nonexistent.

As defined by the World Health Organization (WHO) "occupational health deals with all aspects of health and safety in the workplace and has a strong focus on primary prevention of hazards." Health has been defined as "a state of complete physical, mental and social well-being and not merely the absence of disease or infirmity." Occupational health is a multidisciplinary field of healthcare concerned with enabling an individual to undertake their occupation, in the way that causes least harm to their health. It contrasts, for example, with the promotion of health and safety at work, which is concerned with preventing harm from any incidental hazards, arising in the workplace.

Since 1950, the International Labour Organization (ILO) and the World Health Organization (WHO) have shared a common definition of occupational health. It was adopted by the Joint ILO/WHO Committee on Occupational Health at its first session in 1950 and revised at its twelfth session in 1995. The definition reads:

> The main focus in occupational health is on three different objectives: (i) the maintenance and promotion of workers' health and working capacity; (ii) the improvement of working environment and work to become conducive to safety and health and (iii) development of work organizations and working cultures in a direction which supports health and safety at work and in doing so also promotes a positive social climate and smooth operation and may enhance productivity of the undertakings. The concept of working culture is intended in this context to mean a reflection of the essential value systems adopted by the undertaking concerned. Such a culture is reflected in practice in the managerial systems, personnel policy, principles for participation, training policies and quality management of the undertaking.
>
> —*Joint ILO/WHO Committee on Occupational Health*

Those in the field of occupational health come from a wide range of disciplines and professions including medicine, psychology, epidemiology, physiotherapy and rehabilitation, occupational therapy, occupational medicine, human factors and ergonomics, and many others. Professionals advise on a broad range of occupational health matters. These include how to avoid particular pre-existing conditions causing a problem in the occupation, correct posture for the work, frequency of rest breaks, preventive action that can be undertaken, and so forth.

"Occupational health should aim at: the promotion and maintenance of the highest degree of physical, mental and social well-being of workers in all occupations; the prevention amongst workers of departures from health caused by their working conditions; the protection of workers in their employment from risks resulting from factors adverse to health; the placing and maintenance of the worker in an occupational environment adapted to his physiological and psychological capabilities; and, to summarize, the adaptation of work to man and of each man to his job.

Workplace Hazards

Although work provides many economic and other benefits, a wide array of workplace hazards also present risks to the health and safety of people at work. These include but are not limited to, "chemicals, biological agents, physical factors, adverse ergonomic conditions, allergens, a complex network of safety risks," and a broad range of psychosocial risk factors. Personal protective equipment can help protect against many of these hazards.

Physical hazards affect many people in the workplace. Occupational hearing loss is the most common work-related injury in the United States, with 22 million workers exposed to hazardous noise levels at work and an estimated $242 million spent annually on worker's compensation for hearing loss disability. Falls are also a common cause of occupational injuries and fatalities, especially in construction, extraction, transportation, healthcare, and building cleaning and maintenance. Machines have moving parts, sharp edges, hot surfaces and other hazards with the potential to crush, burn, cut, shear, stab or otherwise strike or wound workers if used unsafely.

Biological hazards (biohazards) include infectious microorganisms such as viruses and toxins produced by those organisms such as anthrax. Biohazards affect workers in many industries; influenza, for example, affects a broad population of workers. Outdoor workers, including farmers, landscapers, and construction workers, risk exposure to numerous biohazards, including animal bites and stings, urushiol from poisonous plants, and diseases transmitted through animals such as the West Nile virus and Lyme disease. Health care workers, including veterinary health workers, risk exposure to blood-borne pathogens and various infectious diseases, especially those that are emerging.

Dangerous chemicals can pose a chemical hazard in the workplace. There are many classifications of hazardous chemicals, including neurotoxins, immune agents, dermatologic agents, carcinogens, reproductive toxins, systemic toxins, asthmagens, pneumoconiotic agents, and sensitizers. Authorities such as regulatory agencies set occupational exposure limits to mitigate the risk of chemical hazards. An international effort is investigating the health effects of mixtures of chemicals. There is some evidence that certain chemicals are harmful at lower levels when mixed with one or more other chemicals. This may be particularly important in causing cancer.

Psychosocial hazards include risks to the mental and emotional well-being of workers, such as feelings of job insecurity, long work hours, and poor work-life balance. A recent Cochrane review - using moderate quality evidence - related that the addition of work-directed interventions for depressed workers receiving clinical interventions reduces the number of lost work days as compared to clinical interventions alone. This review also demonstrated that the addition of cognitive behavioral therapy to primary or occupational care and the addition of a "structured telephone outreach and care management program" to usual care are both effective at reducing sick leave days.

Workplace Fatality and Injury Statistics

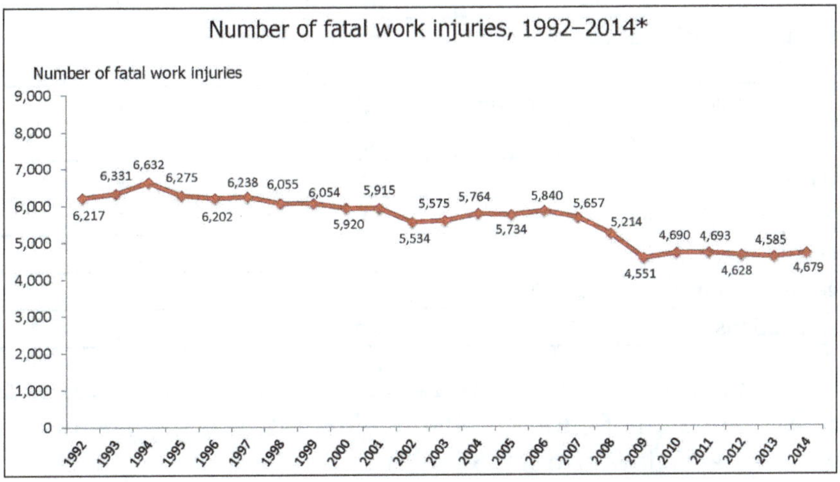

Number of occupational fatal work injuries in the U.S. from 1992 until 2014. Note, 2001 statistics do not include death related to the September 11 terrorist attacks.

The Occupational Safety and Health Statistics (OSHS) program in the Bureau of Labor Statistics of the United States Department of Labor compiles information about workplace fatalities and non-fatal injuries in the United States. The OSHS program produces three annual reports:

- Counts and rates of nonfatal occupational injuries and illnesses by detailed industry and case type (SOII summary data).
- Case circumstances and worker demographic data for nonfatal occupational injuries and illnesses resulting in days away from work (SOII case and demographic data).
- Counts and rates of fatal occupational injuries (CFOI data).

In 1970, an estimated 14,000 workers were killed on the job – by 2010, the workforce had doubled, but workplace deaths were down to about 4,500. Between 1913 and 2013, workplace fatalities dropped by approximately 80%.

The Bureau also compiles information about the most dangerous jobs. According to the census of occupational injuries 4,679 people died on the job in 2014. In 2015, a decline in nonfatal workplace injuries and illnesses was observed, with private industry employers reporting approximately 2.9 million incidents, nearly 48,000 fewer cases than in 2014.

2017 Number and rate of fatal work injuries by major occupation group		
Occupation Group	Fatalities	Fatalities per 100,000 employees
Transportation and material moving	1,443	15.9
Construction and extraction	965	12.2
Service	778	3.3
Management, business, and financial operations	425	1.6
Installation, maintenance, and repair	414	8.1
Farming, fishing, and forestry	264	20.9
Sales and related	232	1.6
Professional and related	229	0.7
Production	221	2.6
Office and administrative support	101	0.6
All occupations	5,147	3.5

A total of 5,147 workers died from a work-related injury in the U.S. in 2017, down slightly from the 2016 total of 5,190. The fatal injury rate was 3.5 per 100,000 full-time equivalent workers, also down from 3.6 in 2016.

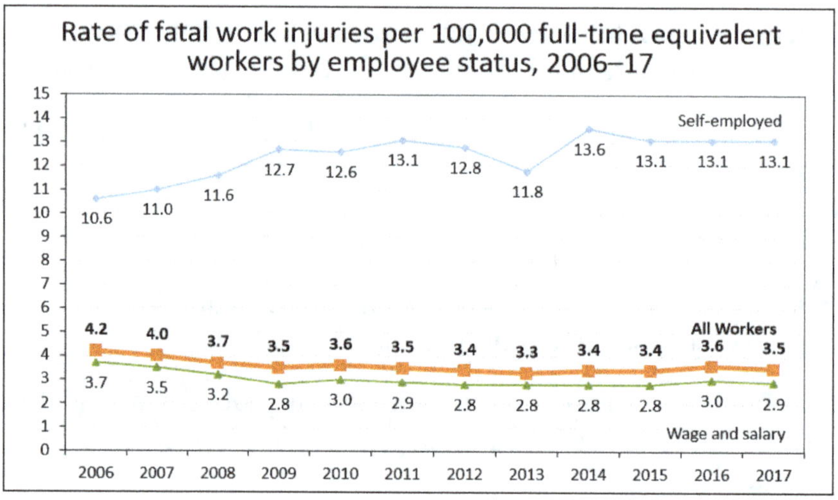

The rate of fatal work injuries per 100,000 full-time equivalent workers by employee status. Rate = (Fatal work injuries/Total hours worked by all workers) x 200,000,000 where 200,000,000 = base for 100,000 full-time equivalent workers (FTEs) working 40 hours per week, 50 weeks per year. The total hours worked are annual average estimates from the Current Population Survey (CPS).

Nonfatal occupational injuries and illnesses by nature, 2017	
Cause of injury and illness	2017 rate per 10,000 full-time employees
Contact with objects or equipment	23.2
Falls, slips, trips	23.1

Over-exertion and bodily reaction	30.0
Violence and other injuries by person or animal	4.0
Transportation incidents	4.9
Exposure to harmful substances or environments	3.8
Fires and explosions	0.1
Total	89.4

In most countries males comprise the vast majority of workplace fatalities. In the EU as a whole, 94% of death was of males. In the UK the disparity was even greater with males comprising 97.4% of workplace deaths. In the UK there were 171 fatal injuries at work in financial year 2011–2012, compared with 651 in calendar year 1974; the fatal injury rate declined over that period from 2.9 fatalities per 100,000 workers to 0.6 per 100,000 workers.

After the destruction of the USSR, the enterprises became owned by new owners who were not interested in preserving the life and health of workers. They did not spend money on equipment modernization, and the share of harmful workplaces increased. The state did not interfere in this, and sometimes it helped employers. At first, the process of growth was slow - due to the fact that in the 1990s this was compensated by mass de-industrialization (factories with foundries and other harmful types of production were closed). In the 2000s, this method of restraining the growth of the share of harmful workplaces was exhausted. Therefore, in the 2010s the Ministry of Labor adopted the Federal law 426-FZ, which equated the issuance of personal protective equipment to the employee to real improvement of working conditions; and the Ministry of Health made significant changes in the methods of risk assessment in the workplace. This explains the "decline" in the proportion of workers working in harmful conditions after 2014 - it happened not in practice, but only on paper.

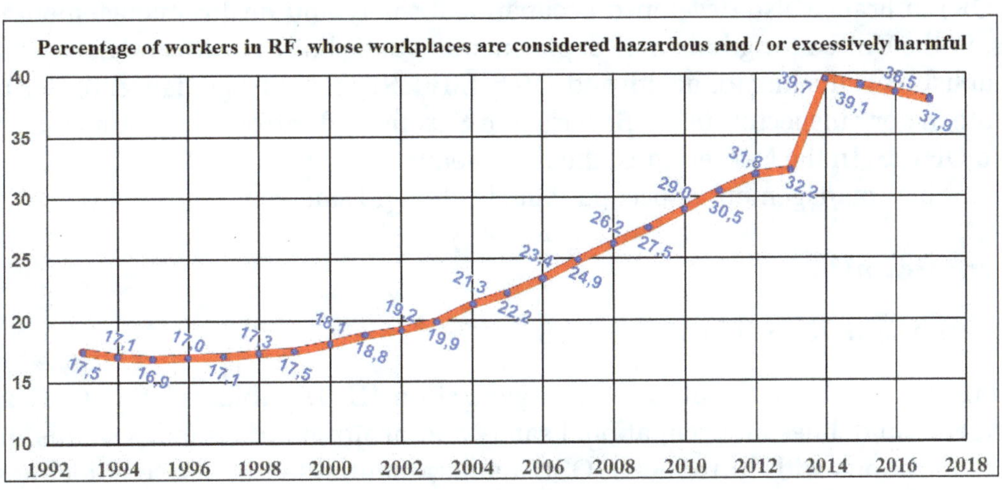

One of the decisions taken by Communists during the reign of Stalin was the reduction in the number of accidents and occupational diseases to zero. The tendency to decline remained in the RF in the early 21st century, and the same methods of falsification are used, so that the real occupational morbidity and the number of accidents are unknown.

Specialists from the Izmerov Research Institute of Occupational Health (the oldest in the world) analyzed information about the health status of workers and the assessment of their working conditions using the new methods of risk assessment. Their findings show that new "methods" do not provide a real picture of working conditions. This is most clearly shown by the results obtained at enterprises producing aluminum. For example, the share of jobs with very harmful working conditions ("labor class" *(health hazard class)* = 3.4) decreased by an order of magnitude (from 11.6% to 1.2%). But the reduction of the level of harmful factors at these enterprises did not happen at all; and the proportion of workers suffering from chronic intoxication with fluorine compounds was 38.7%.

In the opinion of the state inspector, the use of punishment against the guilty manager (disqualification, ban on executive work) is too rare: "The practice of court decisions shows that disqualification of the leader is possible, but for this he or she must kill 5-7 employees, or more". Responsibility for wrong decisions is absent or very low; and punishment of guilty executives in the construction industry usually does not occur.

Management Systems

National

National management system standards for occupational health and safety include AS/NZS 4801-2001 for Australia and New Zealand, CAN/CSA-Z1000-14 for Canada and ANSI/ASSE Z10-2012 for the United States. Association Française de Normalisation (AFNOR) in France also developed occupational safety and health management standards. In the United Kingdom, non-departmental public body Health and Safety Executive published Managing for health and safety (MFHS), an online guidance. In Germany, the state factory inspectorates of Bavaria and Saxony had introduced the management system OHRIS. In the Netherlands, the management system Safety Certificate Contractors combines management of occupational health and safety and the environment.

International

ISO 45001 was published in March 2018.

Previously, the International Labour Organization (ILO) published ILO-OSH 2001, also titled "Guidelines on occupational safety and health management systems" to assist organizations with introducing OSH management systems. These guidelines encourage continual improvement in employee health and safety, achieved via a constant process of policy, organization, planning & implementation, evaluation, and action for improvement, all supported by constant auditing to determine the success of OSH actions. From 1999 to 2018, the occupational health and safety management system standard OHSAS 18001 was adopted as a British and Polish standard and widely used internationally. OHSAS 18000 comprised two parts, OHSAS 18001 and 18002 and was developed by a selection of leading trade bodies, international standards and certification bodies to address a gap where no third-party certifiable international standard existed. It was intended to integrate with ISO 9001 and ISO 14001.

National Legislation and Public Organizations

Occupational safety and health practice vary among nations with different approaches to legislation, regulation, enforcement, and incentives for compliance. In the EU, for example, some member states promote OSH by providing public monies as subsidies, grants or financing, while others have created tax system incentives for OSH investments. A third group of EU member states has experimented with using workplace accident insurance premium discounts for companies or organisations with strong OSH records.

In Australia, the Commonwealth, four of the six states and both territories have enacted and administer harmonised Work Health and Safety Legislation in accordance with the Intergovernmental Agreement for Regulatory and Operational Reform in Occupational Health and Safety. Each of these jurisdictions has enacted Work Health & Safety legislation and regulations based on the Commonwealth Work Health and Safety Act 2011 and common Codes of Practice developed by Safe Work Australia. Some jurisdictions have also included mine safety under the model approach, however, most have retained separate legislation for the time being. In August 2019 Western Australia committed to join nearly every other State and Territory in implementing the harmonised Model WHS Act, Regulations and other subsidiary legislation. Victoria has retained its own regime, although the Model WHS laws themselves drew heavily on the Victoria approach.

In Canada, workers are covered by provincial or federal labour codes depending on the sector in which they work. Workers covered by federal legislation (including those in mining, transportation, and federal employment) are covered by the Canada Labour Code; all other workers are covered by the health and safety legislation of the province in which they work. The Canadian Centre for Occupational Health and Safety (CCOHS), an agency of the Government of Canada, was created in 1966 by an Act of Parliament. The act was based on the belief that all Canadians had "a fundamental right to a healthy and safe working environment." CCOHS is mandated to promote safe and healthy workplaces to help prevent work-related injuries and illnesses. The CCOHS maintains a useful (partial) list of OSH regulations for Canada and its provinces.

Number of full-time OSH inspectors per 100,000 full-time employees	
Italy	17.7
Finland	17.5
Denmark	11.9

United Kingdom	11.1
Norway	10.6
Sweden	10
Belgium	5.3
Netherlands	4.8
Ireland	4.5
Greece	4.1
France	3.5
Spain	2.1

In the European Union, member states have enforcing authorities to ensure that the basic legal requirements relating to occupational health and safety are met. In many EU countries, there is strong cooperation between employer and worker organisations (e.g. unions) to ensure good OSH performance as it is recognized this has benefits for both the worker (through maintenance of health) and the enterprise (through improved productivity and quality). In 1996, the European Agency for Safety and Health at Work was founded.

Member states of the European Union have all transposed into their national legislation a series of directives that establish minimum standards on occupational health and safety. These directives (of which there are about 20 on a variety of topics) follow a similar structure requiring the employer to assess the workplace risks and put in place preventive measures based on a hierarchy of control. This hierarchy starts with elimination of the hazard and ends with personal protective equipment.

However, certain EU member states admit to having lacking quality control in occupational safety services, to situations in which risk analysis takes place without any on-site workplace visits and to insufficient implementation of certain EU OSH directives. Based on this, it is hardly surprising that the total societal costs of work-related health problems and accidents vary from 2.6% to 3.8% of GNP between the EU member states.

In Denmark, occupational safety and health is regulated by the Danish Act on Working Environment and cooperation at the workplace. The Danish Working Environment Authority carries out inspections of companies, draws up more detailed rules on health and safety at work and provides information on health and safety at work. The result of each inspection is made public on the web pages of the Danish Working Environment Authority so that the general public, current and prospective employees, customers and other stakeholders can inform themselves about whether a given organization has passed the inspection, should they wish to do so.

In Spain, occupational safety and health is regulated by the Spanish Act on Prevention of Labour Risks. The Ministry of Labour is the authority responsible for issues relating to labour environment. The National Institute for Labour Safety and Hygiene is the technical public Organization specialized in occupational safety and health.

In Sweden, occupational safety and health is regulated by the Work Environment Act. The Swedish Work Environment Authority is the government agency responsible for issues relating to the working environment. The agency should work to disseminate information and furnish advice on OSH, has a mandate to carry out inspections, and a right to issue stipulations and injunctions to any non-compliant employer.

In the UK, health and safety legislation is drawn up and enforced by the Health and Safety Executive and local authorities (the local council) under the Health and Safety at Work etc. Act 1974 (HASAWA). HASAWA introduced a general duty on an employer to ensure, so far as is reasonably practicable, the health, safety and welfare at work of all his employees; with the intention of giving a legal framework supporting 'codes of practice' not in themselves having legal force but establishing a strong presumption as to what was reasonably practicable (deviations from them could be justified by appropriate risk assessment). The previous reliance on detailed prescriptive rule-setting was seen as having failed to respond rapidly enough to technological change, leaving new technologies potentially un-regulated or inappropriately regulated. HSE has continued to make some regulations giving absolute duties (where something must be done with no 'reasonable practicability' test) but in the UK the regulatory trend is away from prescriptive rules, and towards 'goal setting' and risk assessment. Recent major changes to the laws governing asbestos and fire safety management embrace the concept of risk assessment. The other key aspect of the UK legislation is a statutory mechanism for worker involvement through elected health and safety representatives and health and safety committees. This followed a similar approach in Scandinavia, and that approach has since been adopted in Australia, Canada, New Zealand and Malaysia, for example.

For the UK, the government organisation dealing with occupational health has been the Employment Medical Advisory Service but in 2014 a new occupational health organisation - the Health and Work Service - was created to provide advice and assistance to employers in order to get back to work employees on long-term sick-leave. The service, funded by government, will offer medical assessments and treatment plans, on a voluntary basis, to people on long-term absence from their employer; in return, the government will no longer foot the bill for Statutory Sick Pay provided by the employer to the individual.

In Indonesia, the Ministry of Manpower is responsible to ensure the safety, health and welfare of workers while working, in a factory, or even the area surrounding the factory where labourers work. There are a few rules that control the safety of workers, for example Occupational Safety Act 1970 or Occupational Health Act 1992. The sanctions, however, are still low and the violations of these laws are still at a high rate - with a maximum of 15 million rupiahs fine and a maximum of 1 year in prison.

In Malaysia, the Department of Occupational Safety and Health (DOSH) under the Ministry of Human Resource is responsible to ensure that the safety, health and welfare of workers in both the public and private sector is upheld. DOSH is responsible to enforce the Factories and Machinery Act 1967 and the Occupational Safety and Health Act 1994.

Hardware stores in China specializing in safety equipment.

In the People's Republic of China, the Ministry of Health is responsible for occupational disease prevention and the State Administration of Work Safety for safety issues at work. On the provincial and municipal level, there are Health Supervisions for occupational health and local bureaus of Work Safety for safety. The "Occupational Disease Control Act of PRC" came into force on May 1, 2002. and Work safety Act of PRC on November 1, 2002. The Occupational Disease Control Act is under revision. The prevention of occupational disease is still in its initial stage compared with industrialised countries such as the US or UK.

In Singapore, the Ministry of Manpower operates various checks and campaigns against unsafe work practices, such as when working at height, operating cranes and in traffic management. Examples include Operation Cormorant and the Falls Prevention Campaign.

In South Africa the Department of Employment and Labour is responsible for occupational health and safety inspection and enforcement in commerce and industry apart from mining and energy production, where the Department of Mineral Resources is responsible.

The main statutory legislation on Health and Safety in the jurisdiction of the Department of Labour is Act No. 85 of 1993: Occupational Health and Safety Act as amended by Occupational Health and Safety Amendment Act, No. 181 of 1993.

Regulations to the OHS Act include:

- General Administrative Regulations, 2003.

- Certificate of Competency Regulations, 1990.
- Construction Regulations, 2014.
- Diving Regulations 2009.
- Driven Machinery Regulations, 1988.
- Environmental Regulations for Workplaces, 1987.
- General Machinery regulations, 1988.
- General Safety Regulations, 1986.
- Noise induced hearing loss regulations, 2003.
- Pressure Equipment Regulations, 2004.

In Taiwan, the Occupational Safety and Health Administration of the Ministry of Labor is in charge of occupational safety and health. The matter is governed under the Occupational Safety and Health Act.

2007, official release the document TOSHMS ([Taiwan Occupational Safety and Health Management System]), which defined the basic rule about occupational safety standard.

OSHAD was introduced in February 2010 to regulate the implementation of occupational health and safety in the emirates of Abu Dhabi.

In the United States, President Richard Nixon signed the Occupational Safety and Health Act into law on December 29, 1970. The act created the three agencies that administer it. They include the Occupational Safety and Health Administration, National Institute for Occupational Safety and Health, and the Occupational Safety and Health Review Commission. The act authorized the Occupational Safety and Health Administration (OSHA) to regulate private employers in the 50 states, the District of Columbia, and territories. The Act establishing it includes a general duty clause (29 U.S.C. 654, 5(a)) requiring an employer to comply with the Act and regulations derived from it, and to provide employees with "employment and a place of employment which are free from recognized hazards that are causing or are likely to cause death or serious physical harm to his employees."

OSHA was established in 1971 under the Department of Labor. It has headquarters in Washington, DC and ten regional offices, further broken down into districts, each organized into three sections; compliance, training, and assistance. Its stated mission is to assure safe and healthful working conditions for working men and women by setting and enforcing standards and by providing training, outreach, education and assistance. The original plan was for OSHA to oversee 50 state plans with OSHA funding 50% of each plan. Unfortunately it has not worked out that way. There are currently 26 approved state plans (4 cover only public employees) and no other states want to participate. OSHA manages the plan in the states not participating.

OSHA develops safety standards in the Code of Federal Regulation and enforces those safety standards through compliance inspections conducted by Compliance Officers; enforcement resources are focussed on high-hazard industries. Worksites may apply to enter OSHA's Voluntary Protection Program (VPP); a successful application leads to an on-site inspection; if this is passed the site gains VPP status and OSHA no longer inspect it annually nor (normally) visit it unless there is a fatal accident or an employee complaint until VPP revalidation (after 3–5 years)(VPP sites have injury and illness rates less than half the average for their industry).

It has 73 specialists in local offices to provide tailored information and training to employers and employees at little or no cost. Similarly OSHA produces a range of publications, provides advice to employers and funds consultation services available for small businesses.

OSHA's Alliance Program enables groups committed to worker safety and health to work with it to develop compliance assistance tools and resources, share information with workers and employers, and educate them about their rights and responsibilities. OSHA also has a Strategic Partnership Program that zeros in on specific hazards or specific geographic areas. OSHA manages Susan B. Harwood grants to nonprofit companies to train workers and employers to recognize, avoid, and prevent safety and health hazards in the workplace. Grants focus on small business, hard-to-reach workers and high-hazard industries.

The National Institute for Occupational Safety and Health, created under the same act, works closely with OSHA and provides the research behind many of OSHA's regulations and standards.

Professional Roles and Responsibilities

The roles and responsibilities of OSH professionals vary regionally, but may include evaluating working environments, developing, endorsing and encouraging measures that might prevent injuries and illnesses, providing OSH information to employers, employees, and the public, providing medical examinations, and assessing the success of worker health programs.

In Norway, the main required tasks of an occupational health and safety practitioner include the following:

- Systematic evaluations of the working environment.
- Endorsing preventive measures which eliminate causes of illnesses in the workplace.
- Providing information on the subject of employees' health.

- Providing information on occupational hygiene, ergonomics, and environmental and safety risks in the workplace.

In the Netherlands, the required tasks for health and safety staff are only summarily defined and include the following:

- Providing voluntary medical examinations.
- Providing a consulting room on the work environment to the workers.
- Providing health assessments (if needed for the job concerned).

'The main influence of the Dutch law on the job of the safety professional is through the requirement on each employer to use the services of a certified working conditions service to advise them on health and safety'. A 'certified service' must employ sufficient numbers of four types of certified experts to cover the risks in the organisations which use the service:

- A safety professional.
- An occupational hygienist.
- An occupational physician.
- A work and organisation specialist.

In 2004, 37% of health and safety practitioners in Norway and 14% in the Netherlands had an MSc; 44% had a BSc in Norway and 63% in the Netherlands; and 19% had training as an OSH technician in Norway and 23% in the Netherlands.

Leather craftsman gloves, safety goggles, and a properly fitted hardhat are crucial for proper safety in a construction environment.

The main tasks undertaken by the OHS practitioner in the US include:

- Develop processes, procedures, criteria, requirements, and methods to attain the best possible management of the hazards and exposures that can cause injury to people, and damage property, or the environment.

- Apply good business practices and economic principles for efficient use of resources to add to the importance of the safety processes.
- Promote other members of the company to contribute by exchanging ideas and other different approaches to make sure that everyone in the corporation possess OHS knowledge and have functional roles in the development and execution of safety procedures.
- Assess services, outcomes, methods, equipment, workstations, and procedures by using qualitative and quantitative methods to recognise the hazards and measure the related risks.
- Examine all possibilities, effectiveness, reliability, and expenditure to attain the best results for the company concerned.

Knowledge required by the OHS professional in the US include:

- Constitutional and case law controlling safety, health, and the environment.
- Operational procedures to plan/develop safe work practices.
- Safety, health and environmental sciences.
- Design of hazard control systems (i.e. fall protection, scaffoldings).
- Design of recordkeeping systems that take collection into account, as well as storage, interpretation, and dissemination.
- Mathematics and statistics.
- Processes and systems for attaining safety through design.

Some skills required by the OHS professional in the US include (but are not limited to):

- Understanding and relating to systems, policies and rules.
- Holding checks and having control methods for possible hazardous exposures.
- Mathematical and statistical analysis.
- Examining manufacturing hazards.
- Planning safe work practices for systems, facilities, and equipment.
- Understanding and using safety, health, and environmental science information for the improvement of procedures.
- Interpersonal communication skills.

Differences between Countries and Regions

Because different countries take different approaches to ensuring occupational safety and health, areas of OSH need and focus also vary between countries and regions.

Similar to the findings of the ENHSPO survey conducted in Australia, the Institute of Occupational Medicine in the UK found that there is a need to put greater emphasis on work-related illness in the UK. In contrast, in Australia and the US, a major responsibility of the OHS professional is to keep company directors and managers aware of the issues that they face in regards to occupational health and safety principles and legislation. However, in some other areas of Europe, it is precisely this which has been lacking: "Nearly half of senior managers and company directors do not have an up-to-date understanding of their health and safety-related duties and responsibilities."

Identifying Safety and Health Hazards

Hazards, Risks and Outcomes

The terminology used in OSH varies between countries, but generally speaking:

- A hazard is something that can cause harm if not controlled.
- The outcome is the harm that results from an uncontrolled hazard.
- A risk is a combination of the probability that a particular outcome will occur and the severity of the harm involved.

"Hazard", "risk", and "outcome" are used in other fields to describe e.g. environmental damage, or damage to equipment. However, in the context of OSH, "harm" generally describes the direct or indirect degradation, temporary or permanent, of the physical, mental, or social well-being of workers. For example, repetitively carrying out manual handling of heavy objects is a hazard. The outcome could be a musculoskeletal disorder (MSD) or an acute back or joint injury. The risk can be expressed numerically (e.g. a 0.5 or 50/50 chance of the outcome occurring during a year), in relative terms (e.g. "high/medium/low"), or with a multi-dimensional classification scheme (e.g. situation-specific risks).

Hazard Identification

Hazard identification or assessment is an important step in the overall risk assessment and risk management process. It is where individual work hazards are identified, assessed and controlled/eliminated as close to source (location of the hazard) as reasonably as possible. As technology, resources, social expectation or regulatory requirements change, hazard analysis focuses controls more closely toward the source of the hazard. Thus hazard control is a dynamic program of prevention. Hazard based programs also have the advantage of not assigning or implying there are "acceptable risks" in the workplace. A hazard-based program may not be able to eliminate all risks, but neither does it accept "satisfactory" – but still risky – outcomes. And as those who calculate and manage the risk are usually managers while those exposed to the risks are a different group, workers, a hazard-based approach can by-pass conflict inherent in a risk-based approach.

The information that needs to be gathered from sources should apply to the specific type of work from which the hazards can come from. As mentioned previously, examples of these sources include interviews with people who have worked in the field of the hazard, history and analysis of past incidents, and official reports of work and the hazards encountered. Of these, the personnel interviews may be the most critical in identifying undocumented practices, events, releases, hazards and other relevant information. Once the information is gathered from a collection of sources, it is recommended for these to be digitally archived (to allow for quick searching) and to have a physical set of the same information in order for it to be more accessible. One innovative way to display the complex historical hazard information is with a historical hazards identification map, which distills the hazard information into an easy to use graphical format.

Risk Assessment

Modern occupational safety and health legislation usually demands that a risk assessment be carried out prior to making an intervention. It should be kept in mind that risk management requires risk to be managed to a level which is as low as is reasonably practical.

This assessment should:

- Identify the hazards.
- Identify all affected by the hazard and how.
- Evaluate the risk.
- Identify and prioritize appropriate control measures.

The calculation of risk is based on the likelihood or probability of the harm being realized and the severity of the consequences. This can be expressed mathematically as a quantitative assessment (by assigning low, medium and high likelihood and severity with integers and multiplying them to obtain a risk factor), or qualitatively as a description of the circumstances by which the harm could arise.

The assessment should be recorded and reviewed periodically and whenever there is a significant change to work practices. The assessment should include practical recommendations to control the risk. Once recommended controls are implemented, the risk should be re-calculated to determine if it has been lowered to an acceptable level. Generally speaking, newly introduced controls should lower risk by one level, i.e., from high to medium or from medium to low.

Contemporary Developments

On an international scale, the World Health Organization (WHO) and the International Labour Organization (ILO) have begun focusing on labour environments in developing nations with projects such as Healthy Cities. Many of these developing countries are stuck in a situation in which their relative lack of resources to invest in OSH leads to increased costs due to work-related illnesses and accidents. The European Agency for Safety and Health at Work states indicates that nations having less developed OSH systems spend a higher fraction of their gross national product on job-related injuries and illness – taking resources away from more productive activities. The ILO estimates that work-related illness and accidents cost up to 10% of GDP in Latin America, compared with just 2.6% to 3.8% in the EU." There is continued use of asbestos, a notorious hazard, in some developing countries. So asbestos-related disease is, sadly, expected to continue to be a significant problem well into the future.

Augmented Reality, Virtual Reality and Artificial Intelligence

The impact of technologies on health and safety is an emerging field of research and practice. The opportunities for improving health and safety through use of augmented reality (AR) are now endless. There is emerging technologies for which the range of health and safety implications are not well understood and the impacts of machine learning and its impact on worker health and safety and the health and safety profession is still emerging New technologies and ways of working introduce new *risks* and challenges for *WHS* and workers' compensation, but they also have the potential to make work safer and reduce workplace injury.

Nanotechnology

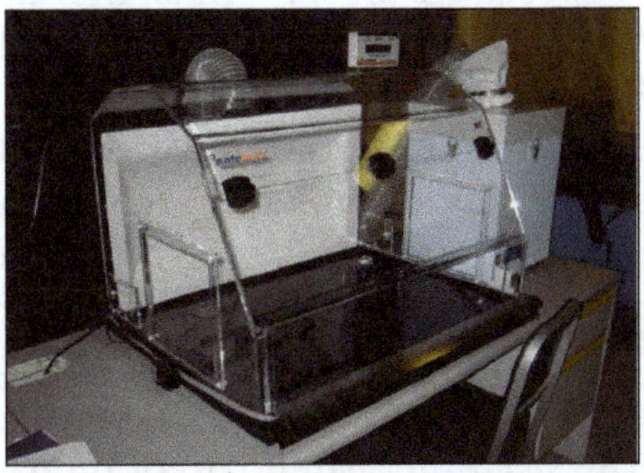

A nanomaterial containment hood, an example of an engineering control used to protect workers handling them on a regular basis.

Nanotechnology is an example of a new, relatively unstudied technology. A Swiss survey of one hundred thirty eight companies using or producing nanoparticulate matter in 2006 resulted in forty completed questionnaires. Sixty five per cent of respondent companies stated they did not have a formal risk assessment process for dealing with nanoparticulate matter. Nanotechnology already presents new issues for OSH professionals that will only become more difficult as nanostructures become more complex. The size of the particles renders most containment and personal protective equipment ineffective. The toxicology values for macro sized industrial substances are rendered inaccurate due to the unique nature of nanoparticulate matter. As nanoparticulate matter decreases in size its relative surface area increases dramatically, increasing any catalytic effect or chemical reactivity substantially versus the known value for the macro substance. This presents a new set of challenges in the near future to rethink contemporary measures to safeguard the health and welfare of employees against a nanoparticulate substance that most conventional controls have not been designed to manage.

Occupational Health Disparities

Occupational health disparities refer to differences in occupational injuries and illnesses that are closely linked with demographic, social, cultural, economic, and political factors.

Education

There are multiple levels of training applicable to the field of occupational safety and health (OSH). Programs range from individual non-credit certificates, focusing on specific areas of concern, to full doctoral programs. The University of Southern California was one of the first schools in the US to offer a Ph.D. program focusing on the field. Further, multiple master's degree programs exist, such as that of the Indiana State University who offer a master of science (MS) and a master of arts (MA) in OSH. Graduate programs are designed to train educators, as well as, high-level practitioners. Many OSH generalists focus on undergraduate studies; programs within schools, such as that of the University of North Carolina's online Bachelor of Science in Environmental Health and Safety, fill a large majority of hygienist needs. However, smaller companies often do not have full-time safety specialists on staff, thus, they appoint a current employee to the responsibility. Individuals finding themselves in positions such as these, or for those enhancing marketability in the job-search and promotion arena, may seek out a credit certificate program. For example, the University of Connecticut's online OSH Certificate, provides students familiarity with overarching concepts through a 15-credit (5-course) program. Programs such as these are often adequate tools in building a strong educational platform for new safety managers with a minimal outlay of time and money. Further, most hygienists seek certification by organizations which train in specific areas of concentration, focusing on isolated workplace hazards. The American Society for Safety Engineers (ASSE), American Board of Industrial Hygiene (ABIH), and American Industrial Hygiene Association (AIHA) offer individual certificates on many different subjects from forklift operation to waste disposal and are the chief facilitators of continuing education in the OSH sector. In the U.S. the training of safety professionals is supported by National Institute for Occupational Safety and Health through their NIOSH Education and Research Centers. In Australia, training in OSH is available at the vocational education and training level, and at university undergraduate and postgraduate level. Such university courses may be accredited by an Accreditation Board of the Safety Institute of Australia. The Institute has produced a Body of Knowledge which it considers is required by a generalist safety and health professional, and offers a professional qualification based on a four-step assessment.

ERGONOMICS RISK ASSESSMENT

As ergonomics increasingly becomes a core component of safety programs around the country, the methods used to evaluate and define the ergonomics risk present in a job develop into a critical element of the ergonomics process. When a company begins to look at ergonomics and how to implement an effective process, the basic job analysis is often the starting point, and the point that defines how a company will approach the analysis and abatement of ergonomics risk.

Identification of ergonomics stressors that are linked with the development of musculoskeletal disorders is a key element of any ergonomics activity. In most cases, stressors successfully can be identified using observational and checklist-driven techniques. The detection of ergonomics risk does not require advanced tools or techniques.

This observational approach often the most efficient method of gathering data on the stressors in the working environment, but the density of this data is limited. There is no measure of exposure, risk or any data that will provide a quantitative measure that can be tracked (i.e. improvement of process). The positive characteristics of this type of stressor identification process are the ease in which it is performed, the low cost of the assessment and quick turnaround times. A simple observation approach often can be used to feed a quick fix of an obvious ergonomics stressor. As the situation becomes more complicated, intricate or costly, the need for a more sophisticated approach may present itself.

When a company is interested in advancing its ergonomics job analysis process, the next level of assessment involves the use of risk assessment tools. Now, the term "tool" is used lightly, in that ergonomics risk assessment methods largely are paper-based, with some methods computerized for ease of use. There seldom are complicated pieces of equipment involved, except for a force gauge in some situations. Prior to using an ergonomics risk assessment tool, a company should ask four simple questions:

- Why should we use an ergonomics risk assessment tool?
- Who will be performing the assessments?
- How do we use the risk assessment tool correctly?
- When should we use a specific ergonomics risk assessment tool?

Why and when should you Perform an Ergonomics Risk Assessment?

Where ergonomics is concerned, there are often three questions asked:

- Which jobs pose the greatest risk?

- How much is too much?
- How can I show improvements were made?

One of the first steps in ergonomics evaluations is to identify the stressors present in the jobs. This identification usually is accomplished with a subjective evaluation. The evaluator may identify such things as high repetition, high force and extreme posture as being present in a job without any measurements. While this type of evaluation may be effective for determining which jobs may need further investigation, the severity of the identified stressors often is difficult to express and document. Furthermore, it is difficult to compare different jobs or tasks within a job to determine a prioritization of ergonomics efforts. This leads to the question: "Which jobs pose the greatest risk?"

Ergonomic interventions may not completely eliminate the stressors. They may be reduced but still be present. Additionally, as long as humans are involved in the workplace, there will be ergonomic stressors placed on those individuals. Therein lays the question: "How much is too much?"

Some interventions may address a stressor identified in the original evaluation and create another stressor. Therefore, once interventions are in place they should be evaluated to ensure they eliminated or reduced the stressors identified in the original evaluation without creating another hazard. This begs the question: "How can improvements be shown and evaluated?"

Some answers to these questions may be found through the use of ergonomics risk assessment tools. The use of quantitative or semi-quantitative evaluation tools provides the evaluator with numeric output with which they may evaluate the risk for the development of MSDs for a given job. This output also may allow them to compare relative risk of multiple jobs or tasks, thereby identifying the jobs or tasks that pose the greatest risk. This may assist the evaluator in the prioritization of ergonomics efforts.

These tools also may provide the evaluator or designer with recommended limits to the stressors present in a job, task or job design. These limits may be used to assist in reducing the risk to safe levels. Furthermore, the results may be used to compare the same job or task before and after an intervention is put in place.

Steps to Conducting an Effective Ergonomic Risk Assessment

Establish a Common Ergonomic Assessment Method and Set of Tools

Every ergonomic assessment your organization conducts should use the same method and set of tools. Standardizing ergonomic assessments throughout the organization ensures an "apples to apples" comparison of MSD risk factors between jobs. Every ergonomics team member should be trained in conducting and properly documenting each assessment using the same set of assessment tools and documentation methods.

Without a standardized ergonomic assessment method in place, your team will struggle to identify and communicate MSD risk factors. Don't make this mistake. Instead, start your assessment off on the right foot by taking an organized approach.

Involve the Workplace Athletes Performing the Job

The workplace athletes performing the job each and every day are uniquely qualified to help you assess the job. They are the expert of their job. Involving them in the assessment process can generate helpful improvement ideas and gets the workplace athlete's buy-in early on. They are much more likely to adopt changes to their work environment down the road if you involve them early and often.

Observe the workplace athletes performing the job and ask them questions about their work. Get their opinion on what causes excessive fatigue and how they would improve the job if they could.

Are there any heavy or strenuous lifting/lowering tasks in the job? Do the hand tools they use have an awkward grip? Is the height of the work comfortable for them? Do they experience fatigue and discomfort doing the job? These are just a few of the questions you can ask to get the conversation about the job going. Take good notes during this subjective portion of the assessment, and remember to take plenty of pictures and even video. They will be helpful to you when you're generating improvement ideas.

Conduct the Objective Portion of the Assessment

Once you have collected subjective data of the job demands by observing and interviewing the workplace athlete doing the job, you should be able to generate a list of job tasks for an objective ergonomic risk assessment.

There are many ergonomic assessment tools freely available in the public domain you can use to evaluate job tasks:

- Lifting/lowering tasks: WISHA Lifting Calculator or NIOSH Lifting Equation.
- Upper Body Posture: Rapid Upper Limb Assessment (RULA).
- Entire Body Posture: Rapid Entire Body Assessment (REBA).
- Pushing/pulling: Snook Tables.
- Hand-Arm Vibration: HAV Calculator developed by.
- Screening tools: WISHA Caution Zone Checklist and WISHA Hazard Zone Checklist.

By using a common set of tools and a standardized method for conducting assessments, you will ensure a consistent result for every assessment and be able to objectively compare tasks and prioritize improvements.

Assess the Data you've Collected

Now that you have collected both subjective and objective data, it's time to take a step back and assess what you've learned so far. Is there injury risk at this job? What is the level of risk? How can the risk be reduced?

Now that you know the problem areas in the job, conduct "what if" analysis and begin to generate improvement ideas to take to the ergonomics team.

Create a Plan Moving Forward

Next, bring your subjective data, objective data, and overall assessment back to your ergonomics team to brainstorm additional solutions and improvement opportunities. Consulting with a multi-disciplinary ergonomics team will bring in a fresh perspective and deeper expertise to help solve problems. At this point, the team should be able to generate several improvement scenarios. Choose the best solution and create an improvement plan moving forward.

Levels of Ergonomic Risk Assessment

There are three basic levels of ergonomic risk assessment:

- Hazard Recognition: A quick screen for MSD hazards at the job level.
- Simple Risk Assessment: A more in-depth screen identifying specific ergonomic risk factors for each body segment at the job level.
- Objective Assessment: A detailed, objective assessment of a job task using a fully quantitative tool.

Time and effort required to complete these assessments increases as you progress from hazard recognition to simple risk assessment to objective assessment.

When planning your ergonomic risk assessments, keep in mind that in order to be as efficient as possible you want to minimize the resources required to make a decision on an MSD hazard.

The goal, after all, is to control hazards by making improvements to the workplace, not necessarily to get the most accurate assessment score as humanly possible. Your approach and the tools you use for assessments should reflect this goal.

Hazard Recognition

The goal of the hazard recognition assessment is simply to identify and document the known presence of observed MSD hazards.

The basic MSD hazards are:

- High forces exerted by workers.
- Awkward postures.
- High repetition.
- Vibration.
- Contact stress.
- Cold temperatures.

A hazard recognition tool can be used during your initial worksite tour and also on an ongoing basis as MSD hazards are observed by supervisors, employees, engineers, and the safety/ergonomics team.

Simple Risk Assessment

The goal of the simple risk assessment is to identify and document levels of MSD risk exposure for each segment of the body, resulting in an overall MSD risk score at the job level as well as a list of tasks for further evaluation using an objective tool.

Objective Assessment

The goal of an objective assessment is to quantify exactly the MSD risk exposure present in a job task.

Valid objective assessment tools include:

- NIOSH Lifting Equation.
- WISHA Lifting Calculator.
- Rapid Entire Body Assessment.
- Rapid Upper Limb Assessment.
- Snook Tables.
- NIOSH Lifting Equation.

The NIOSH Lifting Equation is a tool used by occupational health and safety professionals to assess the manual material handling risks associated with lifting and lowering tasks in the workplace. This equation considers job task variables to determine safe lifting practices and guidelines.

The primary product of the NIOSH lifting equation is the Recommended Weight Limit (RWL), which defines the maximum acceptable weight (load) that nearly all healthy employees could lift over the course of an 8 hour shift without increasing the risk of musculoskeletal disorders (MSD) to the lower back. In addition, a Lifting Index (LI) is calculated to provide a relative estimate of the level of physical stress and MSD risk associated with the manual lifting tasks evaluated.

WISHA Lifting Calculator

Developed by the Washington State Department of Labor and Industries and based on NIOSH research related to the primary causes of back injuries, this lifting calculator can be used to perform ergonomic risk assessments on a wide variety of manual lifting and lowering tasks, and can be also used as a screening tool to identify lifting tasks which should be analyzed further using the more comprehensive NIOSH Lifting Equation.

Rapid Entire Body Assessment

This tool uses a systematic process to evaluate whole body postural MSD and ergonomic design risks associated with job tasks. A single page form is used to evaluate required body posture, forceful exertions, type of movement or action, repetition, and coupling. A score is assigned for each of the following body regions: wrists, forearms, elbows, shoulders, neck, trunk, back, legs and knees. After the data for each region is collected and scored, tables on the form are then used to compile the risk factor variables, generating a single score that represents the level of MSD risk.

Rapid Upper Limb Assessment

This diagnostic tool assesses biomechanical and postural load requirements of job tasks/demands on the neck, trunk and upper extremities. A single page form is used to evaluate required body posture, force, and repetition. Based on the evaluations, scores are entered for each body region in section A for the arm and wrist, and section B for the neck and trunk. After the data for each region is collected and scored, tables on the form are then used to compile the risk factor variables, generating a single score that represents the level of MSD risk.

Snook Tables

The Liberty Mutual MMH Tables (commonly known as Snook Tables) outline design goals for various lifting, lowering, pushing, pulling, and carrying tasks based on research by Dr. Stover Snook and Dr. Vincent Ciriello at the Liberty Mutual Research Institute for Safety. The tables provide weight/force values, for specific types of tasks that are deemed to be acceptable to a defined percentage of the population. This is done by comparing data for each of the specific manual handling tasks against the appropriate table.

HUMAN RELIABILITY

Human reliability (also known as human performance or HU) is related to the field of human factors and ergonomics, and refers to the reliability of humans in fields including manufacturing, medicine and nuclear power. Human performance can be affected by many factors such as age, state of mind, physical health, attitude, emotions, propensity for certain common mistakes, errors and cognitive biases, etc.

Human reliability is very important due to the contributions of humans to the resilience of systems and to possible adverse consequences of human errors or oversights, especially when the human is a crucial part of the large socio-technical systems as is common today. User-centered design and error-tolerant design are just two of many terms used to describe efforts to make technology better suited to operation by humans.

Common Traps of Human Nature

People tend to overestimate their ability to maintain control when they are doing work. The common characteristics of human nature addressed below are especially accentuated when work is performed in a complex work environment.

Stress: The problem with stress is that it can accumulate and overpower a person, thus becoming detrimental to performance.

Avoidance of Mental Strain: Humans are reluctant to engage in lengthy concentrated thinking, as it requires high levels of attention for extended periods.

The mental biases, or shortcuts, often used to reduce mental effort and expedite decision-making include:

- Assumptions: A condition taken for granted or accepted as true without verification of the facts.
- Habit: An unconscious pattern of behavior acquired through frequent repetition.
- Confirmation bias: The reluctance to abandon a current solution.
- Similarity bias: The tendency to recall solutions from situations that appear similar
- Frequency bias: A gamble that a frequently used solution will work.
- Availability bias: The tendency to settle on solutions or courses of action that readily come to mind.
- Limited Working Memory: The mind's short-term memory is the "workbench" for problem solving and decision-making.
- Limited Attention Resources: The limited ability to concentrate on two or more activities challenges the ability to process information needed to solve problems.

Mind-Set People tend to focus more on what they want to accomplish (a goal) and less on what needs to be avoided because human beings are primarily goal-oriented by nature. As such, people tend to "see" only what the mind expects, or wants, to see.

Difficulty Seeing One's Own Error: Individuals, especially when working alone, are particularly susceptible to missing errors.

- Limited Perspective: Humans cannot see all there is to see. The inability of the human mind to perceive all facts pertinent to a decision challenges problem-solving.
- Susceptibility to Emotional/Social Factors: Anger and embarrassment adversely influence team and individual performance.
- Fatigue: People get tired. Physical, emotional, and mental fatigue can lead to error and poor judgment.
- Presenteeism: Some employees will be present in the need to belong to the workplace despite a diminished capacity to perform their jobs due to illness or injury.

Analysis Techniques

A variety of methods exist for human reliability analysis (HRA). Two general classes of methods are those based on probabilistic risk assessment (PRA) and those based on a cognitive theory of control.

PRA-based Techniques

One method for analyzing human reliability is a straightforward extension of probabilistic risk assessment (PRA): in the same way that equipment can fail in a power plant, so can a human operator commit errors. In both cases, an analysis (functional decomposition for equipment and task analysis for humans) would articulate a level of detail for which failure or error probabilities can be assigned. This basic idea is behind the Technique for Human Error Rate Prediction (THERP). THERP is intended to generate human error probabilities that would be incorporated into a PRA. The Accident Sequence Evaluation Program (ASEP) human reliability procedure is a simplified form of THERP; an associated computational tool is Simplified Human Error Analysis Code (SHEAN). More recently, the US Nuclear Regulatory Commission has published the Standardized Plant Analysis Risk - Human Reliability Analysis (SPAR-H) method to take account of the potential for human error.

Cognitive Control based Techniques

Erik Hollnagel has developed this line of thought in his work on the Contextual Control Model (COCOM) and the Cognitive Reliability and Error Analysis Method (CREAM). COCOM models human performance as a set of control modes—strategic (based on long-term planning), tactical (based on procedures), opportunistic (based on present context), and scrambled (random) - and proposes a model of how transitions between these control modes occur. This model of control mode transition consists of a number of factors, including the human operator's estimate of the outcome of the action (success or failure), the time remaining to accomplish the action (adequate or inadequate), and the number of simultaneous goals of the human operator at that time. CREAM is a human reliability analysis method that is based on COCOM.

Related Techniques

Related techniques in safety engineering and reliability engineering include failure mode and effects analysis, hazop, fault tree, and SAPHIRE (Systems Analysis Programs for Hands-on Integrated Reliability Evaluations).

Human Factors Analysis and Classification System (HFACS)

The Human Factors Analysis and Classification System (HFACS) was developed initially as a framework to understand the role of "human error" in aviation accidents. It is based on James Reason's Swiss cheese model of human error in complex systems. HFACS distinguishes between the "active failures" of unsafe acts, and "latent failures" of preconditions for unsafe acts, unsafe supervision, and organizational influences. These categories were developed empirically on the basis of many aviation accident reports.

"Unsafe acts" are performed by the human operator "on the front line" (e.g., the pilot, the air traffic controller, the driver). Unsafe acts can be either errors (in perception, decision making or skill-based performance) or violations (routine or exceptional). The errors here are similar to the above discussion. Violations are the deliberate disregard for rules and procedures. As the name implies, routine violations are those that occur habitually and are usually tolerated by the organization or authority. Exceptional violations are unusual and often extreme. For example, driving 60 mph in a 55-mph zone speed limit is a routine violation, but driving 130 mph in the same zone is exceptional.

There are two types of preconditions for unsafe acts: those that relate to the human operator's internal state and those that relate to the human operator's practices or ways of working. Adverse internal states include those related to physiology (e.g., illness) and mental state (e.g., mentally fatigued, distracted). A third aspect of 'internal state' is really a mismatch between the operator's ability and the task demands; for example, the operator may be unable to make visual judgments or react quickly enough to support the task at hand. Poor operator practices are another type of precondition for unsafe acts. These include poor crew resource management (issues such as leadership and communication) and poor personal readiness practices (e.g., violating the crew rest requirements in aviation).

Four types of unsafe supervision are: inadequate supervision; planned inappropriate operations; failure to correct a known problem; and supervisory violations.

Organizational influences include those related to resources management (e.g., inadequate human or financial resources), organizational climate (structures, policies, and culture), and organizational processes (such as procedures, schedules, oversight).

MANUAL MATERIAL HANDLING FOR SAFETY

Manual material handling tasks can sometimes expose workers to risk factors that eventually turn into costly injuries and lost productivity.

"Manual material handling (MMH) work contributes to a large percentage of the over half a million cases of musculoskeletal disorders reported annually in the United States."

In other words, manual material handling tasks can become a major problem if you don't take proactive measures to reduce injury risk in your workplace.

The good news is that these injuries are preventable.

Reduce Workplace Risk Factors with Ergonomics

Ergonomic risk factors are commonly found in the manual material handling environment.

Ergonomic risk factors are problems with the work environment that cause unnecessary physical fatigue. The three primary ergonomic risk factors are:

- Awkward postures (bending, twisting).
- Highly repetitive motions (frequent reaching, lifting, carrying).
- Forceful exertions (carrying or lifting heavy loads).

A proactive ergonomics improvement process ensures that jobs and tasks are within the worker's physical capabilities. It's about identifying these ergonomic risk factors in your work environment and putting control measures in place to limit exposure.

This process is the foundation for preventing back injuries for manual material handling tasks. An ergonomically designed work environment reduces fatigue and discomfort for workers. This, in turn, limits the risk of an injury occurring.

Make Sure Team Members are Ready to Work with a Pre-shift Warm-up Program

Manual material handling tasks require workplace athletes to be ready for their workday.

Workplace athletes prepare themselves for work in a similar way with "pre-shift stretching" or "pre-shift warm-up stretching". They take a few minutes before they begin their work day by preparing their body and mind for work with a pre-shift warm-up routine.

Well-designed workplace stretching programs (Work Readiness Systems) ensure workplace athletes are physically ready for their work day.

Make Sure Team Members use Proper Body Mechanics and Work Technique

By definition, manual material handling tasks require workers to handle materials using their body. As workplace athletes it's important they use their bodies properly, using good biomechanics and work technique.

When workplace athletes use poor body mechanics and work technique, they introduce unnecessary MSD risk. By educating workers to use better body mechanics and spending the necessary time out on the shop floor to make sure they're getting the job done properly, you are greatly reducing the MSD risk in your workplace.

Educate Team Members on Self-care

Physical wear and tear on the body is a normal part of the aging process. Every day, we go through the process of fatigue and then recovery. Each day we fatigue the body. Each night we sleep as the body's natural process to recover from the day.

Well, with manual material handling workers, it's as important as ever to know how to recover from each workday. Manual material handling tasks are physically demanding on the body and require and above average process in place to recover from the day.

Workplace athletes that do a great job at self-care are able to recover from each workday and minimize the risk of an MSD from forming.

The only way your workplace athletes will know how to properly care for themselves and recover from each workday is if you educate and train themselves on self-care tools and techniques.

Proactively Respond to Early Reports of Fatigue and Discomfort

Fatigue and physical wear and tear is a normal part of the aging process. In manual material handling tasks, there will be additional fatigue and discomfort that is just a natural part of life under these circumstances. Even with a proactive ergonomics process that makes sure the work fits the workers' capabilities, this work day in and day out can take a toll on the workplace athlete's body.

Because cumulative fatigue will eventually turn into an MSD, it's important to encourage early reports of fatigue and discomfort so you can proactively respond and put control measures in place to prevent fatigue from developing into an injury.

ERGONOMICS TRAINING

Ergonomics training is one of the most essential elements of an effective ergonomics process. After all, the success of your ergonomics process hinges on your team's ability to find and fix the ergonomics problems in your work environment.

The effectiveness of your team will depend on how well they are trained and (most importantly) the skills they gain during the ergonomics training process.

Good ergonomic design removes incompatibilities between the work and the worker and creates the optimal work environment. This allows you to efficiently create the best product possible.

Who do you think should be responsible for creating the best product (or delivering the best service) possible?

If you're thinking that should be everyone's job, you're right. Everyone at your company is responsible for the ergonomics process, and everyone needs the knowledge and tools to successfully execute their role in the process and meet their responsibilities. This goes for the CEO and leadership team all the way down the organization to the team members out on the shop floor.

Ergonomics training should be approached from this high-level perspective and given adequate time, attention and resources. Without these things, you won't get the results you're looking for and you'll be missing out on a tremendous opportunity for your organization.

Ergonomics Process Roles and Responsibilities

Ergonomics training content should be segmented based on the roles and responsibilities assigned for each group throughout your facility.

Role: Plant Management and Leadership

- Responsibilities:
    - Regularly communicate and demonstrate management's leadership and commitment to the ergonomics process.
    - Provide authorization of adequate resources.
- Ergonomics training content:
    - The primary objective for this training is to obtain management sponsorship

for the ergonomics and MSD prevention process. Focus on high level aspects of the program, the OHS and business goals you will achieve, roles and responsibilities, and how every team member will be held accountable.

Role: Safety and Ergonomics Team

- Responsibilities:
    - Identify ergonomic risk factors through a systematic ergonomic risk assessment process.
    - Investigate, prioritize and develop solutions for ergonomic improvement opportunities that have been identified.
    - Assist in ergonomics communication and education to all employees.
    - Ensure new job tasks and processes are designed with ergonomics in mind.
- Ergonomics training content:
    - Training for the ergonomics team is about transferring critical ergonomics knowledge and real world skills. These team members have the greatest responsibility to lead the process from risk identification to implementing control measures to verifying success.

Role: Engineering and Facilities Staff

- Responsibilities:
    - Work closely with the safety/ergonomics team to identify ergonomic risk factors, develop solution recommendations with cost-justification support, and implement solutions.
    - Consider ergonomics in new jobs, tasks and equipment design.
- Ergonomics training content:
    - Engineering and facilities staff should work closely with the ergonomics team (and preferably should be represented on the ergonomics team). Take a quantitative approach during these training sessions, focusing on ergonomic design principles and risk assessment methods.

Role: Supervisors

- Responsibilities:
    - Implement and direct ergonomics process within area of responsibility.
    - Encourage early reporting of fatigue and discomfort.

- Observe workers, be alert to non-verbal discomfort cues, and take a proactive approach to ask employees if they are experiencing any difficulty.

- Ergonomics training content:
  - Ergonomics training content for supervisors should focus on the benefits and objective of the ergonomics process. Supervisors should come away with a clear understanding of how they will support the ergonomics process and how crucial their role is in engaging all team members in this process.

Role: Employees

- Responsibilities:
  - Report early signs and symptoms of discomfort to department supervisors.
  - Identifying potential ergonomic risk factors.
  - Provide suggestions for controlling ergonomic risk factors.
- Ergonomics training content:
  - Training objectives for ergonomics awareness training for employees should encourage identification of ergonomic problems at the workstation level. Employees are the real workplace improvement experts. An engaging ergonomics training session will encourage them to participate in the ergonomics process and make their life a little easier on a daily basis.

Ergonomics Training Best Practices

Know your Audience

Great training content always begins with understanding your audience. Each training session should be customized for the roles and responsibilities of your training session audience. Before you create your training content, make sure you've put in the time to understand your audience to ensure you're helping them meet their responsibilities.

Be Hands On

The most effective training uses all the senses to affect learning. Make sure you demonstrate and apply teaching points to create greater understanding and knowledge of the subject. If you can, head out to the shop floor for a practical example or bring an example into the classroom for a hands-on experience. This type of training will help attendees' memory retention and improve their ability to deal with a real world situation.

Be Clear on Roles and Responsibilities

Above all else, don't let ergonomics training attendees leave the room if they aren't clear on their personal role and responsibility in the process. Take it one step further and demonstrate the importance of their role and how it ties into the goal of your ergonomics process. All attendees should be regularly reminded of their role and what the action plan is moving forward.

Get Feedback and Improve

Gather feedback after each training session and always work to get better. An employee survey is a fantastic tool to get feedback on your training sessions. Strive to improve both your training content and delivery.

Ergonomics Training Mistakes

Lack of Credibility

When you walk into the room, your past actions are walking in with you. It is vitally important that you live out every day what you are about to teach in the classroom. The best ergonomics training is delivered by the best ergonomics expert. Credibility is huge – don't take this lightly.

Boring Presentations

But just because it isn't all that exciting doesn't mean you can't approach it with a positive and enthusiastic attitude. You set the tone for the training session, so make sure you're the most enthusiastic person in the room even if the audience doesn't respond the way you had hoped.

Not Being Hands On

Classroom training is important, but practical application of learning material is where knowledge is ingrained into the person and real progress is made. Follow up formal classroom training sessions with one-on-one time out on the shop floor or office workstation. Knowledge is great, but skills development for the real world is an essential element of an effective ergonomics process.

One and Done

The statistics on memory retention are disappointing for trainers. Sadly, much of what you teach in the classroom will be forgotten. For this reason, it is important that training doesn't stop once you leave the classroom doors. Ongoing classroom sessions (as well as the hands-on application training described above) will allow the training content and core learning objectives to sink in over time.

Phoning it In

Don't phone it in! Using the same stale PowerPoint presentation over and over again is a surefire way to go nowhere. Be passionate about continuously improving your ergonomics training skills. Gather feedback on your training program and always work to get better. An employee survey is a fantastic tool to get feedback on your training sessions. Strive to improve both your training content and delivery.

References

- Ergonomic-hazards, prevent-harm/hazards: comcare.gov.au, Retrieved 13 August, 2020
- Examples-of-ergonomic-hazards-in-the-workplace: blog.sliceproducts.com, Retrieved 20 June, 2020
- Controlhazards, SLTC-ergonomics: osha.gov, Retrieved 18 February, 2020
- Ergonomics-risk-assessment-determining-when-why-who-and-how-you-should-perform-one-21905391: ehstoday.com, Retrieved 09 June, 2020
- Concha-Barrientos, Marisol; Nelson, Deborah Imel; Fingerhut, Marilyn; Driscoll, Timothy; Leigh, James (2005-12-01). "The global burden due to occupational injury". American Journal of Industrial Medicine. 48 (6): 470–481. doi:10.1002/ajim.20226. ISSN 0271-3586. PMID 16299709
- Conducting-Ergonomic-Assessment, The-OHS-Wire: ohsonline.com, Retrieved 10 July, 2020
- Manual-material-handling-tips: ergo-plus.com, Retrieved 28 May, 2020
- Burton, C; Chesterton, LS; Davenport, G (May 2014). "Diagnosing and managing carpal tunnel syndrome in primary care". The British Journal of General Practice. 64 (622): 262–3. doi:10.3399/bjgp14x679903. PMC 4001168. PMID 24771836

5

Cognitive Ergonomics

Cognitive ergonomics is the discipline that is associated with the evaluation and designing of tasks, products and environment as well as their interaction with humans. It can be applied in different sectors of aviation, transportation, healthcare system, nuclear power systems and product design. The topics elaborated in this chapter will help in gaining a better perspective of cognitive ergonomics.

Cognitive ergonomics is the discipline of making human-system interaction compatible with human cognitive abilities and limitations, particularly at work. Cognitive ergonomics utilizes the knowledge emerging from the cognitive sciences on mental processes such as perception, attention, memory, decision making, and learning. The methods of these fields of research are applied to gain a better understanding of the factors that affect cognitive function. The practical aim is to improve work conditions and human performance, as well as safety and health, and to avoid human error and unnecessary load and stress.

Cognitive ergonomics is a division of ergonomics (or human factors): A discipline and practices that aim to ensure 'appropriate interaction between work, product and environment, and human needs, capabilities and limitations'. In this human-system interaction, cognitive ergonomics focuses on mental processes, especially on cognitive functions and psychological/behavioural level interactions.

The theoretical background is based on cognitive psychology as well as other cognitive sciences. The goal is to elucidate the nature of human abilities and limitations in information processing. In cognitive ergonomics, these aspects are studied in the context of work and other systems. In recent years, there has also been a trend to exploit the methods of neuroscience also in the field of ergonomics. The term neuroergonomics is used when the focus is on neurological and physiological functions and biological explanations.

Cognitive Processes

In ergonomics and psychology, cognition refers to the mental processes that are involved in processing and handling information, i.e. encoding, maintaining, rehearsing, recalling, and transforming information in the human mind and brain. Human cognition can be divided into several functions that underlie optimal human performance.

It is important to recognise the cognitive functions that are relevant for a specific task or job, and to ensure that the working environment is suitable for these task requirements.

- Sensation and perception refers to perception of stimuli gathered through the senses such as sight, hearing, taste, smell, and touch. For example, in construction work one needs to hear the warning signals and in medical care one needs to be able to discern the symbols on the monitor.
- Attention is the stage where the processing is focused on certain aspects of perceived information or processing may be divided between two or several aspects. For example, in a control room one needs to notice if there has been a significant change in the situation; in a kindergarten a nurse may need to focus his/her attention on several children at the one time.
- Working memory includes a short term memory storage in which information is available for up to 30 seconds. It also refers to the processes with which information is actively rehearsed and manipulated in the mind. For example, a telephone operator has to rehearse the name of the desired person until she/he has connected the call, and laboratory assistant needs to keep track of the order of locations when working with several samples.
- Long term memory is a permanent store for different kinds of information. Semantic memory refers to the storage of knowledge about the world, symbols, and concepts. Episodic memory contains information about events and episodes, whereas events in an individual´s personal life are referred to as autobiographical memories. Procedural knowledge concerns 'knowing how' and skills. For example, all work requires specific knowledge of the field and specific skills, e.g. how to use a machine in a safe way, or how to organise a meeting.

These basic cognitive processes and representations are also relevant when one considers higher level cognitive functions such as language comprehension and production and thinking processes such as problem solving, decision making and reasoning. For example, the job of a communicator requires constantly reading and writing of texts, whereas a worker doing maintenance work has to follow guidelines that need to be read now and then. In addition, the need to solve problems and to make decisions varies between different tasks and occupations. Cognition also includes learning which refers to permanent or long lasting changes in knowledge and skills that is relevant to all occupations. In cognitive science, expertise refers to some superior human ability in a complex cognitive task and can be considered to reflect maximal adaptation to a particular environment.

Studying Cognition

Research on human cognition describes the nature of the human cognitive system. This knowledge of the human part of the system is needed in the design of equipment, appliances etc. It is useful in appreciating the critical aspects when one tries to fit an environment to the human cognitive functions that are relevant to the specific job or task.

Methods of Cognitive Science

Cognitive ergonomics not only utilizes the general knowledge originating from basic and applied studies, but also specific knowledge obtained when studying a specific task and situation. The core method being utilized in cognitive psychology is experimental and behavioural: the question of interest is studied in a controlled (laboratory) environment, by using carefully selected stimulus material, and by ensuring a balanced the order of the conditions that are being studied. Behavioural measures such as response times and percentage of correct responses provide information on a human´s ability to perform efficiently under various conditions. Brain imaging techniques can help to clarify the underlying biological and physiological aspects of cognition. Experimental neuropsychology aims to understand the principles of cognitive processing in both healthy and damaged systems. Simulating human cognition computationally and mathematically is also a method that can be applied in cognitive science.

The aim of the experimental research is to provide reliable results on the specific mechanisms explaining human cognition. One unfortunate effect of this careful experimental control is that only a limited number of issues can be studied within a single experiment. Thus, there are hundreds of thousands of studies sometimes with apparently conflicting results on a myriad of issues. It is challenging to obtain a full perspective of the nature of human cognition and to apply this knowledge. Therefore reliable knowledge on cognition requires complimentary theories and replication of experimental results.

Studying Cognition in Everyday Contexts

Two issues are crucial when results concerning the nature of human cognition are applied in the everyday context, e.g. in the field of ergonomics. First, ecological validity, which means that the results that are obtained also apply outside the laboratory. This requires that the methods, materials, and setting of the study approximate to the real-world task that is being examined. Second, the generalizability of the results, which refers to the concept that the results also can be applied to outside the specific context in which they were obtained. This requires meticulous control of experiments to ensure that they are based on truly generalizable principles of human cognition and performance. The optimal situation is that the study should utilize ecologically valid methods and produce generalizable results.

In addition to objective behavioural and physiological methods, also there are other methods that can shed light on cognitive performance. For example reliable questionnaires, can be used to study the frequency of cognitive failures or memory problems at work, or the work load experienced by the employee. Cognitive task analysis methods try to capture people's thoughts, focus of attention, decision making strategies, and the basis for skilled performance.

There are various methods available for analysing cognitive tasks, e.g. knowledge elicitation and cognitive engineering. These techniques aim to understand what people know and how they know it. Cognitive task analyses collect data via interviews, self-report, observations, and automated collections of behavioural data. They can focus on the present, on events that have happened, or on future prospects. The data can be gathered in real-world or in simulated, even virtual environments. The target can be either typical routine events or rare or challenging events. Data can be analysed and represented in a variety of ways. The goal is to gain an insightful account of the cognitive phenomenon underlying real-world tasks in complex and dynamic work settings.

Cognition at Work

Cognitive functions are subjected to their limits in the same way as the physical characteristics. Even the most adept juggler cannot throw ten apples into the air and catch them all with only two hands. However, the brain's functional capacity limits are not visible and usually cannot be consciously recognized. Therefore, it is essential to apply reliable knowledge on these aspects of human characteristics in order that we can ensure that they are not overwhelmed at work. It is important to note that cognitive limitations will have a less significant impact on performance if the task at hand is learned to such a level that it becomes an automatized skill, since automatized processes do not burden the limited capacity of attention and working memory.

Perception and Attention at Work

Human beings have a limited ability to perceive the environment, and especially to perceive all the details. People do not notice everything that would be relevant in their work and they are easily distracted by co-workers.

There are also many working conditions, such as poor lighting, that may impair a worker´s ability to perceive objects and to focus attention on relevant aspects. Good visual perception requires that the symbols are clearly noticeable: i.e. the size of a text is large enough and that there is adequate contrast between the symbols and the background. Thus good lighting conditions will increase the visibility and the impact of size and contrast.

Good perception conditions make targets visible. Furthermore, they decrease the amount of time that is needed in visual search when a certain symbol is being sought from among other targets. Targets that pop out from the environment are found easier and faster than complex targets that require that the region is scanned serially. If one reduces the number of background objects or grouping targets instead of scattering them evenly then this will also help to direct attention to the relevant objects, e.g. on an operator's desktop or in the vehicle's control board. An efficient way to direct attention and to enhance perception is to provide an alert about an incoming relevant stimulus or its spatial location in the environment before the object appears.

It is important to note that there are several conditions that are distracting and direct attention towards irrelevant objects. For example, the ability to focus visual attention and to maintain information active in visuo-spatial working memory is easily distracted by moving objects and flashing lights. In the auditory domain, a noise that includes detectable speech sounds may impair perception, attention, and other forms of processing of linguistic information. Furthermore, the ability to hear and to follow a conversation is impaired in noisy conditions; this is a fact to be considered when designing communication and warning signals.

New technologies also utilize other sense modalities, such as touch. In principle, the incorporation of multimodal information can be an effective way to divide attention or to direct the focus of attention towards relevant objects. However, every sense modality has its limitations that need to be considered when designing work. Best practices of cognitive ergonomics include:

- Optimizing the size of symbols and text, contrast between objects and background, and lighting conditions.
- Discernibility of targets, grouping of targets, small number of background objects, alerting about relevant stimulus.
- Decreasing auditory and visual noise.

Working Memory at Work

While performing any task, it is crucial to effectively maintain and process all of the relevant information. Human beings have a limited ability to process information at the focus of attention, i.e. there are limits to the working memory system. The capacity of working memory is about 4 items and without rehearsal, information fades from the working memory in less than 30 seconds.

Some of the capacity limitations of working memory can be avoided by decreasing the amount of noise and unnecessary visual information, and by limiting the information to be remembered. If the task or the system requires active maintenance and processing of codes or other details, it leads to unnecessary loading of working memory. In contrast, if there is no need to mentally rehearse trivial details, the capacity of working memory can be used for problem solving, decision making, and other crucial tasks. Therefore, good visualizations and other external memory aids can improve cognitive functioning and performance.

Whereas there is a general capacity to process information in working memory, the capacities of working memory and attention are also modality specific. Thus a system that allows the use of several modalities, e.g. visual and auditory instead of only the visual mode, helps to divide the attention and capacity requirements so that performance can be improved. Wicken's model is a practical way to realize the overlapping demands for information processing and to design work and systems that try to decrease the cognitive load by sharing the load between the non-overlapping resources.

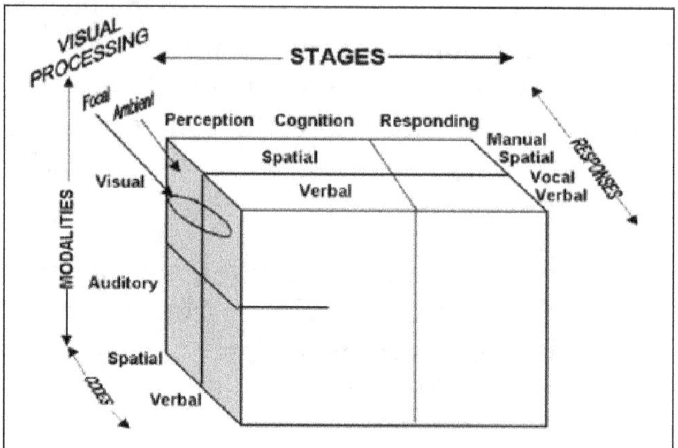

Figure 1. The 4-D multiple resource model.

The 4-D multiple model.

Wicken's model on overlapping demands for information processing defines four dichotomies of non-overlapping resources:

- Modalities: Auditory and visual perception use different resources.
- Stages: Perception/cognition and responding/action use different resources.
- Codes: Spatial and verbal/linguistic activity use different resources.
- Visual processing: Focal and peripheral vision use different resources.

Working memory also is a site for executive functions; one can depict it as a kind of conductor of the orchestra of information processing in the human mind. Many tasks require that people switch their focus of attention or switch between different tasks or perform several tasks at the same time. These situations are cognitively demanding, and problems in the control of information processing may lead to action failures and lapses. For example, people may unintentionally press control switches on machines or they may accidentally throw away or dispose of some item that they will need later.

The costs of task switching have been convincingly demonstrated. Performance, even in simple tasks, is prone to errors and there will be an increase in performance time if the individual must switch focus between tasks rather than finish one task before tackling the next. Underlying cognitive control processes are relevant to a wide variety of tasks that everyone encounters at work and in life in general. Therefore in designing work environments and tasks, it is crucial to strive to have situations that require neither constant switching between tasks nor performing several tasks at a time. Best practices of cognitive ergonomics include:

- Reasonable number of objects/information to be kept in mind.

- Decreasing unnecessary visual information, background speech, and interruptions.
- Use of external memory aids and visualizations.
- Non-overlapping modalities, codes, stages, and responses required in a task.
- Reducing costs of task switching and the need to perform simultaneous tasks.

Memory and Learning at Work

The limitations of long-term memory are mainly related to the slow process of acquiring new knowledge and skills, the difficulties in recalling information and work procedures, and the rapid forgetting of information that has not been rehearsed. However, the capacity of long-term memory storage is unlimited, and at any age, there is 'space' to acquire new knowledge and skills.

According to recent reviews and meta-analyses, the most effective learning techniques are testing and distributed practice of the to-be-learned information/skill. Distributed practice techniques consist of several practice phases instead of one massed practice. The literature of occupational training also considers the importance of evaluating what happens before the training as well as what happens after the training.

The human memory is reconstructive: information is not stored as a perfect recording, but retrieval of information from memory involves using the available information and cues about an event or the topic. The details are reconstructed on the basis of what is familiar, likely, and meaningful, or taking the context into consideration. The ability of human beings to define the source of recalled memories is limited. Therefore it is common to have false memories of actual details, even though the gist of the memory may be correct. Due to this reconstructive nature of memory, written and picture/video documentation is essential when detailed and exact recall is required. Best practices of cognitive ergonomics include:

- Providing enough time for learning knowledge and skills.
- Avoiding forgetting of relevant knowledge and skills by using them at work and by utilizing check lists and other aids.
- Applying effective learning techniques at work if occupational training is the relevant solution.
- Careful documentation of essential and detailed information and decisions.

Thinking and Language Processes at Work

Thinking and communication are complex processes in natural settings. Laboratory studies have shown that human decision making, problem solving, and reasoning doesn't follow normative rules, e.g. those of logical reasoning. Instead, people use rules of thumb that are not cognitively demanding but very often lead to acceptable solutions. However, many typical errors in decision making have been recognized in real life situations.

Several factors affect whether thinking and communication succeed at work and in complex problem solving tasks. Thinking and communication rely on the basic cognitive processes described above. Furthermore, prior experience, knowledge, and skills affect how people evaluate the problems and try to solve them. Mental models are complex representations of situations and events, and they are used as a way to represent relevant information in thinking processes. Many workplace situations are complex and poorly defined. Thus it not may be immediately obvious how to solve a problem or whether a goal has been achieved, for example, how to improve safety attitudes and how large an intervention is needed in a particular case.

Thinking and communication at work often take place in teams and between individuals who have different expectations, roles, knowledge, experiences, educations, and job specific vocabularies. In order that there will be effective communication, it is important that there should be some common ground, i.e. a degree of unified understanding among the team members. It is difficult to change the way people think, but there are some general rules that can help in debunking false assumptions, e.g. focusing on core facts rather than myths, and providing an alternative explanation for why some myth is wrong. Best practices of cognitive ergonomics include:

- Listing information and arguments relevant to the problem to be solved or the decision to be made.
- Using graphics to represent relevant factors and their connections.
- Constructing common understanding by making the content easy to process.
- Debunking false assumptions.

Expertise at Work

It takes time for an individual to develop into expert; it may require years of dedicated practice. Experience and learning lead to superior performance in domain-specific tasks, i.e. tasks that require knowledge and skills relevant to that specific field or domain. The exceptional performance of experts when compared to novices is evident at multiple levels of cognition: finding and recognizing relevant stimuli, encoding and categorisation of material, the organisation of knowledge in long term memory, immediate recall, learning, and thinking.

The superior skill of the expert is not only simply because he/she knows more than others, there also are qualitative differences in processing task-relevant information. Experts represent domain-specific knowledge and problems at an abstract level and concentrate on fundamental concepts, whereas novices focus more on superficial features and dominant objects. Experts are able to select information that is meaningful, that makes sense and is relevant to the task at hand. In problem solving, experts are able to think ahead, i.e. to use forward search to identify those possibilities leading to the best outcome.

Research on expertise has revealed the maximal adaptability of human cognitive skills. For a beginner, many tasks and situations at work are novel and they are thus cognitively more demanding than familiar or automatized tasks. In contrast, experts possess a vast amount of pre-learned knowledge and skills that can be used in deliberate and conscious ways to ensure exceptional performance. However, it seems to take 10 years or 10,000 hours of practice to develop such exceptional skills; this has been demonstrated in many different domains. Therefore, there has to be a trade-off between acquiring exceptional skills and the amount of training necessary to achieve adequate performance. When designing work and tasks, it is crucial to consider the level and kind of expertise required in the task, and the amount of training that is needed if novices of that domain are expected to perform these tasks. In many cases, it is more efficient that employees are able to apply their core expertise at work rather than undertaking many additional tasks that require other skills and understandings. Best practices of cognitive ergonomics include:

- Utilizing the expertise of the employees.
- Providing training for novices.
- Finding a balance between tasks that require training and tasks that are based on a worker's existing expertise.

Cognitive Demands of Work

There are certain conditions that make it even more demanding for a human to perform at an optimal level. The cognitive demands of the tasks and work environments in any job can be significant, e.g. working in changing conditions, doing multiple tasks at the same time, or being subjected to noise or interruptions at work. These conditions impair cognitive performance, and may thus develop into critical work-related factors that can lead to human errors and be responsible for health problems and accidents at work. Therefore in safety-critical domains, it is essential to consider human factors and utilize cognitive ergonomics to ensure performance and safety.

Specific Work Requirements

There are some jobs that overload performance capacity, endangering the safety and health of workers. The specific job demands can be physical, mental and psychosocial, e.g. the work of fire-fighters, police officers, medical specialists, pilots, and air traffic controllers. High-demand jobs are often safety-critical, such as working in aviation, nuclear power, or health care, where the employees are responsible for other people's safety and well-being.

The specific job demands may involve several factors, e.g. unconditional working hours and stress that are known to influence cognitive functioning. It is known that sleep deprivation related to shift work and working during normal sleeping hours exerts detrimental effects on cognitive performance. However, there are significant inter-individual differences in response to the sleep deprivation and night work. In addition, psychosocial stress may impair attention and memory function and increase the rate of errors and accidents at work.

Working in Dynamic Environments

Several working environments are complex and dynamic: the perceptual environment changes constantly, there are moving objects around, and performance requires rapid reactions and decision-making under pressures of time. Professional drivers, air traffic controllers, and firefighters are some of the employees required to have total and accurate situation awareness. They need to know what is going on and they have to understand what to do next in all circumstances.

According to Endslay's model, situation awareness involves three levels:

- Perception refers to awareness of relevant objects, people, systems and other environmental factors.
- Comprehension is related to understanding the meaning of what was perceived: recognizing, interpreting and evaluating the significance.
- Projection refers to the ability to predict the situation in the near future, based on perceiving and understanding the dynamic elements of the environment. Thus situation awareness is a complex phenomenon that depends on several basic and higher level cognitive processes.

Information Technology and Automation

Information and communications technology (ICT) has an increasing role at the work place: in Finland, nearly 75% of employees use a computer in their work and every third of them spends more than four hours of the working day in front of a computer. In service work, sales, and care work, the use of information technology has doubled during the last 10 years. The aim of cognitive ergonomics is to ensure that also the information work with computers is effortless and that ICT improves a worker's ability to perform a variety of tasks instead of causing unnecessary load, errors, and wasting of time.

Using computers does not necessarily decrease cognitive load. In fact, usability problems of information technology may disrupt performance. The increasing numbers of interfaces at work create new cognitive demands on employees: workers need to learn several kinds of applications and use diverse systems. Many tasks require also switching between several applications. If the applications do not have technical connections between them, work may involve moving information from one application to another, a task that a computer can do more efficiently than any human being.

The increase of information technology has also led to automation, e.g. in production, manufacturing, and traffic. Automation means that workers are responsible for monitoring and controlling the processes. As the complexity of systems increases, and they come to be operated by groups of people, it becomes more and more difficult to understand how the overall system works. There are examples from aviation, financial trading, and cloud computing that demonstrate accidents and errors that happen when technology fails, and people are not able to understand the system and to diagnose the problem. It is therefore necessary that technology provides people with the appropriate information, and workers learn and practice skills that make it possible to intervene should something go wrong.

Nature of Work in Future

The nature of work has changed during the last decades, and the pace of change is likely to accelerate. The workforce is aging, work practices are changing, the transition to the provision of information and services requires new skills from employees, and new technologies affect how people work. Technology can impact on training methods and improve learning, and may offer new ways to modify the environment to make it more compatible with human abilities.

New enhancement technologies can even provide opportunities to improve an individual's ability to learn and perform in cognitive tasks, even in old age and in extreme conditions. Nonetheless, modulating the environment is the key method in ergonomics. Even if new technologies allow enhancement of individual's abilities and skills, these technologies should not be considered as alternatives to improving poor work conditions; i.e. the well-being and health of employees has to be considered as a key component of work.

Towards Optimal Cognitive Functioning at Work

The aim of cognitive ergonomics is to design work conditions and environments that enhance cognitive functioning and human performance at work, and as a consequence improve productivity, safety, and health at work.

Human Cognitive Abilities and Skills are Limited but Adaptive

Cognitive functions have their limits: in many cases, human beings have a limited capacity to perceive, focus and divide attention, learn, memorize, make decisions, solve problems, and communicate. On the other hand, the ability of humans to adapt in order to perform different tasks is exceptional. When designing work conditions one needs to make a trade-off between skills and limitations: people are able to overcome many cognitive limitations through learning, but this takes time.

It is Easier to Change Work Conditions than the Human Cognitive System

Today, there are few safe methods which can change the human cognitive system and the way people process information. However, there are numerous general principles and good practices of visual and cognitive ergonomics and the ergonomics of working hours, organisational ergonomics, and physical ergonomics that help to avoid unnecessary cognitive load at work and that improve human performance. In practice, even if the focus of an intervention and design is on cognitive ergonomics, it is important to ensure that the solutions and proposals for changing a specific case also fulfill the requirements of physical and organisational ergonomics.

Better Work for Everyone

The individual differences and the wide spectrum of cognitive performance are evident in working life. Most conventional jobs employ people that do not come from selected populations, and no special cognitive capacity and skills are required, nor does working presume long training periods or high level of expertise. Furthermore, some workers may also have specific cognitive limitations, such as learning difficulties or other cognitive deficits. It is thus necessary to design work for all and to consider accessibility issues.

In the future, the greater amount of ageing workers will become a factor that may affect the diversity in work ability. Cognitive variables that are critical to performance in several occupations can begin to display age-related effects after 45 years of age, although individual variation is great. There are age-related reductions in visual function and hearing at least to some extent. Some mental processes which are critical for many jobs, i.e. working memory and executive functions, as well as dual task performance and task switching, appear to be most affected by age. Higher level cognitive functions also seem to decline with age, although practice and experience enhance performance in individuals of all ages.

It is accepted that older workers can adapt and compensate for a loss of capacity, and thus a high level of expertise may diminish the detrimental effects of age at least to some extent. Furthermore, there is no definitive evidence for the belief that work ability decreases with age. In addition, the between-individual and within-person variation in cognitive functioning increases with age. Therefore, chronological age is not an appropriate factor for assessing an individual's cognitive performance and work ability, but instead there is a need for methods to estimate an individual's functional age. These issues are especially relevant when deciding about the work abilities of ageing workers doing high-demand jobs.

Applications

"The first domains investigated by cognitive ergonomics were nuclear power plants, air traffic control systems, and medical anesthetics. Those situations feature complex environments (e.g., where there are many controls and switches—or many factors—coming into play) and where exceptional focus is needed so as to make decisions in potentially life-threatening situations. In the years following, many studies were conducted in "softer" domains such as banking, office work and leisure activities. The principles proved transferable between such environments."

So, the primary focus of cognitive ergonomics is on work activities which:

- Have an emphasized cognitive component?
- Are in safety critical environments?
- Are in complex, changeable environments?

Disciplines for better user Experience

Products designed to match the cognitive capabilities and limitations of users are simple, clear, and easy to use, contributing to a superior overall user experience. This is the ultimate goal of the designer of any system. But before we get to the disciplines to building a better user experience, first it's important to understand what influences a user's experience.

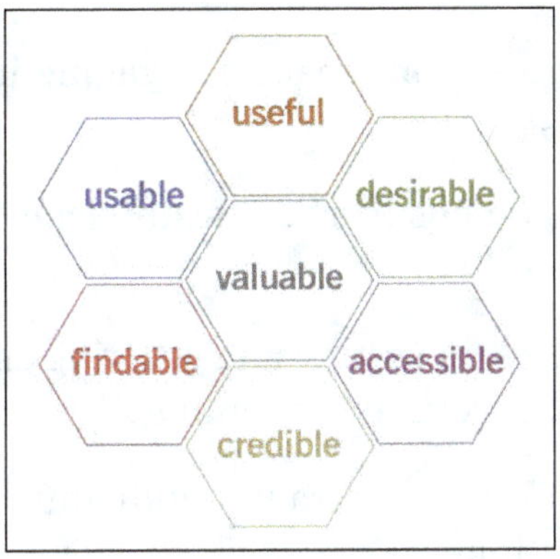

According to user experience expert Peter Morville a good user experience is:

- Useful.
- Usable.
- Desirable.
- Findable.
- Accessible.
- Credible.
- Valuable.

Disciplines to Build a Better user Experience

There are ten disciplines to building a better user experience:

- Project Management focuses on planning and organizing a project and its resources. This includes identifying and managing the lifecycle to be used, applying it to the user-centered design process, formulating the project team, and efficiently guiding the team through all phases until project completion.
- User Research focuses on understanding user behaviors, needs, and motivations through observation techniques, task analysis, and other feedback methodologies.
- Usability Evaluation focuses on how well users can learn and use a product to achieve their goals. It also refers to how satisfied users are with that process.
- Information Architecture focuses on how information is organized, structured, and presented to users.
- User Interface Design focuses on anticipating what users might need to do and ensuring that the interface has elements that are easy to access, understand, and use to facilitate those actions.
- Interaction Design focuses on creating engaging interactive systems with well thought out behaviors.
- Visual Design focuses on ensuring an aesthetically pleasing interface that is in line with brand goals.
- Content Strategy focuses on writing and curating useful content by planning the creation, delivery and governance behind it.
- Accessibility focuses on how a disabled individual accesses or benefits from a site, system or application.
- Analytics focuses on the collection, reporting, and analysis of website data.

NEUROERGONOMICS

Neuroergonomics is the application of neuroscience to ergonomics. Traditional ergonomic studies rely predominantly on psychological explanations to address human factors issues such as: work performance, operational safety, and workplace-related risks (e.g., repetitive stress injuries). Neuroergonomics, in contrast, addresses the biological substrates of ergonomic concerns, with an emphasis on the role of the human nervous system.

Neuroergonomics has two major aims: to use existing/emerging knowledge of human performance and brain function to design systems for safer and more efficient operation, and to advance this understanding of the relationship between brain function and performance in real-world tasks.

To meet these goals, neuroergonomics combines two disciplines—neuroscience, the study of brain function, and human factors, and the study of how to match technology with the capabilities and limitations of people so they can work effectively and safely. The goal of merging these two fields is to use the startling discoveries of human brain and physiological functioning both to inform the design of technologies in the workplace and home, and to provide new training methods that enhance performance, expand capabilities, and optimize the fit between people and technology.

Research in the area of neuroergonomics has blossomed in recent years with the emergence of noninvasive techniques for monitoring human brain function that can be used to study various aspects of human behavior in relation to technology and work, including mental workload, visual attention, working memory, motor control, human-automation interaction, and adaptive automation. Consequently, this interdisciplinary field is concerned with investigations of the neural bases of human perception, cognition, and performance in relation to systems and technologies in the real world—for example, in the use of computers and various other machines at home or in the workplace, and in operating vehicles such as aircraft, cars, trains, and ships.

Approaches

Functional Neuroimaging

A central goal of neuroergonomics is to study the way in which brain function is related to task/work performance. To do this, noninvasive neuroimaging methods are typically used to record direct neurophysiological markers of brain activity through electrical activity Electroencephalography (EEG), Magnetoencephalography (MEG) or through indirect metabolic Positron-emission tomography (PET) and neurovascular measures of neural activity including Functional magnetic resonance imaging (fMRI), Functional near-infrared spectroscopy (fNIRS), transcranial Doppler (TCD) sonography. Typically, neuroergonomic studies are more application-oriented than basic cognitive neuroscience studies and often require a balance between controlled environments and naturalistic settings. Studies using larger room-scale neuroimaging setups such as PET, MEG, and fMRI, offer increased spatial and temporal resolution at the expense of increased restrictions on participant's actions. Using more mobile techniques such as fNIRS and EEG, research may be conducted in more realistic settings including even participation in the actual work being investigated (ex: driving). These techniques have the advantage of being more affordable and versatile, but may also compromise by reducing the number of areas recorded and the ability to image neural activity from deeper brain regions. Together the application of both controlled lab experiments and the translation of findings in realistic contexts represent the spectrum of neuroimaging in neuroergonomics.

Neurostimulation

Neurostimulation methods may also be used apart, or in conjunction with neuroimaging approaches to probe the involvement of cortical regions in task performance. Techniques such as transcranial magnetic stimulation (TMS) and Transcranial direct-current stimulation (tDCS) can be used to temporarily alter the excitability of cortical regions. It is proposed that stimulating a cortical region (particularly with TMS) can disrupt or enhance that regions function, permitting researchers to test specific hypotheses related to human performance.

Some studies have shown the promise of using transcranial magnetic stimulation (TMS) and transcranial direct-current stimulation (tDCS) to improve cognitive skills during tasks. While initially used to treat various neurological disorders such as Parkinson's disease or dementia, the scope of TMS is expanding. In TMS, electricity is passed through a magnetic coil that is positioned near the person's scalp. Results from studies show that noninvasive brain stimulation leads to 20 more minutes of sustained vigilance performance.

Psychophysiology

Psychophysiological measures are physiological measures (blood, heart rate, skin conductance, etc.) which change as part of psychological processes. Although not considered as a direct neural measure, neuroergonomics also promotes the use of physiological correlates as dependent measures when they can serve as an index of neural activities such as attention, motor, or affective processes. These measures can be used in conjunction with neuroimaging measures, or as a substitute when the acquisition of neuroimaging measures is too costly, dangerous, or otherwise impractical. Psychophysiology is a distinct field from neuroergonomics, however the principals and objectives can be considered complementary.

Applications

Mental Workload Assessment

Using an fMRI, mental workload can be quantified by an increase in cerebral blood flow in regions of the prefrontal cortex (PFC). Many fMRI studies show that there is increased PFC activation during a working memory task. Equally important as measuring mental workload, is evaluating the operator vigilance, or attentiveness. Using TCD to monitor blood flow velocity in intercranial arteries, it was shown that a decrease in blood flow was associated with a decrease in vigilance and depletion of cognitive resources.

Adaptive Automation

Adaptive automation, a novel neuroergonomic concept, refers to a human-machine system that uses real-time assessment of the operator's workload to make the necessary changes to enhance performance. For adaptive automation to work, the system must utilize an accurate operator-state classifier for the real-time assessment. Operator-state classifiers such as discriminant analysis and artificial neural networks show an accuracy of 70% to 85% in real-time. An important part to properly implementing adaptive automation is figuring out how big a workload needs to be to require intervention. Implementing neuroergonomic adaptive automation would require the development of nonintrusive sensors and even techniques to track eye movement. Current research into assessing a person's mental state includes using facial electromyography to detect confusion.

Experiments show that a human-robot team performs better at controlling air and ground vehicles than either a human or robot (i.e. the automatic target recognition system). When compared to 100% human control and static automation, participants showed higher trust and self-confidence, as well as lower perceived workload, when using adaptive automation.

In adaptive automation, getting the machine to accurately reason how to respond to the changes and get back to peak performance is the biggest challenge. The machine has to be able to determine to what extent it must make the changes. This is also a consequence of the complexity of the system and factors such as: how easily can the sensed parameter be quantified, how many parameters in the machine's system can be changed, and how well can these different machine parameters be coordinated.

Brain Computer Interfaces

A developing area of research called brain-computer interfaces (BCIs) strives to use different types of brain signals to operate external devices, without any motor input from the person. BCIs provide promise for patients with limited motor capabilities, such as those with amyotrophic lateral sclerosis. When the user engages in a specific mental activity, it generates a unique brain electrical potential that is processed and relayed into a signal for the external device. BCIs using signals from EEGs and ERPs have been used to operate voice synthesizers and move robotic arms. Research for BCIs began in the 1970s at the University of California Los Angeles, and its current focus is towards neuroprosthetic applications. BCIs can be substantially improved by incorporating high-level control, context, the environment, as well as virtual reality into its design.

Stroke Rehabilitation

As of 2011, there has been an effort to applying a rehabilitation robot connected to a non-invasive brain-computer interface to promote brain plasticity and motor learning following a stroke. Half of stroke survivors experience unilateral paralysis or weakness, and approximately 30-60% of them do not regain function. Typical treatment, post-stroke, involves constraint-induced movement therapy and robotic therapy, which work to restore motor activity by forcing the movement of the weak limbs. Current active therapy cannot be utilized by patients who suffer complete control loss or paralysis, and do not have any residual motor ability to work with.

With a focus on these underserved patients, a BCI was created that used the electrical brain signals detected by an EEG to control an upper-limb rehabilitative robot. The user is instructed to imagine the motor activity while the EEG picks up the associated brain signals. The BCI uses a linear transformation algorithm to convert the EEG spectral features into commands for the robot. An experiment done on 24 subjects tested a non-BCI group, which used sensorimotor rhythms to control the robot, against the BCI-group, which used the BCI-robot system. The results from the brain-plasticity analysis showed that there was a decrease in beta wave activity in the subjects of the BCI-group, which is associated with a change in movement. The results also showed that the BCI-group performed better than the non-BCI group in every measure for motor learning.

Virtual Reality

Virtual reality could allow for testing how human operators would work in dangerous environments without actually putting them in harm's way. For example, it would allow the testing of how fatigue or a new technology would affect a driver or a pilot in their specific environment, without the possibility of injury. Being able to evaluate the effects of some new workplace technology in virtual reality, before real life implementation, could save money and lives. Bringing virtual reality technology to the point where it can accurately mimic real life is difficult, but its potential is vast.

Healthcare Training

Healthcare training programs have adopted virtual reality simulation (VRS) as a training tool for nursing students. This computer-based three-dimensional simulation tool allows for nursing students to practice various nursing skills repeatedly in a risk-free environment. A nursing program at a major Midwestern state university agreed to utilize a VRS module for teaching the insertion of an intravenous (IV) catheter, and complete an evaluation on the effectiveness of the program. The VRS composed of a computer program and a haptic arm device, which worked together to simulate the feel of vascular access. On the computer screen, the user would have to select the equipment for the procedure in the correct order. The user then palpates the veins of the haptic arm, and virtually inserts the IV catheter. The program provides immediate feedback by notifying the user when he/she misses a step and needs to restart the procedure.

Results of evaluation pointed to the VRS an "excellent learning tool" for increasing a student's knowledge on the procedure. All eight of the nursing faculty who participated agreed to this much, and that they would recommend that students work with the VRS before performing the IV catheter insertion on real patients.

This tool allows educators to expose students to an extensive range of real-life patient conditions and nursing experiences. The central advantage of the VRS program is the availability of a variety of case scenarios, which allow students to increase their awareness of differences in patient responses to IV catheter insertion. From the standpoint of the student, the virtual reality simulation helps bridge the gap between nursing theory and practice.

Applications for Neurocognitive Disabilities

Neuroergonomic assessments have tremendous potential for evaluating the psychomotor performance in an individual with a neurocognitive disability or following a stroke or surgery. They would allow for a standardized method for measuring the change in neurocognitive function during rehabilitation for a neurocognitive disability. In terms of rehabilitation, it would allow for the efforts to be goal-oriented. These tests could be applied for measuring change following operational procedures such as neurosurgery, carotid endarterectomy, and coronary artery bypass graft.

Driving Safety

One of the main application domains of neuroergonomics is driving safety, especially for older drivers with cognitive impairments. Driving requires the integration of multiple cognitive processes, which can be studied separately if the right kinds of tools are used. The types of tools used to evaluate cognition during driving include driving simulators, instrumented vehicles, and part task simulators.

The Crossmodal Research Laboratory in Oxford is working on developing a system of warning signals to grab the attention of a distracted driver, in an effort to make driving safer for everybody. The research has found that using auditory icons, such as a car horn, is a better warning signal than a pure tone. On top of that, spatial auditory cues work better at redirecting the driver's attention than non-spatialized auditory cues. Cues that integrate multiple senses, such as an audiotactile signal, grab attention better than unisensory cues. Others have evaluated different types of in-vehicle notifications (i.e., auditory icons, speech commands) designed for task management in autonomous trucks for their relevance to separable neural mechanisms; this serves as an effective method to clarify often conflicting findings drawn from behavioral results alone.

Neuroergonomic Methods

Neuroergonomic studies rely heavily on existing neuroimaging techniques to understand brain structures, mechanisms, and functions during work. Neuroimaging techniques applicable to neuroergonomics fall into two general categories, those that are direct indicators of neuronal activity in response to stimuli, such as electroencephalography (EEG) and event-related potentials (ERPs), and those that provide indirect metabolic indicators of neuronal activity, such as functional magnetic resonance imaging (fMRI), positron emission tomography (PET), and functional near infrared spectroscopy (fNIRS). EEG represents summated post-synaptic electrical activity of neurons firing in response to motor/cognitive stimuli as recorded on the scalp, and thus offers excellent temporal resolution of electromagnetic brain changes, on the order of milliseconds. In comparison, fMRI and PET techniques, that provide information on cerebral blood flow in response to neuronal activity, have low temporal resolution (on the order of about 10 s), but offer excellent spatial resolution (1 cm or better) and unlike EEG, they provide valuable information on location of the neural signal generated.

Since neuroergonomics distinguishes itself from traditional neuroscience in that it evaluates brain functions in response to work, it is important that the neuroergonomic methods provide the flexibility to assess brain function in naturalistic work settings. Some neuroimaging techniques are better designed for and adapted for assessing brain functions in mobile work environments than others. The pros and cons of neuroergonomic methods are discussed in reference to three criteria: (1) temporal resolution, (2) spatial resolution, and (3) degree of immobility. Figure illustrates how these neuroimaging techniques compare against each other based on the three criteria.

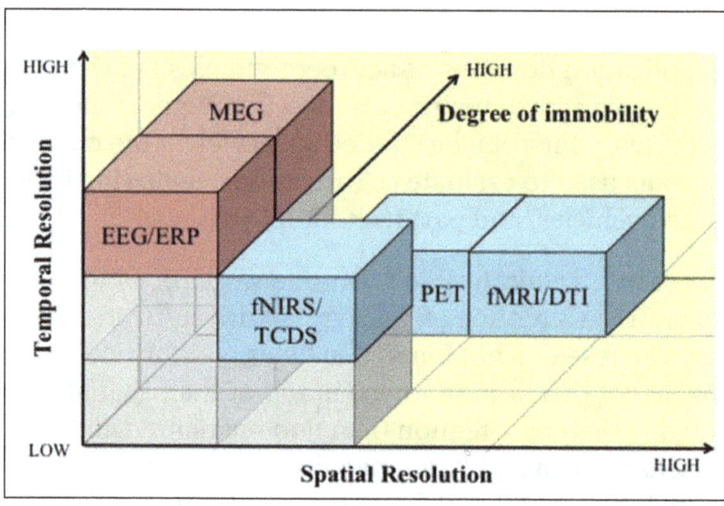

A comparison of electromagnetic (pink) and hemodynamic (blue) neuroimaging techniques for use in neuroergonomics based on temporal resolution (x-axis), spatial resolution (y-axis), and degree of immobility (z-axis). EEG, electroencephalography; ERP, event-related potentials; MEG, magnetoencephalography; fNIRS, functional near infrared spectroscopy; TCDS, transcranial Doppler sonography; fMRI, functional magnetic resonance imaging; DTI, Diffusion tensor imaging; PET, positron emission tomography.

List of Neuroergonomic Techniques and their Major Features

Method	Measures/stimulates	Portability/ mobility	Cost	Spatial resolution	Temporal resolution
MRI	Gray matter volume	None	High	High	NA

DTI	White matter integrity	None	High	High	NA
fMRI	Relative blood oxygenation	None	High	High	Low
fNIRS	Oxyhemoglobin and deoxy-hemoglobin	High	Low	Moderate	Low
TCDS	Cerebral blood flow velocity	Moderate	Low	Low	Low
EEG	Summated post-synaptic electrical activity	Moderate	Low	Low	High
ERP	Stimulus or response-related electrical activity	Moderate	Low	Low	High
TMS	Brain activation or inhibition	Low	Moderate	High	High
tDCS	Brain activation or inhibition	High	Very low	Low	Low

Electroencephalography signals are the spatial summation of current density induced by synchronized post-synaptic potentials occurring in large clusters of neurons measured at the scalp. The EEG is recorded as differences in voltage between active electrodes at different positions on the scalp, such as the frontal, parietal, temporal, and occipital lobes of the brain according to the International 10–20 System, and a reference electrode, typically the ear. EEG signals comprises of different frequency bands, each associated with various cognitive and physical states. Spectral analyses of EEG signals can be conducted to assess power in different frequency bands: delta (0.5–3 Hz), theta (4–8 Hz), alpha (8–13 Hz), beta (13–30 Hz), and gamma (40–50 Hz). Another commonly computed EEG-driven spectral metric (i.e., brain) used in conjunction with muscular output (i.e., body) is corticomuscular coherence (CMC). CMC reflects "communications" between the brain and muscle and is determined as the coherence between sensorimotor cortex activation obtained from EEG and muscular activation as measured by electromyography (EMG) during motor activities.

Electroencephalography-derived ERPs represent the brain's neural response to specific sensory, motor, and cognitive events. ERPs represent the outcome of signal averaging of EEG epochs time-locked to a particular stimulus or response event. To evaluate mental workload or examine human error, ERP waveforms are examined for changes in the amplitude and latency of different ERP components, typically defined as positive or negative peak activity (such as the P3 and N1 components) or slowly rising activity such as the lateralized readiness potential. To assess neural bases of motor activities, motor-related cortical potential (MRCP) ERP components have been studied that are characterized by a slowly rising negative potential, called Bereitschaftspotential (BP) or readiness potential, which is followed by a sharp rising negative potential, known as negative slope. As the onset of MRCP occurs prior to the onset of the motor activity, MRCP is considered to indicate pre-motor activity, which involves specific brain regions that prepare for a desired motor behavior.

Electroencephalography-driven metrics, both spectral and temporal, in evaluating brain function during naturalistic complex tasks are relatively unobtrusive so that it does not interfere with the operator's work performance. Its compact size and low cost, compared to other neuroimaging techniques such as fMRI and PET, makes it fairly well suited for use in both laboratory and field conditions. While artifacts attributed to movement, eye blinks, and physiological interference accompany EEG data, several algorithms have been developed to allow for the removal of noise in the EEG signal in real time or during post processing of the data. Recent developments in making "field-friendly" EEG systems include "dry" electrode caps, which do not need extensive participant preparation time, as well as wireless systems that do not require the participant to be tethered to cables. These technical developments have enhanced the relevance and value of EEG for mobile applications.

Cerebral hemodynamic techniques such as fMRI and PET provide valuable information on source locations of distinct neural activation patterns associated with simple and complex cognitive, motor, and affective functions. While PET uses injected radioactive tracers to measure the blood flow in response to stimuli, based on their respective magnetic characteristics fMRI focuses on the resulting contrast between oxygenated and deoxygenated blood called the Blood Oxygenation Level Dependent or BOLD signal. Both fMRI and PET have been fundamental in advancing our knowledge on brain functions and mechanisms during simple, and relatively static, cognitive and motor tasks. By leveraging high spatial resolution offered by fMRI measurements, reliable techniques for the fMRI-EEG integration have been made possible that offer greater spatio-temporal resolution of imaging dynamic brain activity as well as significant improvement over the conventional fMRI-weighted EEG source imaging techniques. At the same time, fMRI and PET present several limitations in studying brain functions, such as the required supine position that may yield altered hemodynamic changes than seated or standing positions, limited mobility, and restrictions on synchronized brain-body measurements. Moreover, the increasing need to examine brain activation patterns in complex tasks more representative of natural everyday situations have led researchers to adopt alternative neuroimaging techniques that offer better mobility features.

Functional near infrared spectroscopy is a non-invasive optical technique for measuring cerebral hemodynamics similar to PET and fMRI but with lower spatial resolution. By utilizing the tight neurovascular coupling between neuronal activity and regional cerebral blood flow fNIRS measures regional cerebral hemodynamic changes (i.e., changes in oxy- and deoxy-hemoglobin levels). Since oxygenated and deoxygenated blood can be contrasted by their different optical absorption properties, fNIRS detects the levels of these blood parameters in response to neuronal activity. fNIRS is portable, inexpensive, and has shown to be an effective tool in quantifying cortical activation during static and dynamic motor movements, without causing substantial movement artifact issues. While fNIRS measurements, particularly oxygenated hemoglobin levels, have shown to be strongly correlated to the fMRI BOLD signals, albeit with relatively lower signal to noise ratio, unlike fMRI and PET its effectiveness in mapping neural activations across closely connected regions or within deep cortical areas is limited due to its relatively lower spatial resolution. Multimodal imaging approaches using both fNIRS and EEG systems have demonstrated that fNIRS is capable of enhancing event-related desynchronization-based EEG measurements significantly.

While fNIRS enables measurement of oxygenated and deoxygenated hemoglobin levels in cortical regions, transcranial Doppler sonography (TCDS) uses ultrasound to image cerebral blood flow to the brain hemispheres. TCDS uses an emitter attached to the head to direct ultrasound toward the middle cerebral artery (MCA) within the brain, and a receiver then records the frequency of the sound wave reflected by red blood cells moving through the artery. The magnitude of the change in frequency (the Doppler shift) varies directly proportional to the velocity of blood flow within the artery. In response to increased task-related neuronal activity, MCA blood flow velocity increases to remove by-products of the metabolic exchange, which is captured using TCDS. TCDS has become increasingly popular in cognitive neuroergonomic studies of vigilance and mental workload. However, because cerebral blood volume and blood flow velocity is influenced by systemic changes such as heart rate and blood pressure during exercise, TCDS is less popular in assessing task-related neuronal activity in physical neuroergonomic studies of fatigue.

In contrast to the excellent temporal resolution offered by EEG techniques (on the order of milliseconds), magnetic resonance imaging (MRI) provides a structural image of the brain and offers excellent spatial visualization of deep internal parts, such as the hippocampus. While MRI provides static images of the brain that is critical in examining structural changes in the brain due to diseases (such as tumor), its application in studying structural changes in the brain over time (i.e., plasticity) has provided important information on learning and training. A relatively newer MRI technique, called diffusion tensor imaging (DTI), uses MRI to target the diffusion of water molecules in the axons that make up white matter in the brain and allows for the computation of fractional anisotrophy (FA). FA values can range from 0 to 1, where 0 indicates non-directional (isotropic) and 1 indicates perfectly directional (anisotropic) diffusion. Higher FA values are thought to reflect greater integrity of white matter linking different cortical and subcortical regions of the brain. Several recent studies have assessed the effectiveness of cognitive and motor training on white matter integrity using the DTI technique. In general, the MRI technique does not offer any mobility features, but an MRI static image can be overlaid with more dynamic fMRI images (i.e., blood oxygenation) so that areas of activation can be associated with particular brain regions.

The electromagnetic and hemodynamic neuroimaging techniques discussed thus far are based on sensing brain activity while a human operator is engaged in cognitive or physical work. As such, all such techniques are correlational, thus it may be difficult to establish causal links between brain activity and performance using these methods. Researchers have therefore turned to non-invasive stimulation techniques that modulate brain activity, such as transcranial magnetic stimulation (TMS) and transcranial direct current stimulation (tDCS), in order to establish such causal associations. These techniques allow for temporary inhibition or activation of specific brain regions thereby allowing researchers to examine the causal role of different brain regions in various cognitive functions. TMS and tDCS can also be used to modulate brain activity so that the performance of a given cognitive or motor task is improved. Alternatively, these techniques can also be applied not to enhance performance over baseline, but to reduce or eradicate a normally occurring performance limitation, such as performance decrements that occur in vigilance tasks.

- Transcranial magnetic stimulation uses a magnetic coil that is positioned over the participant's scalp over a brain region of interest to send electrical current that changes the magnetic field perpendicular to the head. This induces current flow in the underlying cortical issue, sufficient to alter neural firing. The spatial resolution of TMS is relatively high, particularly when the participant's MRI scan is available to guide the TMS coil placement. The temporal resolution is also high, since the TMS pulses can be delivered with millisecond precision. However, due to the equipment setup TMS does not offer a sufficient degree of mobility needed for neuroergonomic assessment in naturalistic work settings. Whereas TMS uses changing magnetic pulses, tDCS uses small DC electric current (1 or 2 mA) with electrodes attached to the scalp. A positive polarity (anode) is typically used to stimulate neuronal function and enhance performance, and a negative polarity (cathode) is used to inhibit neuronal activity. Compared to TMS, tDCS has low spatial and temporal resolution, but has the advantage that it is portable and very inexpensive and thus is more likely to be adopted in applied neuroergonomic studies.

Physical Work

Ergonomics began as the science of work to maximize productivity, particularly in physical work environments, but has since then expanded to become a scientific discipline concerned with the understanding of the interactions among humans and other elements of a system, in order to optimize human well-being and overall system performance. Physical ergonomics focuses on human physical capabilities and limitations, pertaining to anthropometry, physiology, and biomechanics of the human body, as they relate to physical work. Traditional ergonomic evaluations focus solely on peripheral outcomes, such as force or muscle activity, and disregard the contributions of the brain during work. Physical neuroergonomics is an emerging field of study that focuses on the knowledge of human brain activities in relation to the control and design of physical tasks, by taking into consideration an operator's physical, cognitive, and affective capabilities and limitations. Here we consider how neuroergonomic methods have been employed to evaluate different physical work parameters (such as force production and repetition) and physical fatigue (localized muscle fatigue and whole body fatigue).

Physical Work Parameters

The primary goal of ergonomics is to ensure that work demands are always lower than operator capacity, and the conventional assessment of work demands include measuring biomechanical and physiological outcomes, such as joint torque, muscle activity, and heart rate, in laboratory and field settings. There has been recent interest in assessing physical work using neuroergonomic methods in controlled laboratory conditions; however, there is a clear lack of neuroergonomic studies in assessing physical work in actual field/work settings. Like any new field, physical neuroergonomics research first needs to understand the capabilities, limitations, and considerations of existing neuroimaging techniques on simulated work environments that can help build the knowledge base necessary to perform research in naturalistic work environments.

Since physical work can involve both static and dynamic work at different intensities, repetitions, and durations, which in turn can affect autonomic responses, different work parameters can influence the type of measurement technique adopted. For example, dynamic or ambulatory tasks, such as walking or lifting, cannot be assessed using fMRI due to mobility constraints. More appropriate neuroimaging methods to evaluate ambulatory physical work are EEG, ERP, and fNIRS. Of these, EEG appears to be the most common neuroimaging technique since it provides excellent temporal resolution. Effective artifact removal techniques are available that allow for its use in evaluating dynamic tasks. For example, EEG-derived MRCP has provided valuable information on the role of cortical motor commands (represented by the MRCP) on the control of voluntary muscle activation. MRCP from the supplementary motor area and the contralateral sensorimotor cortex has shown to be highly correlated with force production and rate of force production during isometric elbow-flexion, and associated muscle activity. Of note, a recent fNIRS investigation has demonstrated obesity-related alterations in neural patterns of force control (i.e., lower prefrontal cortex activation associated with decreased joint stability) that can shed some light on the increased incidence of injury rates and higher work absenteeism in obese workers. High repetition is one of the major work-related risk factors that contribute to the development of musculoskeletal disorders. To evaluate the effects of repetition that involves flexion and extension of a joint, traditional ergonomic methods focus on muscular responses such as EMG. In a study investigating thumb flexion and extension movements, EEG-derived MRCP findings from the supplementary motor area and contralateral motor cortex demonstrated that extension and flexion result from separate corticospinal projections to the motor neurons. Thumb extensions resulted in lower EMG but elicited greater brain responses than flexion movements. This particular finding may be important to our understanding of the etiology of musculoskeletal disorders due to repetitive motion. Real work environments are seldom static, and can require operators to focus not only on the physical work demands but also on the necessary visual/auditory cues associated with the tasks. Such tasks, which are dynamic and require visuomotor control, have shown to increase corticomuscular coupling at higher EEG frequencies (i.e., gamma bands), indicating the adaptive role of cortical oscillations in rapidly integrating visual (or new) information with the somatosensory information. These findings have important implications for task analysis and design, particularly for work tasks that require visual feedback or fine or precise control of body motions.

Physical Fatigue

Fatigue is defined as the inability to maintain required power after prolonged use of the muscles, and can be affected by central (i.e., motivation, cortical activity, etc.) and peripheral (i.e., changes in muscle contractile properties) mechanisms. Neuroergonomic methods can help examine the role of central brain mechanisms in fatigue development. Based on the work tasks, fatigue in the workplace can be broadly categorized as localized muscle fatigue, which is the fatigue of specific muscle groups during tasks such as assembly line work or precision work, and whole body fatigue, which is more cardiorespiratory in nature that can occur during manual materials handling tasks. Commonly used ergonomic indicators of localized muscle fatigue include a reduction in force generating capacity and a decrease in EMG power spectrum. However these measures do not delineate the contributions of central fatigue from peripheral fatigue. Using EEG-derived MRCP, Johnston et al. demonstrated a significant increase in the activity of the BP component and the motor potential (MP) component of the MRCP, associated with a decline in force production and reduced EMG activity during a fatiguing grasping task. These increases in the early components of MRCP may reflect development of compensatory cortical strategies to accommodate for the inability to maintain the desired force levels due to peripheral fatigue. Supporting this, Liu et al. advocated that muscle fatigues well before the brain does; in essence that peripheral fatigue occurs before central fatigue. They demonstrated, by estimating the changes of source locations of high-density EEG signals using a single moving current dipole model, that handgrip muscle fatigue was associated with shifting of brain activation centers from one location to another when neurons in the previous location become fatigued. These studies collectively demonstrate the application of EEG in examining the neural correlates of localized fatigue development of smaller muscles during relatively static, or immobile, tasks.

Of the various neuroimaging techniques, EEG offers the greatest flexibility and mobility features that make it an attractive candidate in assessing whole body fatigue. By simultaneously obtaining information on eye movements and spontaneous EEG signals, Kubitz and Mott demonstrated increased brain activation (i.e., decreased alpha activity and increased beta activity) during a fatiguing cycling task. While technical advances have been made in minimizing mechanical artifacts from high-density EEG signals during whole body movements, fNIRS has gained rapid attention in evaluating whole body fatigue owing to its methodological advantages over EEG. First, fNIRS provides information on the location of the neural signal generated, whereas with EEG signals, source localization has to be computationally derived. Second, there are no time-sensitive requirements in examining whole body fatigue when compared to fast reaction time tasks; slower hemodynamic responses of fNIRS are thus appropriate when compared to fast EEG responses. As such, fNIRS responses have shown to be less affected by movement artifacts than EEG signals. Several fNIRS studies have reported a significant decrease in relative levels of oxygenated hemoglobin in the prefrontal cortex, accompanied by muscular impairment, at exhaustion during submaximal and maximal fatiguing contractions. In particular, Thomas and Stephane demonstrated that oxygenated hemoglobin levels in the prefrontal cortex during incremental cycling exercise increased in the early stages, but decreased markedly in the last stage until exhaustion. These findings imply that prefrontal cortex activation is associated with reduction in motor output at the cessation of exercise. However, these fatiguing tasks are accompanied by cardiorespiratory changes in the autonomic system that can affect fNIRS responses. Depending on the research questions asked, such systemic influences on cerebral hemodynamic responses may be desired or undesired. Obrig and Villringer emphasize the importance of analyzing deoxygenated hemoglobin levels as an indicator of "neuronal activation" over the more commonly used oxygenated hemoglobin values. They argue that oxygenated hemoglobin levels are acceptable neuronal activity indicators when cerebral autoregulation is intact, i.e., cerebral blood flow is in homeostasis. Increases in oxygenated hemoglobin during exercise can be attributed not only to neuronal activation but also to exercise-induced increased blood flow to the brain, and as such a decrease in deoxygenated hemoglobin is the most valid parameter. Thus, neuroergonomic investigations of fatigue need to consider these systemic influences, and perhaps collect peripheral measurements such as arterial blood pressure and heart rate to ensure that appropriate inferences are made from fNIRS signals.

Cognitive Work

The field of human factors and ergonomics had its origins in time-and-motion studies conducted in the early 1900s. With the advent of World War II, increasing attention was paid to evaluation of human psychological processes during work performance, but the dominant approach was behaviorism, or stimulus-response psychology. The advent of the cognitive revolution in the late 1950s lead to the introduction of the cognitive approach in human performance assessment from the 1960s to the present day, but there was still a relative neglect of brain mechanisms. Advances in neuroimaging and related methods that lead to the development of the field of cognitive neuroscience lead to the argument that neural measures should also be considered in human factors and ergonomics. Since that time, the neuroergonomic approach has been applied to a number of different issues in cognitive ergonomics.

Mental Workload

The assessment of human mental workload is one of the most widely studied topics in ergonomics. If operator mental workload is either too high or too low human-system performance may suffer in work environments, thereby potentially compromising safety. Hence, workload must be assessed in the design of new systems or the evaluation of existing ones. Behavioral measures, such as accuracy and speed of response on secondary tasks, or subjective reports (such as the NASA-TLX) have been widely used to assess mental workload. However, measures of brain function offer some unique advantages that can be exploited in mental workload assessment. Among these is the ability to extract covert physiological measures continuously in complex system operations in which overt behavioral measures may be relatively sparse.

The dominant theory of human mental workload is resource theory. This theory postulates that except for highly overlearned "automatic" tasks, task performance is directly proportional to the application of attentional resources. The theory also proposes that the degree of overlap of multiple pools of resources determines the pattern and amount of interference when two or more tasks are performed simultaneously (such as driving and talking on the cell phone). Dual-task studies have provided abundant support for resource theory, but one criticism is that the theory is circular, which can be linked to the lack of an independent measure of resources. This criticism can be countered if neural measures of mental resources can be identified.

Measures of cerebral hemodynamics, such as fNIRS and TCDS, have provided validation for the resource construct.

There are many factors, such as cost, ease of implementation, intrusiveness, etc., that must be taken into consideration when selecting neuroergonomic techniques for mental workload assessment. Some of these factors (e.g., cost) may rule out the use of neuroergonomic methods in favor of simpler indexes such as subjective measures. Some workers may also not wish to be "wired up" for physiological recording, so operator acceptance must also be carefully considered. However, with increasing miniaturization and development of dry electrode, wireless, wearable systems, some of these concerns are diminishing.

Vigilance and Mental Fatigue

The evaluation of operator vigilance and mental fatigue in work environments is a topic closely related to workload assessment. The widespread implementation of automation in many work environments, including air and surface transportation and health care, while often leading to a reduction in operator workload, can also increase workload because of the resulting need for monitoring the automation. The typical finding in vigilance studies is that the detection rate of critical targets declines with time on task. Vigilance decrement was originally attributed to a reduction in physiological arousal but more recent neuroergonomic research using TCDS and fNIRS have attributed it to resource depletion. Warm et al. reported a series of studies of TCDS and vigilance. A consistent finding is that the vigilance decrement is paralleled by a decline in blood flow velocity over time, relative to a baseline of activity just prior to beginning the vigilance session. The parallel decline in vigilance performance and in blood flow velocity is found for both visual and auditory tasks. These findings have been interpreted using resource theory. A critical control finding in support of resource theory – as opposed to a generalized arousal or fatigue model – is that the blood flow change occurs only when observers actively engage with the vigilance task. When observers are asked to simply watch a display passively without having to detect targets for the same amount of time as in an active vigilance condition – a case of maximal under-arousal – blood flow velocity does not decline but remains stable over time.

The deleterious effects of loss of operator vigilance can countered with reduced work hours and more frequent rest breaks, but this may not be practical in all work settings. Another mitigating strategy is to use cueing. Detection performance in vigilance tasks can be improved by providing observers with consistent and reliable cues to the imminent arrival of critical signals, with the extent of the decrement being reduced or eliminated. With cueing, observers need to monitor a display only after having been prompted about the arrival of a signal and therefore can husband their information processing resources over time. In contrast, when no cues are provided, observers are never certain of when a critical signal might appear and consequently have to process information on their displays continuously across the watch, thereby consuming more of their resources over time than cued observers. If the vigilance decrement stems from resource depletion due to need to attend continuously to a display, then pre-cues should reduce the decline in cerebral blood flow velocity as measured by TCDS. This was confirmed in a study by Hitchcock et al. They used no pre-cues or pre-cues that were 100, 80, or 40% reliable in pointing to an upcoming critical event in a simulated air traffic control task. Performance efficiency remained stable when perfectly reliable cues were provides but declined over time in the remaining conditions, so that by the end of the vigil, performance efficiency was clearly best in the 100% group, followed in order by the 80, 40%, and no-cue groups. Blood flow declined in the no cue control condition, but there was a progressive reduction in the extent of the decline with progressively more reliable cues. There was no decline when the cues were perfectly reliable. This pattern of change in blood flow exactly matched that of performance.

In addition to cueing, non-invasive brain stimulation could also be used to mitigate vigilance decrement and mental fatigue. Nelson et al. applied 1 mA anodal tDCS to either the left or right prefrontal cortex while participants performed the same vigilance task used by Hitchcock et al. tDCS was applied either early or late during the course of the vigilance task. Compared to a control group that showed the normal vigilance decrement, the early stimulation group had a higher detection rate of critical signals. The late stimulation group initially exhibited a vigilance decrement, but this was reversed following application of tDCS. These initial findings are highly encouraging, but need to be followed up with additional research to examine the long-term effectiveness of tDCS as a method to alleviate vigilance problems at work.

Training and Neuroadaptive Systems

While the goal of ergonomic design is to avoid having workers exposed to extremes of workload and to loss of vigilance, this may not always be possible in certain work settings where unexpected events, equipment failures, or other unanticipated factors lead to a transient increase in the task load imposed on the human operator, or long work hours impose demands on operator vigilance. Adaptive automation offers one approach to deal with these issues. In this approach, the allocation of functions to human and machine agents is flexible during system operations, with greater use of automation during high task load conditions or emergencies and less during normal operations, consistent with the approach of dynamic function allocation. The adaptive automation concept has a long history, but neuroergonomic methods for its implementation have been considered relatively recently.

Several methods to implement adaptive systems have been examined, including neuroergonomic measures to assess the operator's functional state. Many studies have used EEG because of its ease of recording and (relative) unobtrusiveness (compared, say, to secondary tasks or subjective questionnaires). EEG also has the property of being a very high bandwidth measure, offering the possibility of sampling the human operator at up to about 30 Hz. Workload adaptive systems need to assess operator state in real time, or near real time, so that task allocation or restructuring can be implemented in cases of overload or underload. A number of different statistical and machine learning techniques have been used for this purpose. These include discriminant analysis, artificial neural networks, Bayesian networks, and fuzzy logic. These have been implemented in real time and typically provide accuracies of 70–85%.

Implementing neuroergonomic adaptive systems in real settings poses significant challenges. A major issue concerns the detection and removal of artifacts in real time. Furthermore, while initial success has been achieved in using computational techniques to classify workload on the basis of EEG and other neuroergonomic measures, the reliability and stability of these methods within and across individuals needs to be more rigorously tested. Finally, the operational community must be involved in the design of adaptive systems to ensure user acceptance and compliance.

Neuroergonomic Assessment of Concurrent Physical and Cognitive Work

Both physical and cognitive neuroergonomics have helped advance our understanding on the role of the human brain during physical and cognitive work, respectively.

Only a small number of studies have investigated the interaction between physical and cognitive work, which is a big concern since "work" places combined physical and cognitive demands on operators, never either one in isolation. High cognitive demands can influence physical work; and physical activity can in turn influence cognitive processing. In comparison to traditional evaluation techniques in either physical or cognitive ergonomics domain, neuroergonomic methods offer a great advantage in assessing these combined demands. For example, using EEG signals Kamijo et al. investigated the influence of exercise intensity on cognitive function using the P300 ERP component. They suggested that exercise influenced the amount of attentional resources devoted to a given task and that the changes in P300 amplitude followed an inverted U-shaped behavior of differences in exercise intensity.

When examining the impact of cognitive demand on physical capacity, a few studies have attributed decreased muscle endurance in presence of a cognitively stressful situation to lower motivation, increased neuromotor noise impairing joint steadiness, or neuronal interference at the prefrontal cortex that is involved in cognitive processing and isometric motor contractions. In particular, using fNIRS to monitor cerebral oxygenation during handgrip exercises, Mehta and Parasuraman demonstrated that concurrent handgrip exercises in cognitive stressful conditions were associated with lower oxygenated hemoglobin levels in the bilateral prefrontal cortex at exhaustion when compared to the handgrip exercises at the same intensity levels (i.e., no changes observed in peripheral muscular responses of EMG and force exerted) under no stress. Quite similarly, using EEG- and EMG-derived corticomuscular coupling measure, Kristeva-Feige et al. reported that corticomuscular coupling decreased significantly during a cognitively stressful condition despite no changes observed in traditional measures such as EMG and force production. These studies collectively emphasize the importance of obtaining brain (or central) responses along with the more conventional ergonomic measurements to accurately understand the "total" demands placed on humans during work that requires both physical and cognitive processing. Future investigations on comparing these brain-body responses with the more traditional performance or subjective measures are also needed to understand the underlying neural "cost" of operator functional state. Such studies are also needed so as to develop evaluation tools (surveys, heuristic checklists) that are predictive of the neural and physiological cost associated with optimizing work tasks, which can be used by designers or supervisors to quantify operator workload and fatigue.

Mobile Brain Imaging Considerations for Workload/Fatigue Assessments

One of the key distinctions between neuroergonomics and neuroscience is that neuroergonomics is the study of brain and behavior "at work." Thus, it is extremely important that neuroergonomic methods are capable of examining human operators at their naturalistic work settings. Recent efforts in developing mobile brain imaging (MoBI) techniques, which consider the physical and environmental impact on human cognitive processing, show great promise. For example, Gramann et al. reviewed the implications and feasibility of a newly developed MoBI system that was previously employed in examining cognitive processing during human stance and locomotion. In particular, their MoBI investigation included simultaneous brain-body measurements from a 256-channel EEG system and kinematic and kinetic outcomes that are otherwise employed during conventional gait biomechanics using motion capture systems and force plates. In their review, Gramann and colleagues identify key requirements for MoBI methods that include: (1) robust mobile sensor technology to measure brain activity, (2) comprehensive "wireless" body measurement system, and (3) powerful computational software to collectively processing and analyze both brain-body responses. While developing an ideal MoBI system may be a challenging goal, understanding current limitations in mobile brain-body imaging and addressing them, albeit painstakingly, is a critical step toward achieving this goal. Future investigations can also include developing similar mobile brain-body imaging systems for hemodynamic neuroimaging techniques, utilizing either fNIRS or TCDS to provide brain imaging measures, and using peripheral measurements such as heart rate and blood pressure to document physiological whole-body responses.

COGNITIVE ERGONOMICS OF OPERATIONAL TOOLS

Control systems have become increasingly more powerful over the past decades. The availability of high data throughput and sophisticated graphical interactions has opened a variety of new possibilities. But has this helped to provide intuitive, easy to use applications to simplify the operation of modern large scale accelerator facilities?

A "tool" is something that helps you to achieve a goal. It is called an "ergonomic tool" if it has been tailored to be used by humans, taking into account our physical and cognitive limitations. These days the operator in an accelerator control room pursues his goals exclusively by means of computer applications. The discipline that deals with the design of ergonomic computer applications is human computer interaction (HCI). For the software industry this field has continuously gained in importance over the last few decades. The branch of human-computer interaction that deals specifically with the analysis of cognitive processes is known as cognitive ergonomics. It deals, for example with diagnosis, decision making and planning: all required of operators in modern industries. At the same time human-computer interaction has been widely ignored in the development of modern control systems for accelerators.

One of the most important figures of merit for accelerator operation managers is beam availability. The contributions of the different systems to beam interruption time for the Swiss Light Source (SLS) in 2009. There appears to be no contribution from "bad operational tools", but "operator faults" do account for 3% of the down-time.

The operational applications at the SLS are the only means of the operator to interact with the accelerator; therefore an operator fault is most likely an unintended action of the operator: he did not properly predict the consequence of his action. Or we could say that the application failed to communicate the risks of the action to the operator in a timely manner.

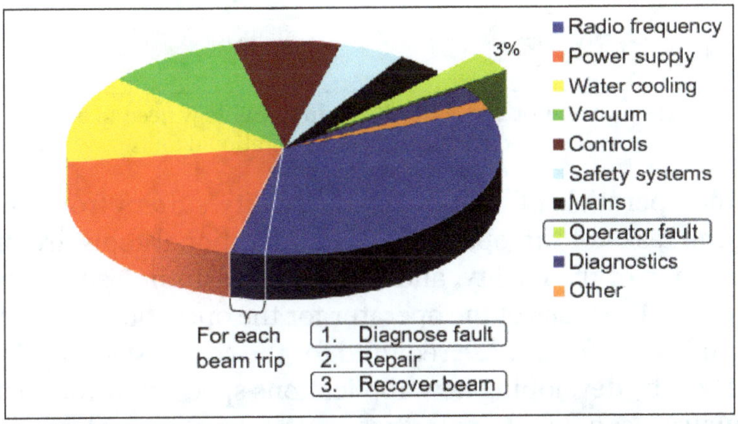

Beam failure statistics of the Swiss Light Source for 2009. Operational tools do affect the number of operator faults and the time to diagnose faults and recover beam.

The design of ergonomic operational tool does not just help to prevent operator faults. Every beam interruption is handled by the operator in three phases: first, he has to diagnose the fault; then he takes care that anything preventing him from making beam gets repaired and finally the operator has to recover the beam. The actual repair is often not in the responsibility of the operator, only the delegation of the repair. But as well for the proper diagnosis before as for the beam recovery after the repair he is in charge. He'll depend on his operational tools to solve these tasks quickly and efficient. If the actual repair time is on average in the same order as the time required for failure diagnosis and beam recovery, then the quality of the operational tools for these two tasks can have a significant impact on the operation statistics.

Human-computer Interaction

Three aspects need to be understood for the design of good user interfaces. They are shown in figure: the goals to be achieved (the tasks), the user that has these goals (the operator) and the technology to build the user interface (the control system).

A thorough understanding of the user of operational tools, the operator, is vital to create ergonomic tools for the accelerator operation. Unfortunately many developers of operational tools are not aware that this knowledge is important. Therefore this should be the main focus of this contribution.

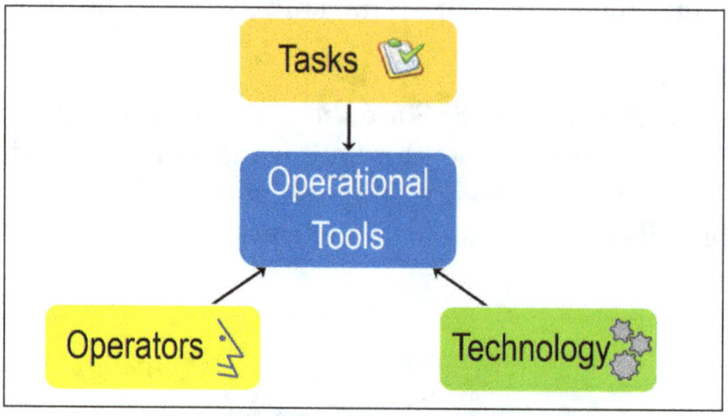

Tasks, operator and control system technology need to be understood for the design of operational tools.

In some cases the operation of an accelerator facility suffers from an inappropriate specification of the tasks of the operators. The operational tools are often developed for the commissioning of the facility, and therefore are optimised for the flexibility required for this phase. The tasks of the operator for the operation of an accelerator facility can differ significantly from those required for the commissioning. Problems of this type are often solved by developing new applications specifically for operation later on. A formal task analysis can help to prioritise on the development of operational tools. The task analysis section will introduce into this technique.

The technology to develop the operational tools compromises all aspects of the user interface of the control system: from input devices like a mouse, over GUI development software to the means of visualisation.

Interaction Design

The operator will act on his tools by the means of discrete control, like buttons, and continuous handles, like sliders. His actions are driven by his goal and his knowledge on how to achieve it. This knowledge can be like a path, where the operator follows step-by-step a defined procedure, or rather like a map, if the operator has a deeper understanding of his task, making him autonomous to find the way to his goal based on his knowledge. The information presented by his tool will be perceived by him either as a sharp picture, showing exactly the information he needs or rather fuzzy with room for interpretation.

A good tool should support the operator in all aspects: it should present a selection of actions appropriate to the task and easy to use by the operator, it should present all information relevant to the task in a way appropriate for the perception by the operator and it should provide all necessary knowledge required to perform the task such that they are comprehensible by the operator.

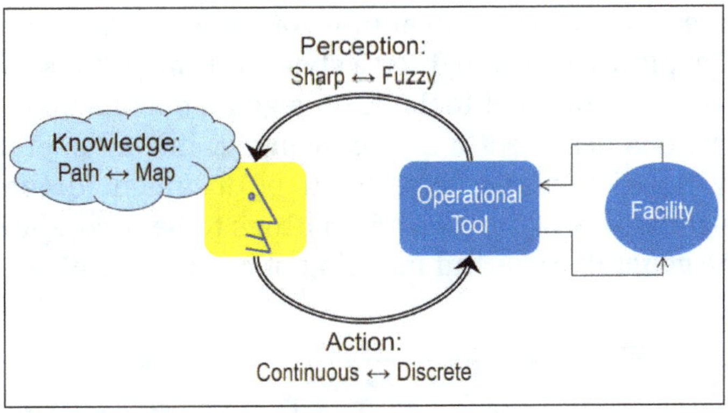

Simple interaction model of the operator, his operational tools and the accelerator facility.

Human-computer interaction research used the theory of perception to derive guidelines for the design of effective and efficient user interfaces. The cognitive limitations of humans defining how user interfaces needs to be designed to support the user in pursuing his goals.

User Interface Design Guidelines

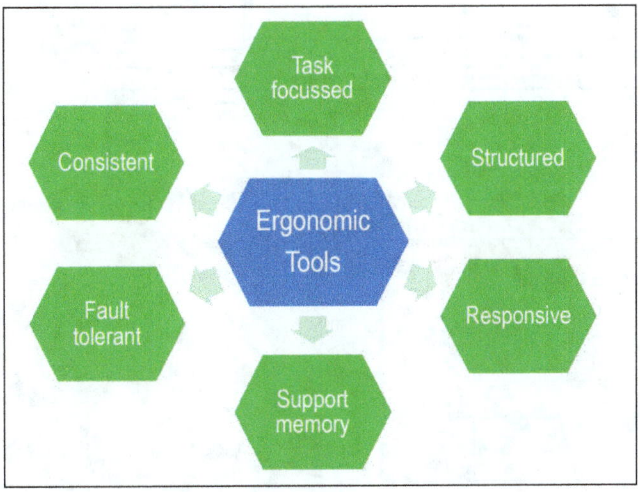

Design concepts for ergonomic user interfaces.

While guidelines for user interfaces are formulated differently in different reference publications for user interface design, they have a great overlap in their concepts. We will briefly introduce these concepts in the following. Simple strategies will be provided to apply them to the design of operational tools.

Consistency and Structure

It is obvious that consistency of the user interface has many advantages for the user. Exceptions are difficult to remember and variations in the style and layout can easily lead to confusion. Consistency is often reached without special measures, when the operational tools are created by a small number of people working closely together. If a larger number of people are involved, then a style guide helps to implement consistency in the design of the operational tools. A style guide documents a desired common style for all applications designed in a given context, like all operational tools of an accelerator facility. A variety of style aspects can be documented: the general layout of screens, the types and styles of handles and buttons to be used, the standards for the display of data, the general usage and meaning of colour and symbols or the vocabulary to be used.

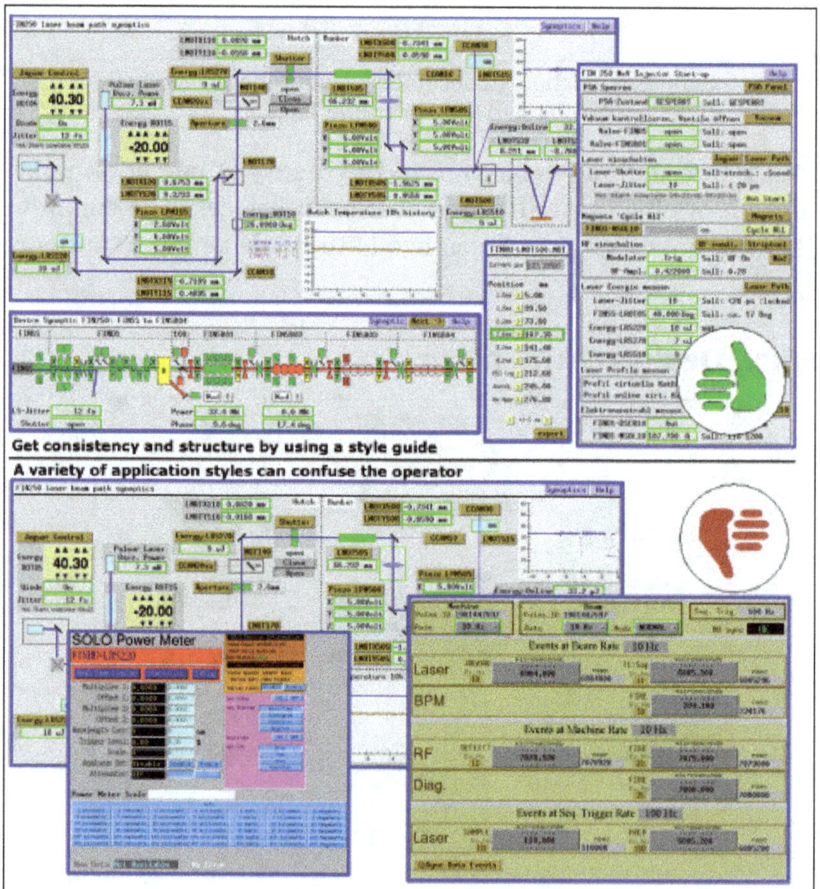

Use a style guide to make all operational tools similar to use. This increases the confidence of the operator in his tools and reduces the number of operator faults.

The benefit of standardisation derives from the limitations of our perception. People are unlikely to mix up a picture of a close friend with the picture of a similar looking stranger, but we do confuse sometimes buttons labelled "edit" and "exit", in particular if they are at the same location in two similar looking screens. Colour can be spotted very easily, for example a red word in a black on white text, but we have difficulties to distinguish different shades of red. We can spot relevant information quickly if it is presented in a clear, visual structure, but to find a specific word buried in a long text is very hard. The reasons for this are simple: we are good at things that helped our ancestors over the past hundred thousand years to survive. Reading text was no such thing within that time scale. And a red apple had a different shade of red anyway, depending on the light. These needs to be taken into account in the style guide: have a standardised layout and few defined handles and formats to provide structure. Define few colours with specific meanings and select colours that are easy to distinguish. Have a glossary of button and text labels following the simple rule: "same name, same thing, different name, and different thing".

In addition the vocabulary should be simple and unambiguous to the operators. Reading requires us to concentrate on the text that will hinder us to concentrate on the task. Use structure, colour and symbols to minimise the amount of text the operator has to read while performing his task. Many symbols have a known meaning, like a red triangle with an exclamation mark. Using them, e.g. for error messages, will catch the eye of the operator. Be careful to use "eye-catcher", like blinking text or pop-up windows: they do get the attention of the operator, but they can distract him from the task.

A style guide should best be ready before you start developing applications. Then it is not much extra work to adhere to it. But even after all applications have been developed, it is still a good idea to create and implement a style guide. Because many changes, like button labels or colours are very easy to change and the effort will pay off compared with the long term benefit for operations.

Task Focused

A good tool should help you to achieve a goal. All your concentration should be on the task to accomplish the objective. People get easily distracted and an operator has many possible distractions: alarms to handle, telephone calls to receive, staff coming into or leaving from the control room. Therefore the tool should help the operator to stay focused on the task despite the distractions. There are several methods to help the user to focus on the task. In multi-step procedures it is useful to show which steps have been done and which still have to be done. The application should appear focused: display only actions relevant for the task and show all information useful for the task but no unrelated information.

The application itself should never distract the user from the task. Therefore it should use the task specific vocabulary, not the terminology of the application programmer. A message "division by zero, abort" will likely confuse the operator, while "the selected scan range of the measurement is zero, please select a valid scan range and retry" tells him clearly what went wrong and what he needs to do to continue his task.

Fault Tolerant

Even the best tool cannot fully prevent the operator from making errors. But ergonomic operational tools should make it hard for the operator to create significant failures and they should make it easy for him to recover from his errors. That way the operator will not just do fewer errors significant to operation. He'll as well feel more secure in using his tools. And his learning curve, while he's trying out new tools, will be much steeper, if he feels secure to try things out.

The confidence in his tools will even have an impact on the performance of the machine. Let's consider an SLS operator who tried to optimise the pre-accelerator with no success. He then decides to restore a saved machine setting from last week. This turns out to produce zero transmission, because - he then remembers - something had been changed yesterday on the pre-accelerator. He then learns that nobody saved the new setting. He'll be busy for an hour to restore transmission. Everyone will tell him afterwards that he should have followed the proper procedure by saving the machine settings before making many changes.

This kind of stress is likely not helping him to learn the proper procedure; it is rather probable to make the operator reluctant to optimise the pre-accelerator again. It happened at the SLS, too. But we introduced an "Undo" button at the application to restore a machine setting. This allows the operator to recover to the state before the machine settings were loaded from the file. When restoring the saved settings does not produce the desired result, he can easily get back to the previous setting. In the example he would have saved the new setting after the "Undo": this would have prevented a significant fault of the accelerator, would have reminded him of the proper procedure and would have increased his confidence in continuing the optimisation.

Responsive

Our brain has time requirements in order to perceive causality. If we click a button and nothing happens for ten seconds, then we will not be confident that things that happen afterwards are related to our actions. The following time requirements have been identified for human computer interaction:

- 0.1 sec: Immediate reaction to user input, e.g. a button appears "pressed" or a wheel-switch "turns".
- 1 sec: Status feedback if a process has not completed.
- 10 sec: Estimate time, if a process takes longer.
- 100 sec: The typical time to make critical decisions.

A tool does not need to be fast in performing the task to meet those time requirements. It just needs to respond quickly to user input and if the task takes longer it needs to keep the user informed about the process. Human computer interaction scientist found that responsiveness has a high impact on user satisfaction. More important for the control room is that a responsive application clearly tells the operator what it is doing and if his attention is currently required. If it is not he can use his time for something else;

fix problems to improve the performance, return phone calls to improve communication or have a cup of coffee to improve operator satisfaction.

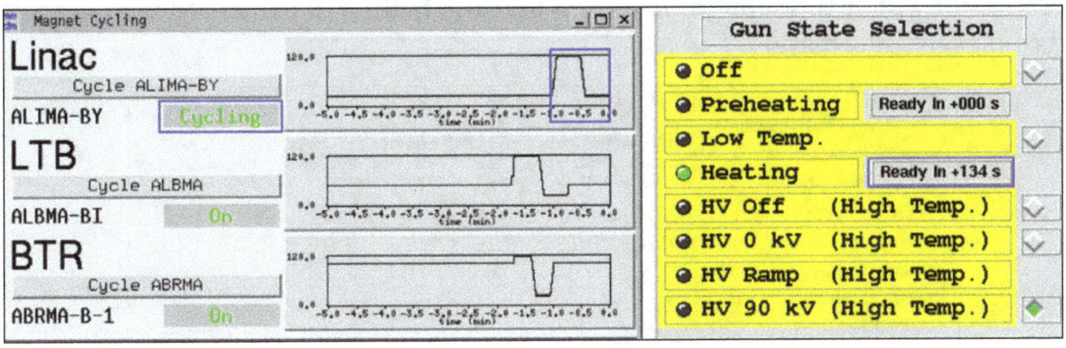

The magnet cycling application on the left shows the magnet current as visual feedback to the operator and the status "Cycling" while the process is still ongoing. The control panel of the electron source on the right shows a countdown to forecast the end of the heating process.

Support Memory

The obvious approach to support the long term memory of an operator in performing a task is to have a thorough documentation of all the steps necessary to perform it, with a direct link from the tool to the document. Practice shows, that this works initially, most operators will read the documentation to learn the task. Some will prefer to learn the task from other operators. Once they learnt the task, only very few will read the documentation again. That should be taken into account when the documentation is updated: the operator needs to be informed about what parts have been updated and when.

There are additional methods to support the memory of the user. Each tool should clearly state its purpose, e.g. by a descriptive title. It is often useful to provide links to related tools, to help the operator to find the tool he's looking for. Our memory works by association, therefore it will be much easier for the operator to select the proper action from a list of choices, than to recall the proper action from memory. If the number of choices is very large it is often useful to sort them by the expected frequency of usage: make those choices most visible that will be needed frequently.

A tool should provide the operator with all information required for the task. Do not expect the operator to collect the necessary information from other tools. This is particularly important during critical decision making: under stress the operator will base his decision on the available information, if the decision needs to be collected from several tools he'll may miss important information and make a bad decision.

If a tool is used to recover from a failure, then it should support documenting the failure. Do not expect the operator to type in the failure information into the electronic logbook after the failure! It is error prone and a waste of the operator's time. Figure shows how the magnet power supply control application at the SLS allows saving the information of the fault into the electronic logbook. This procedure is convenient for the operator but will at the same time assure that the fault is documented with complete and consistent information.

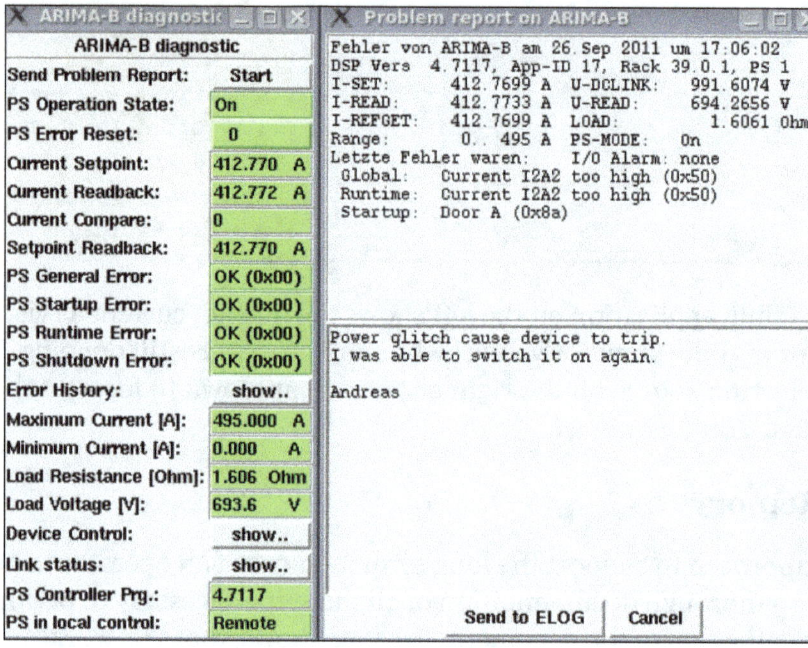

A problem report can be issued from the magnet power supply diagnostics application. It collects all information of the last failure and allows the operator to add a comment and save it the electronic logbook.

References

- Cognitive-ergonomics: oshwiki.eu, Retrieved 18 April, 2020
- COGNITIVE-ERGONOMICS-OF-OPERATIONAL-TOOLS-264877799: researchgate.net, Retrieved 10 August, 2020
- 784-ergonomic-aspects-of-human-computer-interaction, visual-display-units-item: iloencyclopaedia.org, Retrieved 14 May, 2020
- Cognitive-ergonomics: ergo-plus.com, Retrieved 04 January, 2020

Permissions

All chapters in this book are published with permission under the Creative Commons Attribution Share Alike License or equivalent. Every chapter published in this book has been scrutinized by our experts. Their significance has been extensively debated. The topics covered herein carry significant information for a comprehensive understanding. They may even be implemented as practical applications or may be referred to as a beginning point for further studies.

We would like to thank the editorial team for lending their expertise to make the book truly unique. They have played a crucial role in the development of this book. Without their invaluable contributions this book wouldn't have been possible. They have made vital efforts to compile up to date information on the varied aspects of this subject to make this book a valuable addition to the collection of many professionals and students.

This book was conceptualized with the vision of imparting up-to-date and integrated information in this field. To ensure the same, a matchless editorial board was set up. Every individual on the board went through rigorous rounds of assessment to prove their worth. After which they invested a large part of their time researching and compiling the most relevant data for our readers.

The editorial board has been involved in producing this book since its inception. They have spent rigorous hours researching and exploring the diverse topics which have resulted in the successful publishing of this book. They have passed on their knowledge of decades through this book. To expedite this challenging task, the publisher supported the team at every step. A small team of assistant editors was also appointed to further simplify the editing procedure and attain best results for the readers.

Apart from the editorial board, the designing team has also invested a significant amount of their time in understanding the subject and creating the most relevant covers. They scrutinized every image to scout for the most suitable representation of the subject and create an appropriate cover for the book.

The publishing team has been an ardent support to the editorial, designing and production team. Their endless efforts to recruit the best for this project, has resulted in the accomplishment of this book. They are a veteran in the field of academics and their pool of knowledge is as vast as their experience in printing. Their expertise and guidance has proved useful at every step. Their uncompromising quality standards have made this book an exceptional effort. Their encouragement from time to time has been an inspiration for everyone.

The publisher and the editorial board hope that this book will prove to be a valuable piece of knowledge for students, practitioners and scholars across the globe.

Index

www.ingramcontent.com/pod-product-compliance
Lightning Source LLC
LaVergne TN
LVHW080627210926
848485LV00003B/219